From: STEVEN NEWMAN
450 N. CHARITY ST.
BETHEL, OHIO 45___
U.S.A.

MALAYSIA #1
TAIPING
JUNE 2, 1985

DEAR FOLKS,
THE BARE-CHESTED PLANTATION WORKER STOOD SUPPORTED BY TWO
OF HIS FRIENDS. HIS EYES WERE WIDE AND UNFOCUSED. AROUND THEM
THE AIR WAS ELECTRIFIED WITH THE SOUNDS OF CHANTING. FIERCE
WAVES OF HEAT UNDULATED FROM
THE MAN'S SH--
20-FOOT-LONG PIT OF COALS AT

JANUARY 19, 1984
OUJDA, MOROCCO

DEAR FOLKS,
HOW DO I EVEN BEGIN TO DESCRIBE THA___
10 DAYS CROSSING THE STARK SAND DU___
OF EAST MOROCCO? SO MU___ $1
NESS, AND MYSTERY HAVE ___
I CAN DO TO REMEM___
NOT THE 10 ___
IT ___

A TEEN-AGED
___ Tam___
APRIL 3, 1984
NICASTRO, ITALY

Australia 33c
Australia
WARRA___ 27 MY 0___

OVERSEAS EXPRESS
EXPRESS
MAIL
PAR AVION

DEAR FOLKS,
IMAGINE YONKERS, SOUTHERN CALIFORNIA, AND THE CASTS OF ABOUT
___ THROWN TOGETHER INTO ONE SMALL AREA OF TER-
100 BAD HOLLYWOOD ___ AND YOU'LL HAVE A GOOD IDEA
RACED BROWN MOUNT___ ___ HAD ANY NOTION
___ WHAT MY 10 DA___
___ I WAS GOIN___
___ AND SLEE___
AFTER

STEVEN
450 ___
BE___

___GRAD
02.07.84.14
000
81000

J.RUEY, E___
J___

DEAR FOLKS,
THE EYES OF THE TWO YOUNG MEN NARROWED AND
TWO HATEFUL TOMCATS. THEIR ARMS COCKED AND THE
OTHER TO ADVANCE. BARE FEET DANCED NERVOUSLY OVE___
DIRT, AS THE PACE OF THOSE SAME QUARRELING CATS ___
___ ___ OF THE DAY. ___ ___ING FROM

SEPTEMBER 28, 198___
LIMOGES, FRA___

DEAR FOLKS,
YOU DON'T RUSH FRANCE... AND FRANCE DOESN'T R___
IT'S AS SIMPLE AS THAT.
I.F. THERE'S A MORE COMPLICA___
THROUGH, IT ___

STEVEN NEWMAN
___ NORTH CHARITY ___
___, OHIO 45106
U.S.A.

To: DOROTHY HARVEY
CAPPER'S ___
616 J___

malaysia
Bunga Raya
20¢
Malaysia

HARVEY

LETTERS FROM STEVEN

Stories from the first solo walk around the world

Steven M. Newman

CAPPER'S BOOKS
TOPEKA, KANSAS

Published by
Capper's Books
616 Jefferson, Topeka, Kansas 66607

Acknowledgments:

Front Cover Photograph of Steven Newman by Jeff Hinckley
Copyright © 1987 by *The Columbus Dispatch*
Reprinted by Permission of *The Columbus Dispatch*

Front Cover Map Copyright © 1987 by Rocky Boots
Reprinted by Permission of Rocky Boots

Photographs on Pages 347, 348, 349, 350, 354
Copyright © 1987 by Rocky Boots

Photographs on Page 341 Copyright © 1987 by Tanya Philpot

Photographs on Page 348 (top right; bottom left)
Copyright © 1987 by The Associated Press

A.P. Story on Page 346 Copyright © 1987 by The Associated Press

Book Design by Ron Joler

Cover Design by Kathy J. Snyman

Typeset by Karen Jaramillo

First Printing, September 1987

ISBN 0-941678-09-1 Softcover Edition
ISBN 0-941678-10-5 Hardcover edition

Printed in the United States of America

*For the moms all over this world who made me their son,
especially the one I came home to.*

FOREWORD

Steven Newman's solo Worldwalk is the stuff of which legends are made. No person in the history of humankind had ever walked around the world alone, that is, until April 1, 1987, when Steven Newman took the final step up to the porch of his home in Bethel, Ohio, thus completing his four-year, twenty thousand mile odyssey.

Imagine it . . . a person walking around the world alone. Walking because he believes that is the only real way to get a full sense of our world. Walking because it is the best way to meet the people of the world. Walking without a companion. Walking without a sponsor. Walking not knowing what the day and night ahead would bring. Walking to see what the world would teach him. Walking in order to allow a world of experiences flood through him, and through his stories, through us.

LETTERS FROM STEVEN is the true story of Steven Newman's journey through twenty countries on five continents. This book is comprised primarily of letters that he wrote as he walked, ninety-three letters previously published in *Capper's*, written for its readers so they could experience with him the adventure of our world. For the most part, these letters are reprinted here unchanged, except for those changes that Steven wished to make for the sake of accuracy and for expansions of several stories that were originally published in shortened versions. And at Steven's wish, and to our delight, we have also included six of his previously unpublished letters, as well as eight excerpts from his diaries, and many of his photos.

The letters in this book are more than just letters home— because Steven Newman is more than an adventurer and journalist. He is also a natural storyteller in the grand tradition. His letters are stories, true stories that because of the strength of his vision and his storyteller's art, "ring true." The stories he tells about the people he meets, and their lands and cultures, spring to life with a turn of the phrase, or the telling gesture, or simply through his exuberance in telling them. I think the reason that his stories are so moving and the experiences so immediate and real is that he writes fearlessly about the world, that is, he is not afraid to reveal what he sees and what he feels. And in that sense his stories are revelations of our world and of him.

When Steven Newman stepped onto the front porch of his home in Bethel, Ohio, on April 1, 1987, he accomplished not only a monumental personal achievement, he also completed a significant historical event. The true stature of his achievement and this event becomes clear when you fully consider the fact that he is the only person who has ever lived to have actually walked alone around our world. Of all the billions and billions of people who have lived on our earth, he is the only one ever to walk solo around it. That is a staggering thought, a monumental achievement, truly a significant historical event.

But that is not why Steven Newman walked around the world. Important though they may be, personal achievement or an historical first are not what his Worldwalk is about. It is, simply, about people. Steven Newman walked around the world because he hungered to experience it fully, as it really is. He walked from land to land because he wanted to learn about the peoples of our world, and he wanted to learn about himself and what it means to be a human being. Through his letters you can see him growing in his recognition of our world as a place of awesome physical and spiritual beauty, and his recognition of the common bonds that peoples in all lands share— the same desire to live fully, the same love of family, the same wonder at the miracle of life. You can see his growing recognition that love, not hate, is the strongest force in our world. And that is the true jewel that this courageous adventurer brings home from his Worldwalk. If his journey teaches us one thing, it is that we as adults can experience life with the same openness, exuberance, interest, playfulness and joy in just being alive that we felt as children.

It is in this spirit, the spirit of excitement, acceptance, and adventure that we invite you to walk along with Steven on this grand odyssey, and to experience the world in a fresh way through his letters collected here in this, the first book by the first person ever to have walked solo around the world.

Ron Joler
Capper's Books

PREFACE

In 1983, while making final preparations for my walk around the world, I contacted editors of newspapers and magazines to see if they would be interested in publishing stories that I planned to write during my journey.

Perhaps the most positive and enthusiastic response I received was from Dorothy Harvey, editor of *Capper's Weekly* (since renamed *Capper's*). Dorothy suggested that I share the adventures of my solo walk around the world with the readers of *Capper's* by writing a letter to them for each issue. I thought it was a wonderful idea, and, thus, my column in *Capper's*, "Letter From Steven," was born.

I felt honored to have my stories included in *Capper's,* an old tabloid publication about which Carl Sandburg once said, "*Capper's Weekly* is to American journalism what folklore is to the nation's literary verse." And I felt that Dorothy's idea of a letter format was perfect. I thought it would be a casual, yet very personal and indeed intimate way of telling the stories of my walk around the world.

Soon after I began my walk and my letters began to appear in *Capper's*, I began receiving the first of thousands of letters from my readers, which made it very clear to me indeed, that I was not walking alone. And as I met more and more people in many lands, people who, like my readers, were also fascinated by the idea of a single human being actually walking around the world alone, I soon realized that my letters, my stories belonged not just to my original readers, but to everyone with a love for our world, an adventurous heart, and the will to dream.

My dream of walking alone around the world was born in a nine-year-old's excitable mind. I'll never forget the day over twenty-four years ago when my dream was born. It was during one of those frequent Ohio rainy afternoons, when my imagination was lost in the pages of a stack of old issues of *National Geographic Magazine.* Though the covers of that dignified periodical may have been worn and faded at the time, the beauty of the glossy photographs inside was still unmistakably very much alive. I knew then and there that someday I had to visit all of those exotic lands and meet all those smiling faces.

Even now, almost a quarter century later, I can still remember so clearly that night's restlessness caused by the magic of those paper windows to the world "out there." When my mother came into my bedroom to calm the thoughts swirling in my nine-year old head, I remember looking up at her from beneath my blanket and saying, "Mom, when I grow up I know exactly what I'm going to do—I'm going to become a writer and walk around the world!" At which point she chuckled and replied, "Oh, you mean you'll be a soldier of fortune?"

"Yeah," I answered, not at all sure what a soldier of fortune was, but sure that it sounded pretty exciting.

Well, that little boy did grow up to become the writer he had envisioned. But, the other half of my childhood dream of walking around the world became lost and nearly forgotten in a journalistic career, and in a world of headlines and news reports about assassinations, wars, nuclear arms and terrorism. Like, I imagine, almost everyone else, I began to think of the world as a fearful place, where hatred and violence far outweigh the influence of love and compassion.

Then, one day in 1977, I was sitting at my reporter's desk at the *Casper Star-Tribune* in Wyoming, when I realized how terribly little I knew about the daily lives and dreams of everyday people in other parts of the world. Sure, I knew what the newspapers and television said about our world. But what were those people really like? I couldn't believe that they were all that different from me. Nor could I bring myself to join the chorus of fear and cynicism that seemed to be sounding everywhere anymore from discussions of American society and the world in general. But how could I find out for sure?

My dormant childhood dream sprang back to life. Within a few weeks I quit what looked to be a promising career, and began preparing and planning for what others said was the most foolish act imaginable (but which I viewed as the biggest undertaking of my young life) . . . to walk alone around the world, and to meet people throughout the world one by one, day after day. What followed were six years of hard work laying the foundations upon which to pursue a dream which surely must have appeared to any rational person to be impossible.

My preparation included toiling for three and one-half

years as a roughneck on drilling rigs in Wyoming and Montana to save enough money to finance the walk (during that time my right hand was partially severed in an accident and was considered by the doctors for six frightening months to be permanently crippled). I camped alone for most of yet another year in the deserts and mountains to toughen myself mentally and sprititually. I visited other nations' embassies in Washington, D.C., to get their advice and suggestions for walking through their countries. I spent hundreds of hours in libraries scrutinizing maps and reading accounts of other adventurers who had walked various parts of our world. And, after making arrangements with newspapers and magazines for the publication of my stories, I finally returned home to Bethel, Ohio, to break the news to my mother and father (I think all parents could imagine the conflict they would feel in their hearts at hearing such news from their son).

At last, all that remained was to put that pack on my back, lace up my hiking boots, and venture forth, walking toward the rising sun to seek the answers to all those questions in my heart.

Now, four years, thirty-nine million steps, and a wonderful walk later, I have accomplished my dream, and many of my questions about people and our world have been answered. This book is the story of my walk around the world, a story of people and their ways, a story written letter by letter as the world unfolded before me. And this, my first book, is also part of the dream that is the Worldwalk.

No one's dream is ever realized without the help of others. And in that regard, few have ever been as blessed as I have. I could not have accomplished my Worldwalk without the faith and support of my family and friends, or without the tremendous love of all those thousands of people around the world who shared their homes when I was homeless, who shared themselves when I was lonely, and who shared their tables, however modest, when I was hungry. Most of all, I would like to thank them, the people of the world who shared their lives and their dreams with me.

I would also like to thank the folks at *Capper's* who shared in my walk by bringing a "Letter from Steven" to their readers each issue for four years, and for responding to the hundreds of requests from their readers for the publication of this book. In particular, I want to thank Ron Joler for his work on this book, and for all of the late, late nights we spent at his Lawrence, Kansas home fitting together the pieces of this world puzzle.

And, finally, I want to thank those thousands of readers who followed my walk year after year, letter by letter—but for them I would have walked alone. And you, dear reader, I wish last of all to thank you for curling up with this book and walking with me around world.

Steven M. Newman

CONTENTS

May the blessing of light be with you—
 light outside and light within.

May sunlight shine upon you and warm your heart
 'til it glows like a great peat fire
 so that the stranger may come and warm himself by it.

May a blessed light shine out of your two eyes
 like a candle set in two windows of a house,
 bidding the wanderer to come in out of the storm.

May you ever give a kindly greeting to those whom you pass
 as you go along the roads.

May the blessing of rain—the sweet, soft rain—fall upon you
 so that little flowers may spring up to shed their sweetness
 in the air.

May the blessings of the earth—the good, rich earth—
 be with you.

May the earth be soft under you when you rest upon it,
 tired at the end of the day.

May earth rest easy over you when at the last you lie under it.

May earth rest so lightly over you that your spirit
 may be out from under it quickly,
 and up, and off,
 and on it's way to God.

An old Irish blessing

LETTERS FROM STEVEN

THE EASTERN
UNITED STATES

STEVEN'S ROUTE

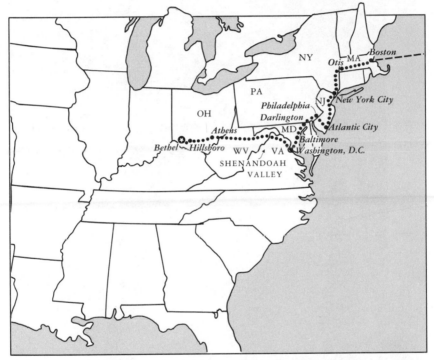

The first part of my journey saw me crossing the Appalachians on up to New England. I was surprised to find the eastern United States—which is such a highly populated region—to be so beautiful, and to be largely unpopulated forest and farmland. From Boston, after a last second change in my flight destination in the British Isles, I flew on to London.

The walk ahead through the eastern United States
114 days
April 1, 1983 - July 23, 1983
1,117 miles

Here I am, a "fledgling" Worldwalker, just several miles into my journey.

Bethel, Ohio
March 22,1983

Dear Folks,

In nearly every man and woman dwells a Sinbad, a spirit which forever longs to explore the unknown and to experience adventure in its rawest forms.

I am no different. In a few days I will take my first steps into an adventure which has dominated my imagination since early childhood—walking around the world.

This walk is something I can't deny myself, for I have an insatiable desire to know more about the world. I have made sacrifices to be able to follow this dream. But ahead of me lie three to five years of joys, lessons, mysteries and perils, the likes of which only a handful of men and women in history have experienced. I will cross twenty-one countries, fifteen thousand miles of deserts, jungles, mountains, rivers and farm-lands.

My trek will take me through America, the British Isles, Europe, North Africa, the Middle East, Asia, and Australia. If I somehow survive the elements, bandits, dangerous animals and loneliness awaiting me, I may become the only man to have ever circled the world alone on foot.

Yet I'm not out to set a record, but I do need the chance to appease the Sinbad in me. I hope that through these letters I write to you, your imagination will be rekindled, and together we will rediscover a world as full of romance, beauty, kindness and adventure as the world we have read about in the days of Marco Polo or Sir Francis Drake.

Steven

Hillsboro, Ohio
April 4, 1983

Dear Folks,

Only three days into the walk and the kindness of strangers has been incredible. It helps me forget the physical pain.

When blisters and sore back muscles become unbearable, someone drives up or comes out of a house to help. Most have read newspaper stories of my walk around the world or have seen it on Cincinnati television. People's eagerness to help never ceases to surprise me.

The first day I signed autographs, waved at a hundred honking autos, ate brownies and cookies handed to me by farm wives, and drank a dozen cups of tea.

One man pulled over and handed me ten dollars to buy another pair of shoes later on. Then a woman drove up with a carload of children—they gave me sandwiches and lemonade. The most surprising gift of all was from the young lady who pulled over to the side of the road and gave me a big kiss. Now what did I ever do to deserve *that?*

The first night, I stayed in Mt. Orab, Ohio, with the family of an unemployed auto factory worker. The second night I slept on a living room floor in Fayetteville.

Easter was cold and rainy and by evening, miserable. The owner of a tiny Tastee Freeze in Hoagland recognized me and invited me inside for a Big T Burger and fries. His kindness and the food prodded me on down the road another mile where I found an old barn with a clean dirt floor and a roof that didn't leak. Wearily, I peeled off my soaked jeans, shirt and socks and crawled into my sleeping bag, every muscle in my body feeling old and stiff. All I could think was—In three days I've only gone 50 miles—50 long, painful miles! How am I ever going to make the other 14,950? Then, I slipped into one of the deepest sleeps I've ever known.

I know the miles will come faster and easier once my feet and muscles begin to match my enthusiasm for this walk. These factors, along with the kindness of others, will help me get down the road.

Steven

Guysville, Ohio
April 18, 1983

Dear Folks,

I thought I'd never make it to Athens, Ohio, my first major stop. The route (old U.S. 50) I've chosen to take from Bethel, Ohio, to Washington, D.C., is one of the hilliest and curviest highways anywhere. Consequently, my legs felt as if they were going to fall apart long before I'd reach the eastern edge of Ohio.

The blisters disappeared—more or less—after the second day out, but then it seemed that that something else painful would crop up every day. If it wasn't the knees, it'd be an ankle or perhaps my back.

After about seventy miles I had the good sense to lighten my pack by about twenty-five pounds. So many things that I had thought were indispensable at the start of the trip suddenly didn't seem so important anymore. Back to Bethel, via UPS, went such things as cooking gear, tent, jacket, and fishing gear.

My poor back and knees hurt so much I even contemplated ridding myself of my sleeping bag. Yet I held back, because I knew I won't always be able to find persons willing to put me up for the night.

And sure enough, two nights later I needed the sleeping bag. I was in a particularly lonely stretch of back hill country in the middle of Vinton County, Ohio's poorest county. It was raining, cold, windy and dark when I finally decided to call it quits for the day. Although there were no farmhouses to be seen on any of the surrounding hills, I spotted an abandoned church about a quarter of a mile off the road.

Carefully I crossed a flooded field to the empty white building and stepped into its black and musty interior. All day I had been warned by strangers not to stop in Vinton County, for it was said to be a violent place because of its high unemployment (21 percent) and poverty.

Adjoining the church was a cemetery and several of the oldest, deadest trees I'd ever seen. Needless to say, I hardly slept a wink, for all night all I could hear were ghouls and murderers and thieves creeping up on me over the old floor boards.

5

In the gray morning, however, I was still in one piece, and much of the noises I'd heard had been nothing more than trees scraping the tin roof in the wind or rats scurrying through the litter piled in the corners.

Furthermore, I found the people to be extremely friendly and compassionate, even though they were extremely poor. Although the homes in this Appalachian region were more often than not lifeless looking, their inhabitants had hearts of gold, particularly the very poorest.

Many of the homes I was invited into didn't have plumbing, and all were heated by wood or coal stoves, yet the treatment I received was as good as any king could have wished.

When I finally reached Athens, after nine days and 140 miles, I'd made a lot of friends and learned again how helpful my fellow Americans are.

Steven

Capon Bridge, West Virginia
April 30, 1983

Dear Folks,

How it saddens me to realize that this will be my last day in West Virginia. So much beauty I have discovered in both its people and its scenery, that I wish I could just lay down my pack and stay here in these lush Appalachian Mountains for at least one lifetime.

Truly West Virginia—"Wild and Wonderful West Virginia"—is, in spite of all its poverty, one of this country's brightest gems. And the beauty I talk of is of the simple, unselfish kind—the best kind.

Although it has taken me nearly eleven days to cross northern West Virginia's 215 miles of mountains and valleys, those were days that seemed to fly by, because of the never-ending kindness shown me.

I must admit, however, I had my doubts when I first entered the state at Parkersburg. Like the dark waters of the Ohio River that flow by that city of forty thousand, the first few people I met on the streets and in the shops were rather expressionless and cold.

Furthermore, the city and outlying towns I passed through those first few rainy days were comprised mostly of gray and decaying buildings. A general sense of extreme poverty prevailed, and I looked upon all the shuttered homes and shops and the piles of junk stacked everywhere as signs of a people who no longer cared, who found little to be proud of anymore.

How wrong I was! Even though the state has the nation's highest unemployment rate—22 percent—and the people scattered about its moist and heavily-forested mountains live very simple lifestyles, they have managed to maintain a friendliness towards strangers that would put most so-called "do-gooders" to shame. Their autos may be rusty and their homes small, but their hearts are as big and shiny as the sun itself.

Because it is mostly a rural state and most of its young people have migrated to the larger cities of neighboring states to seek work, nearly every home I approached for water, food, or shelter was occupied by elderly people, nearly always in their seventies or eighties.

With memory of the last great Depression still fresh in their minds, the old people never failed to help me even though sometimes they had so little to share. They remembered how in their younger days everyone had had to depend upon others for a lot of life's basics, and it gave them great pride and joy to know they had helped me make it a little further down the road.

Indeed, incredible as this may sound, I had to pay for only two meals during my entire trek across the state. Almost as if I were some long lost son returned, many of those who invited me in fed and pampered me to the point of making me feel a little embarrassed.

And the young people? I finally started meeting many of them once I had crossed to the eastern side of the Appalachians. And what a joy it was to find that the younger West Virginians are as friendly and inwardly contented as the old people of the mountains.

Even as I write this letter, a dozen canoes drift by me down the beautiful Capon River. Each canoe holds one or two young people who are laughing, smiling and waving, their eyes as full of kindness as the flowered hills watching over me.

You know something, West Virginia? I miss you already.

Steven

Winchester, Virginia
May 4, 1983

Dear Folks,

As I have read so often in the written accounts of other wanderers, it is the poor and the elderly who generally are the most eager to assist the passing stranger. Perhaps they see in my lonely and haggard figure some reflection of their own struggles. Or maybe they are more likely to take a closer look at those around them, and like Estaline Mantz did early this morning, perhaps wonder if it could be more than just a mere human being passing by.

It was while walking down a secluded foggy road in the Shenandoah Valley that I heard Estaline's distant shouts. I looked up to the side of a broad grassy hill, to the front porch of a lone white cottage, and saw a very old and tiny lady with shining hair and the bluest eyes I have ever gazed into. "Yoo-hoo! Yoo-hoo!" she was yelling, with an excited wave. "Young man, have you had any breakfast?"

I responded that I hadn't eaten since noon the day before and had spent the night sleeping in an abandoned farm house.

"Well, you get up here and eat breakfast!" she demanded. Both the firmness in her voice and the way she stamped her foot on the porch's floor boards made me feel like a naughty child. I went up to her directly, lest she call the sheriff on me for refusing to eat any breakfast!

She lived all alone and yet did not hesitate to invite me into her simple home, where she sat me down to a huge breakfast. It seemed she could not feed me enough food to satisfy herself, and more than once I thought I caught her looking at me as if I reminded her of someone she loved dearly. Later, as I stood on the porch with my tall pack on my back, I asked her why she had invited me in, why she so readily trusted a complete stranger.

She was actually quite shy—she lowered her eyes and looked over the still misty valley as if both embarrassed and trying to collect her thoughts. After a few minutes she looked back at me and said ever so softly, "When I was a little girl, my mother used to read to me from the Bible. Her favorite passage was the one that said God sometimes sends angels to us disguised as men to test our charitableness. Well," a slight red came to her face, "I'm eighty-eight years old and my eyesight is not so good anymore.

"And when I looked out the screen door into the forest and saw this tall figure coming through the fog, I could feel my heart suddenly beating faster. No one ever walks down that road so early in the morning. I watched you coming closer, and when I saw there was something very big and long on your back, I thought surely this must be one of the angels coming to test me."

Her right hand shot up to her face, as if she might giggle. Instead, she nervously gripped her chin and continued with both frustration and relief in her voice, "I thought I was seeing wings on your shoulders. And there was no way I was going to let you go by without feeding you. For I've been so good all these many years, and—darn it!—I'm just too old now to be blowing my chance of getting into heaven.

"Why, I might *never* have another chance to feed an angel!"

Even though she was being very serious and sincere, there was no way to keep from having a good chuckle at her expense. After all, it wasn't every day that I got to be an angel.

When I stepped off her porch to continue my journey across Virginia's wonderfully bright green pastures, I felt extremely warm inside. Not only did I have a full stomach, but a bigger heart, too. Perhaps my chances of stepping through those pearly gates in the sky weren't all the greatest at the moment, but her's certainly were. And, how nice it was to realize I'd been one of the angels she'd stopped to help her on her path to find those gates.

Steven

Darlington, Maryland
May 11, 1983

Dear Folks,

Walking across northern Virginia in the springtime may be the closest I'll ever come to finding heaven on this earth.

What an incredibly peaceful region with lush rolling hills, quiet lanes perfumed with pink and white dogwood trees, and apple trees with blossoms whiter than the sun! The large, old stone farmhouses are surrounded by stone walls and white picket fences.

Like the land, the people radiated contentment. Smiling and waving "Good day" seemed as natural to them as breathing. No one knew who I was or why I was walking, yet you'd have thought they'd known me all my life.

It seemed unreal that only a little over one hundred years ago, Americans—some in blue uniforms, others in gray—were spilling their blood on those soft pastures.

I took my time passing through the beautiful upper Shenandoah Valley knowing too soon I would be on the hot, hard cement and in the roaring traffic of Washington, D.C. I savored the countryside and delighted in seeing one thoroughbred horse farm after another.

Mark Twain would have been proud of the Huck Finn in me—no pressures, no responsibilities, nothing but warm sunshine and blue skies and flowered meadows. I could hardly resist the temptation to kick off my boots and fall asleep on the banks of each brook I crossed.

Eventually I arrived in Washington where I spent five days in the suburb of Chevy Chase resting at the home of a retired Naval officer and his gracious wife.

Then on to Baltimore with its blocks of cement block and brick houses and littered streets. In Baltimore I stayed with young Jesuit volunteer social workers who lived in an old convent in the Little Italy section of the inner city. There I learned of the high unemployment in that port city and that, despite city government claims, poverty is very common.

As I walked north from Baltimore on my way to Philadelphia, I passed many doorways in which I saw the hard faces of the jobless and the restless.

Now, back in the countryside of northern Maryland, on the banks of the Susquehanna River, once again life seems to be at peace.

Steven

Atlantic City, N.J.
May 28, 1983

Dear Folks,

I am sitting on a bench on a still-sleepy Atlantic City Boardwalk, watching and listening to the restless ocean. The hazy sun is just peeping up from the Atlantic, and except for a few hungry seagulls and a couple of joggers, this stretch of the boardwalk along the casinos is probably as deserted as it ever gets.

Last night I stayed in a rescue mission in a room with twenty-nine other transients—a sleepless night, with all the hacking and snoring and drunks stumbling against my bed.

I had no intention of coming anywhere near Atlantic City. My plan was to go in a line from Washington to Baltimore, Philadelphia, New York City, and Boston. Then a week ago I received a phone call from a freelance writer who wanted to interview me.

She asked if I could meet her in "A.C." I said yes—mistakenly thinking that the old resort city was somewhere along the ocean close to New York City. Later, when I looked on a map, I saw it is 60 miles southeast of Philadelphia. I had a strong urge to call back and tell her to forget the interview. The idea that for the first time on the walk I'd be going backward instead of forward was most disturbing. However, my curiosity got the better of me, so I left the "City of Brotherly Love," to go to New Jersey, the "Garden State."

Philadelphia can best be pictured as an "inverted donut." Surrounding the city is a light area of lush countryside and expensive suburbs which suddenly turns into a wide ring of dark ghettos of trash-filled streets, tens-of-thousands of unemployed poor, and probably a like number of abandoned buildings. In the center, the light area returns again in the form of new office towers, green parks, sparkling water fountains, tree-lined boulevards, and well-preserved, stone-pillared libraries and museums.

But now I'm in Atlantic City, which looks like a sprawling junkyard of seedy motels and bars, graced only by a string of pearls someone threw along its eastern edge—the Boardwalk with its casinos and trinket shops.

All the way across south New Jersey, it was a rare moment when anyone said "Hello." I was puzzled and disappointed to be treated as if I were distrusted and disliked.

Several locals I talked with said there has been a recent large influx of unemployed and unskilled transients into south New Jersey looking for work in the booming "casino row" of Atlantic City. So, ironically, south New Jersey finds itself with more unemployment and crime than ever before.

"We who've lived here all our lives are scared anymore," said the owner of a bar halfway between Philadelphia and Atlantic City. "It ain't like twenty years ago when people waved and stopped to talk. It's a rougher bunch now, we can't trust no one."

He needn't have told me. Many homes and businesses I passed were unkempt or abandoned and guarded by vicious attack dogs.

The biggest disappointment of my walk so far would have to be New Jersey. But time, like the waves of the ocean, has a tendency to alter a lot of things—opinions included.

Steven

I found most New Yorkers to be friendly and caring people, like these two old gentlemen.

New York City, New York
June 12, 1983

Dear Folks,

I walked into the explosive sights and sounds of New York City five days ago and was swept into another dimension—where time never rests, where the imagination is bombarded constantly by stimuli—like a gargantuan arcade.

From the moment I left the Staten Island ferry and ventured into the deep canyons of Manhattan's skyscraper forest, it was "sink or swim." All eighty blocks from lower Manhattan's Wall Street district to Central Park, I was swept along in a river of three-piece suits, briefcases, shopping bags, and loud tape players hanging from shoulders of gyrating teen-aged boys.

Several days before, traveling Route 9 from New Jersey, I'd been told that there are 9.5 million people living in New York City. On the day I arrived I was sure every one of them had decided to come downtown. I stood behind the steaming wagon of a sidewalk frankfurter vendor in awe of the mass of humanity and architecture that engulfed me.

I marvel at the vitality reverberating from every street and avenue. The city moves and breathes every minute of the day and night.

Walking from First Avenue to Eighth Avenue yesterday, I passed a Puerto Rican Street Carnival, the banks of six nations, airline offices of ten countries, dozens of restaurants offering cuisine ranging from French to Indian, and street vendors hawking everything from Italian ice desserts to Greek newspapers.

It would be wrong to think New York's Manhattan district is some sort of materialistic circus, where money and vanity obliterate the human side. Contrary to those who portray the city as cold and selfish, I found New Yorkers to be as healthily "human" as people anywhere. The problem is that in a city as overpowering as New York, the numbers and grandness tend to distract one's attention from the personal drama played out on every corner.

Before I entered the city, I was apprehensive about my safety. I had been told repeatedly the city was crime-ridden, the people rude and concerned only with themselves. I envisioned silent, smileless faces. Wrong. For every grouch I've passed in New York, I've seen ninety-nine others laughing or in lively conversation.

It's true that New Yorkers—as do most Americans—love their money and possessions—it's just not true that they won't help one another.

I'll tell you what happened my first evening on Staten Island. I stopped at a gas station to get a drink of water, and before I could leave, two teen-age boys pumping gas there had each given me twenty dollars, one large pizza, two soda pops and a beer—and I didn't ask for anything but the water.

And what of the crime?

"Don't believe that at all!" a wild-eyed Yugoslavian cab driver laughed. "I dare you to walk anywhere in Manhattan— yes, even Central Park—at any time of day or night and see if anything bad happens to you."

I did. And as usual the purveyors of fear were wrong. Other than a few passes from streetwalkers, absolutely nothing happened.

Sure, you must use common sense and caution in some places. But the horror stories about New York City crime are mostly exaggerations.

I felt safer in Manhattan at two in the morning than I've ever felt in other metropolitan inner-city areas. Maybe it was the masses of people on the streets every hour of the day.

I believe that America's big cities are very much alive and growing—and so are the people in them.

Steven

Great Barrington, Massachusetts
June 22, 1983

The Mount Washington Forest was one of the quietest and most poetically beautiful areas I had seen to date on the walk. I therefore decided to "hide away" in the depths of its maples, oaks, beeches, white birches, pines and hemlocks for a few days to catch up on my journals.

As always, I continue to fall way behind on my daily notes and must play catchup. In a place like this, however, it is actually a welcome burden.

I probably got no more than two miles from the small wooden home of the Reverend Chase when I decided to hike into the forest. I cut through a small meadow on the east side of the road, and walked deep into the thick forest until I found a secluded knoll that overlooked a clear and fast-moving, little stream.

With the only sounds being the songs of birds and the spilling of the brook's waters over several small falls, I was able to concentrate deeply on my memories of the past few weeks. I might have stayed longer in my secret paradise of fleeting sunrays and coolness, but for the fact that I ran out of peanut butter and cookies—hence, no more food.

So, it was with much regret at still not being caught up on my notes that I ventured back onto the open road. When I left the woods, it was late this evening, and although night was quickly coming, I could not help but take my time, for there was so much beauty and peace to be absorbed. Especially when I considered that Boston and the unfamiliarity of Europe were now at most but a handful of weeks away.

In a sense, this was to be the quiet before the storm.

On this enchanting mountain I found a peace that I had not really seen in any other region I'd crossed, except for maybe in Northern Virginia, in the Upperville area.

I felt frustrated at having to leave all this heaven behind, and like some kid who is mesmorized by the strangeness of a fair, I didn't want to return to the "ordinary" world, so to speak.

Adding to all the splendor of the evening were clusters of

mountain laural bushes covered with delicate-petaled, white blossoms, often accented by feather-like ferns growing profusely from the moist forest floor.

At one wide bend in the two-lane road, where the road cut through a thick stand of pine trees, I came upon several fragile white-tailed deer who let me get within fifty feet before they bounded off into the trees.

When I walked whistling through the bend, one of the deer snorted at me from the trees in a manner that seemed to say, "How *dare* you disturb us!"

The only signs of man I saw were an occasional small home or vacation cabin set back into well-cared-for yards. Oh, yes, and the white unceasing flags of No Trespassing signs, too.

As the individual leaves turned into shadowy clumps, and finally into dark, black walls stopped by a ceiling of stars, the air became even more scented with a transcendental kind of atmosphere.

It seemed that life here was so rich, so high in quality, that I could live forever just by breathing the air and its aromas of wildflowers and ripe leaves.

Surely nothing ever died in this area of the material world. Surely I had stumbled upon a secret of which only a few people, such as the Chases, were aware, and were not about to share with any other mortals.

So this was the fairyland called New England that I'd heard so much about all my life and that I'd seen in so many colorful photos?

Well, one thing was sure—even after so few miles . . . I loved it! And obviously by the look of things, so did the gods.

Magic, magic everywhere. I could see it, smell it, taste it, hear it with every step. Even with the pack, I felt as if I could just take a deep breath and float away, away, away . . . right to the stars.

Surely I was bewitched. For why the crazy laughter—the tears in my eyes—the goosebumps—the sensation of being a leaf caught in a gentle breeze?

Even Genghis Kahn would have been a Reverend Chase if he'd had lived here, I marvelled wonderously.

In my many years of living in the West, I'd seen mountains that were awesome, others that were evil, and others that commanded respect. But none that had poured forth such gentle love as this little one.

I just knew that if I could ever live here, I'd never again have to labor for the inspiration needed to create.

Near the bottom of the mountain, I gazed in a bewitched way at a broad, grassy meadow, the texture and color of black velvet. Sprinkled over its sensuous cloth were many glowing fireflies, and above that, like diamonds on yet another cloth of even finer black velvet, countless twinkling stars.

I imagined that if I were to just simply step off the asphalt into that black void of embers and diamonds, I would become weightless and be able to fly about from one glowing jewel to another with but a twitch of a finger or toe.

And yet . . . and yet, a bit of sadness was in my heart at the same time. For, looking at the fireflies, it occurred to me that I'd not thought of the mysterious little insects as "magical" since I'd been a little boy of perhaps six or seven. How terrible to think that I'd forgotten that magic could be in something as ordinary as an insect.

To think I'd ever found *anything* to complain about, when so much wonderment was right at my very fingertips every second of every day.

Call it a spell, call it foolishness, call it what you want, but I just *had* to go out into that panorama of black and light, to try and capture one of those fireflies. It was something I'd spent countless hours doing as a pajama-clad boy long, long ago. And I thought that perhaps—just perhaps—I could recapture a little of that fun now, if I could just wrap my finger around one of those glows.

I set my pack against a telephone pole and waded off into the universe, my eyes darting quickly from one tiny exploding pinlight to another.

The first one I lunged for eluded my grasp as easily as if it'd never been there in the first place. But then another flashed inches from my left shoulder and he was instantly mine.

Funny, I thought as I stared at him breathing light across my open palm, but I could have sworn it was so much harder to catch them. This had been too easy, too quick. Not at all the same as when as a boy I'd chased after some for what seemed miles, my one hand holding up my pajama bottom, the other trying not to shake too hard the jar of fireflies I had already captured.

Ah, but of course. *That* was the secret of the fireflies . . . the chase! Then, as now, the fun had been the pursuit of something, not the capture itself. Only I'd been too young then to realize this. All I'd known then was that when I crawled into bed with my jar of crawling lanterns, I had felt so contented, so alive.

It was not the fireflies, light itself, but the vigorous pursuit of that light, that had been the cause of all the energies rushing through my limbs.

I blew on the insect, and it rejoined the other stars.

Standing there with the entire universe revolving around me, I thought of all the incredible profusion of life I'd seen so far on my walk across eastern America. From every inch of space not artificially covered by man, I'd seen so much life showing itself to the heavens.

Even where man had spread his liquid stone and sticky tar, there had still been plants daring enough to try a life in the cracks that had appeared.

More and more, I was convinced man could never wipe life off this planet. He may kill himself, but there will always be *something* taking birth somewhere.

I put the pack back on and continued on to the main highway north of the park. It suddenly occurred to me I was hungry. I'd fed the mind, now it was the body's turn.

In Great Barrington, I barely made it in time to a little supermarket. There, I purchased some more bread and peanut butter and jelly, and a milk, and ate dinner at around eleven-thirty on the steps of a big church across the street. I was back in civilization, like it or not.

Otis, Massachusetts
June 24, 1983

Dear Folks,

Boston draws nearer, and my heart beats faster with excitement. I am a few days walk from that seaport city.

In Boston, my last stop in the United States before Europe and the rest of the world, demands upon my time will be heavy.

If I were just walking, everything would be simple. I would probably be well into France by now.

But, alas, no sooner do I get another two hundred miles down the road than I find I have fallen behind in my journals, in letters I need to write to newspapers to inform them of my impending arrival, in the growing batches of taped interviews I must carefully label.

I also interview people for the books I will be writing later, tape conversations for National Public Radio, do an occasional magazine article, search out interesting subjects to photograph, and fill three journals for each day—the first, recording mileage and places visited, the second, describing people I meet, and the third, summing up personal feelings and adventures.

That's not all. I have almost daily meetings with the media and city officials, take time to explore each area I visit, and finally, "domestic chores"—laundry, personal hygiene, feeding my never-quite-filled stomach, and at the end of the day, searching out a hayloft, an old building, or a cut field to bed down in.

Then there's walking. I must walk at least seven hours to get in twenty-five miles a day. No wonder I go from seven in the morning until ten or eleven at night! Reviewing my mileage log, I find that for nearly every day I walk, I have spent another "resting" and catching up on my work.

I'm not complaining. I'm madly in love with the whole project and falling more deeply in love with it by the hour. How can I not? Writing, traveling and meeting people are three of my greatest loves, and—like some incredible dream come true—I'm filling each of my waking minutes with all three.

Even now I pinch myself from time to time to remind

myself that this is all very real, that I'm not dreaming.

And now the magic of Ireland looms just over the horizon. How blessed can one person be?

Steven

DATE	TIME START	TIME STOP	LOCATION	MILEAGE	TOTAL MILES
8-19-83	6:45 a.m.	11:30 a.m.	Bolton, England, center of town. Ate lunch then went to home of Hilary Blinkhorn to stay weekend. Bolton — Blinkhorn Apt. in Bolton	11 miles	1,467 miles
8-20-83	—	—	Bolton — REST — Blinkhorn Apt in Bolton	—	—
8-21-83	—	—	Bolton — REST — Blinkhorn apt in Bolton	—	—
8-22-83	9:00 a.m.	10:30 p.m.	Apx 2 miles south of Chapel-en-le-Frith. Dinner in town, slept in field, (had to take bus into Manchester)	34 miles	1,501 miles
8-23-83	9:15 a.m.	10:00 p.m.	2.5 miles south of Matlock. Slept in field west of highway.	23 miles	1,524 miles
8-24-83	7:15 a.m.	9:15 p.m.	Nottingham, England. 40 Ebers Road, apt. of Janice Perry. Slept in bushes in someone's side yard.	30 miles	1,554 miles
8-25-83	9:30 p.m.	10:30 pm	3 mile south of Nottingham.	4 miles	1,558 miles
8-26-83	10:15 a.m.	9:30 p.m.	Apx 1 mile south of Oakham. Slept by hedge on west side of A6003.	27 miles	1,585 miles
8-27-83	8:15 a.m.	10:45 pm	3 miles south of Kettering. Slept beneath hedge on farm field west of 509.	15 miles	1,610 miles
8-28-83	8:00 a.m.	11:30 pm	3 miles south of Leighton Buzzard. Slept by water trough behind hedge on w side of A4146.	30 miles	1,640 miles
8-29-83	8:30 a.m.	2:45 p.m.	Hamel Hempstead Police Social & Athletic Club. Slept in woods on N. edge of city. words on N. edge of H. Hempstead	13 miles	1,653 miles
8-30-83	—	—	Hemel Hempstead — REST — center of Beaconsfield, England.	—	—
8-31-83	3:30 pm	12:15am	Slept in home being used by Chris Fellingham.	17 miles	1,670 miles
9-1-83	9:00 a.m.	11:15 pm	2.5 miles south of Bray, England on Ascot road. Slept in field west of road.	13 miles	1,683 miles
9-2-83	9:15 a.m.	4:30 p.m.	Camberley News Office, center of town. Slept in horse stable on King's Ride Road.	14 miles	1,697 miles
9-3-83	4:30 p.m.	10:00 pm	.5 mile north of South Warnborough. Slept in big barn on east side of road.	15 miles	1,712 miles
9-4-83	7:00 a.m.	9:45 pm	West Meon, England. Slept in home of Peter Atkinson.	16 miles	1,728 miles
9-5-83	10:30 a.m.	12:00am	Community center field about 7 miles n-nw of Portsmouth. Slept in field by center. By A27.	15 miles	1,743 miles
9-6-83	7:30 a.m.	9:45 a.m.	Center of Portsmouth, England. Slept in vacant field near Royal Marine Museum & Barracks. Portsmouth Barracks again letters, notes	7 miles	1,750 miles
9-7-83	—	—	Portsmouth — REST — beside historic church, no feet letters	—	—
9-8-83	—	—	Portsmouth/ — REST — no feet letters, vacant lot	—	—
9-9-83	—	—	Portsmouth/ Cherbourg, Fr. — REST — by amusement park, notes, letters	—	—
9-10-83	9:45 a.m.	9:00 pm	Start at docks in Cherbourg, France. Stop for night 3 km s. of Briquebec. Slept in field, D900. 24 km	16 miles	1,766 miles
9-11-83	8:45 a.m.	10:30 pm	2 km north of Periers, France. Slept in field, in tent, behind hedges east of D900. 45 km	28 miles	1,794 miles
9-12-83	9:00 a.m.	8:30 p.m.	3 km west of Gauray, France. Slept in field north of D7. 45 km	30 miles	2,024 miles

This is a sample page from my Log Book, in which I recorded the technical aspects of every day on the Worldwalk. Included in each day's entry were: the date, the time I started walking, the time I stopped walking, the miles/kilometers covered that day, and the total miles walked on the entire journey to that point. I also included where I camped or stayed and a concise description of the day's main events. As you can see, I spent many a night in my sleeping bag in those dewey English pastures.

AUSTRALIA

DATE	TIME	LOCATION	YOUR NAME & ADDRESS	SIGNATURE	
14/2/85	5.17		John Maxwell 1205 Edmondst, Baulkham hills NSW	9/6 Edmond St 639-4760 Baulkham hills NSW	TOUR BUS TOURIST
2/11/85	3.15		B. N. Artmann (Vic) 127 Fitfscue Ave Seaford	B. Attman	TOUR BUS TOURIST
2/11/85	3.5		R R Gardner Lane Cove N.S.W. Aust	R Gardner	TRUE BUS DRIVER
2/11/85	3.15	Oodnadatta Track Stuart Hwy	Brian McLauchlin C/- Aust Pacific Tours	B. McLauchlin	YOUNG TRAINEE
8/11/85	5.45	Marla Bore	David Abel C/- Address Below	D. Abel	YOUNG TOURIST
8/11/85	3.45	Marla Bore	Malcolm Hessey P/O Box 121 Humpty Doo. N.T	M. Hessey	YOUNG TOURIST
9/11/85	7.35 pm	32.375 km S. of Marla Sarda Bluff	Shaun Davidson 2 Perkins St Whyalla. SA	S. Davidson	YOUNG HIGHWAY INSPECTOR
9/11/85	7.36 pm	32.375 km Marla Sarda Bluff	Justin Mann Edward St. Birdwood, SA	J. Mann T.Q.I.	YOUNG HIGHWAY INSPECTOR
11.11.85	1054 am	15 km South of Mt Willoughby	Nadine Bartel 12 North St Collingwood Melbourne	N. Bartel	TOURIST ON BUS
11.11.85	10.58 am	as above	Enid Svenson 1/60 Threechain Rd Port Pirie SA 5540	E. Svenson	GIRLFRIEND OF ABOVE
12-11-85	8.00 am	between Mt. Willoughby and Coober Pedy	Peter Diehl Ulanen str. 27. 4000 Düsseldorf	P. Diehl	GERMAN TOURIST
12-11-85	8.00 pm	70 ks North of Coober Pedy	Geoff Ball 40 Howard St Windsor Gdns Adelaide 5087	G. Ball	GREASEY OR MENTAL
14.11.85	10.00 am	23 miles North Coober Pedy	95 Sycamore Cresent Hawthorndene SA	K. Martin 2783847	OWNER OR DRIVER
14/11/85	10.00 am	The Shell Patch 23 miles NW Coober Pedy	135 Bridgewater Drive Kalamunda (Perth) WA 6076	Paul W	YOUNG...
14/11/85	12.00 Pm	Harry Crocodile's Nest Coober Pedy	Mr. M Schaffner (Mar) 8482 Wila Ch. Schinkenad	M. Schaffner	YOUNG SWISS TRAVELLER
16/11/85	10.17	Harry Crocodiles Nest Coober Pedy	Paul Herman Bannholde (Switzerland)	B. Herman	FRIEND OF ABOVE
18/11/85	10.25	Harry Crocodiles Nest Coober Pedy	Max 17... Hamburg (Switzerland)		CROCODILE HARRY?
19.XI.85	8000	"Crocodile's Nest"	Aron Blumental Coober Pedy, 5723. S.A.	A Blumental	EXTENSION COLLEGE WORKER
20.11.85	11.50	T.A.F.E.	Chrissy Reynolds P.O. Box, Coober Pedy SA 5723	C. Reynolds	EXTENSION COLLEGE DIALEKT
20.11.85	11.32	AS ABOVE	Hayden Keech C/- Dept of TAFE Coober Pedy	H. Keech	AUSSIES
22-11-85	10.56	10 km North Ingomar	Monica & Peter Robinson 51 Andromeda St Rockingham WA	P. Robinson	LOVELY TO MEET YOU STEVE
22-11-85	14.41	81 km South Coober Pedy MT. Sandy	Christine Pleic 9th Aust.	C. Pleic	ROAD CAMP COOK
24-11-85	12.09 pm	75 kms South of Road Camp (MacMahon)	Lynette Honeybust RR 1 Box 195 Godwin Mich 28344	L. Honeybust	AMERICAN TOURIST
"	"	"	Bill Schneider 29316 Lancaster #107 Southfield Mich 48034	Bill S	AMERICAN TOURIST

In addition to my Log Book, I kept what I called my Witness Book. Like the Log Book, I kept the Witness Book to document my route through each of the twenty nations I crossed. Whenever I passed through any village, town, or city, I always had someone, usually an official or professional person, verify with their signature that I had walked through there. Also included were the signatures of persons with whom I stayed. By the way, Crocodile Harry is not a fictional character like the movie character Crocodile Dundee—you'll meet Harry during my Australian letters.

Boston, Massachusetts
July 12, 1983

Dear Folks,

At last I'm in Boston, the final American stop on the first leg of my world walk. I'll visit friends here and on Nantucket Island this week, then hope to be on my way to the Emerald Isle, Ireland, next week.

I think I could not have chosen a much better place than Massachusetts in which to spend my last weeks in America. The land and the people have exceeded my expectations in terms of scenery and friendliness.

Being one of the first areas in our country to be settled, I expected crowded cities, suburbs, shopping centers and highways. Instead, the state is mostly forest and clean, well-preserved villages which still reflect their colonial heritage.

The heavily-forested mountains of western Massachusetts were undoubtedly the most poetic I have crossed thus far. The thick stands of maple, beech, oak, pine, and white and silver birches provided ever-present shade or birdsong or just a secluded spot for a nap.

Surprisingly, traffic was light on the rural roads I traveled. Amazing when one considers that western Massachusetts is but an hour or two by car from New York City or Albany, northern New Jersey, Boston, and Hartford, Conn.

Although I was told that many lakes and streams were affected by acid rain, they looked clean. And what a blessing on those humid, hot days when I frequently jumped into the water to keep from boiling over.

From Springfield in central Massachusetts, I found much of the urban sprawl I'd been expecting, but it was never as bad as in New Jersey. Wisely, people of Massachusetts have incorporated parks and woods into their urban areas.

Thoughtfulness seems to be natural in the "Bay State." One example was on July 5. The Springfield morning newspaper carried a story about me in which the writer mentioned that I had lost twenty pounds on the walk. That morning I was to leave for Boston. I never made it past the suburbs.

So many people, particularly older people, came to see me on the sidewalks to invite me inside for something to eat, that

I never had a chance to get going.

By the end of the day I was stuffed with milkshakes, hamburgers, ham-and-cheese sandwiches, and cake and ice cream, and also had a nice, warm bed to sleep in, which, as my Irish luck would have it, couldn't have come at a better time, for it poured rain that day.

Steven

The walk thus far
114 days
April 1, 1983 - July 23, 1983
1,117 miles walked

THE BRITISH ISLES

STEVEN'S ROUTE

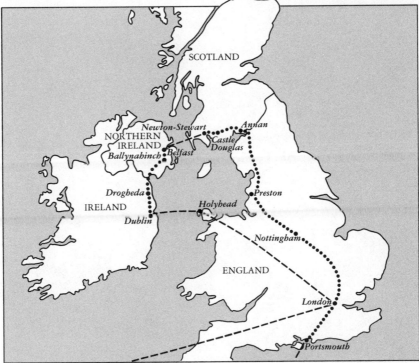

Because I took a bargain flight from Boston to London, rather than the standard fare flight to Dublin, I had to do additional traveling to get to my planned starting point of my walk through the British Isles. From London, I took a bus to Holyhead, Wales, and from there I took a ferry boat directly to Dublin, where I took the first steps on the foreign leg of my journey.

The walk ahead through the British Isles

48 days
July 24, 1983 - September 9, 1983
633 miles

A walkway built into a farmer's fence to allow free passage across his land. Walkways are common in England where the law provides the pedestrian the right of way to cross any property he wants.

London, England
July 25, 1983

Dear Folks,

My first glimpse of the British Isles was not of the jagged coastline of Ireland, as originally expected, but of hedge-rowed meadows in south England.

I had planned to go directly from Boston to Dublin. However, that plan was discarded at the last minute when I discovered I could reach the British Isles for less than $175 ($23 from Boston to Newark International Airport, then $149 to London) on a new economy airline called PEOPLExpress.

I couldn't resist trying the economy airline—especially when regular airlines wanted nearly $500 for a one-way ticket from Boston to Dublin. Common sense told me that train or bus from London to Dublin added to the PEOPLExpress fare couldn't be anywhere near $500. So, true to the spirit of the trek, I decided to risk the economy flight. The risk was that the airline's once-daily flights to London were booked solid until October. That meant I'd have to wait on standby at the Newark terminal hoping someone would cancel his flight and free a seat for me.

London is a popular vacation spot for Americans, so I was apprehensive about the number of other standby passengers I'd find. I visualized waiting at the terminal several days—the "daily" flights to London were only five days a week.

I soon found my worries to be groundless and my luck to be as good as ever.

No sooner had I walked up to the PEOPLExpress's London ticket counter and placed my backpack beside all the other luggage piled there, than a sunburned middle-aged man in shorts and sneakers approached me. "Would you be wanting a reservation, chap?" he asked in a voice heavy with an English accent.

"Why, yes!" I answered eagerly.

He laughed, and with a smile as long as the counter itself, said, "Me son Michael and me daughter Laraine and I come to try standby, too, and found out at one of their other counters that the's 'ad four cancellations to London. If ya 'urry, per'aps ya can grab the last one!"

I glanced at the many other standby hopefuls, dozing in chairs or on the floor, waiting for the ticket counter to open in four hours, and thought, Naw, surely someone else has had the sense to ask at one of the other ticket counters.

"Come, come, you'd best 'urry." It was his beautiful daughter, now tugging at my arm. I followed her to the airline's Melbourne-Florida ticket counter, the only one open at the midnight hour, and asked if the London flight had any empty seats.

"Yes, sir, we do," the clerk replied triumphantly after a check on the computer. "One to be exact."

"I'll take it!"

Laraine smiled. Her father laughed. Even the ticket clerk seemed to take delight in my reaction. With a flourish, he handed me my boarding pass and said, "Your flight attendant will collect the fare after you take off. You can pay cash, with personal check or traveler's checks. Have a nice flight!"

Twelve hours later as our stuffed 747 cruised above the Atlantic at 35,000 feet, I asked Laraine why they had picked me out of all the other standby people to tell about the remaining cancellation.

She pushed her long blonde hair to one side, and said with what I took to be a bit of English humor, "You were the only one awake."

Steven

London, England
July 25, 1983

My first glimpse of my first foreign country, outside of Mexico, was of the soft pastures around London, viewed through gaps in the fog beneath the 747 I was flying in. Somehow it all seemed *too* cliche—the fog, the hedges, the green pastures—and yet there it was, only a few thousand feet below and coming closer every second.

Every one of the other 399 passengers seemed to be buzzing with excitement, and there I sat as calm as a statue. Strange. But then perhaps the magnitude of the project is such that I realize I can't be getting too excited over every little thing, or else I'll wear myself out in no time.

It was not until my luggage was secured that events began to happen which helped to make me realize what an undertaking I was stepping into.

First there was the passport inspector.

"How long do you plan on visiting?"

"Five weeks," I replied without hesitation.

"You say on your card you'll be in Dublin, Belfast, and London."

"Yes. I plan on walking from Dublin to the others."

"Walk! Why?"

"I'm a writer and want to learn about the people in a special manner."

He stamped the passport and handed it back. "Well, the best to you—I expect to be reading about you," he said in such a cheery voice that I couldn't help but grin from ear to ear.

I glanced at the rectangular stamp mark—it was good for six months.

"Thanks."

He winked and flashed the thumbs up. I nodded, very impressed by the cheerfulness exhibited on his part. And yet in the back of my mind I felt a sudden, unexpected twinge of apprehension.

The door to my American past had just clicked shut—I had "officially" entered into the foreign phase of the walk. From here on out I was on my own to a degree I had never really

31

experienced in America. Home was no longer just a car or bus ride away, if I was to find myself in trouble.

Home, it hit me, was no longer here, but *over there*, as far away in time and distance as once the rest of the world had been. And it was only going to get further and further away, at least for a while.

In the afternoon I returned to Earl's Court, after making the rounds of such tourist-packed sights as the Westminster Abbey, Parliament Building, Fleet Street, the Tower of London (which is actually the original fortified city of London, not a tower), and the adjoining Tower Bridge (which I had always thought was "London Bridge").

On the whole, what struck me the most about the city was the overbearing grayness of it. The gray sky, gray soot-coated buildings, black taxis, dark blue and gray-suited businessmen (especially in the Fleet Street district), and the smoggy air all combined to make London hopelessly neutral. Sad to say, the most colorful feature of the city was the Thames River—not its parks and boats, mind you, but the unbroken stream of trash which floats down it out to some doubtlessly growing mound beneath the Atlantic.

More and more as the day wore on I grew anxious to be in Ireland with its green countryside. Quite frankly, one day of stone gray and overcast skies was all I cared for.

From Earl's Court I travelled by train to Uxbridge on the western edge of the Greater London area. Then from Uxbridge to Oxford by bus.

Since no more buses were going westward from Oxford after eleven, I slept that night in the center of the town, in some bushes beside a large parking lot. Twice during the night patrolling Bobbies with noisy walkie-talkies strapped to their belts woke me with their cackling and heavy footsteps.

Each time, however, their flashlight beams passed over and around me, and I escaped detection.

Holyhead, England to Dublin, Ireland
July 27, 1983

The giant, multi-decked ferry ship didn't leave for Ireland until three a.m., after it had unloaded what seemed to be the entire population of Ireland. Sleeping in the noisy, packed waiting room was out of the question, so I entrusted my pack to a young Swedish couple and took to roaming the streets of the old sea town.

Like any coastal fishing town, the smell of rot and fish was as heavy as the fog. Combine that, however, with the dark dress and expressions of the Welsh, especially in the dead of night, and you begin to wonder after so long from which shadowy alleyway it is that an attacker is going to leap.

Down about the middle of a street running along the docks, I spied the flashing neon sign of a fish-and-chips shop, and I made for it, not so much because I was hungry, but more because it looked warm and free of suspicious shadows.

I took my order of fish and chips (french fries) and sat on the step of the tiny place to eat them. They were the first fish and chips I'd ever had outside of the United States and they were almost too delicious to be true.

In America the fish had always been small and previously frozen. The piece I had now was a good one-foot long and six inches wide and as fresh as the water slapping against the dock pilings. The fries were not thin and limp and lukewarm but, rather, thick and crisp and so hot I had to wait over five minutes before my tongue could tolerate them.

At least a dozen times while I was eating, locals walking past smiled amusedly and asked, "Enjoyin' yer fish and chips, are ya?"

How in the world could they tell I was an American eating my first English fish and chips? It was quite obvious by their looks I was doing something out of the ordinary and funny. I tried crossing my legs, eating with my left hand, not blowing on the fries, but they kept on smiling and asking. Finally I just concentrated on enjoying my meal and only answered with a grunt each time the question was put to me.

While returning to the ferry station, a teen-aged boy with

thick muscles and unkempt black hair stepped from a doorway to block my path. He stood perhaps only to my chin, but he acted as if he was the bigger man.

"Wha' be yer name?" he asked me in a voice only Satan could have thought friendly.

"Steve," I answered, all the while watching his hands.

"Would ya be takin' the boat to Dun Laoghaire tonight?" I nodded.

"Steve, do ya 'ave a quid to gi' me fer a box?"

"A box?"

"Smokes."

I'd forgotten that here many of the brands of cigarettes are packaged in cardboard, instead of paper and cellophane.

"Well . . . " I started to shake my head no.

"Are ya on 'olidays?" he pressed.

"You could say that."

"Why Ireland?"

"Never been there."

"Better ya take yer 'oliday in this country."

"Why?"

He edged closer and spoke with a tone of disgust. "The Irish are a lot of dumb trash. There's nothin' over there worth seein' or speakin' to."

"I take it you don't care for the Irish too awful much."

He laughed harshly. "'Tis aren't no secret that there's not much love lost between the Irish and the British." His voice grew louder, more serious. "Ever' time they kill another of our men, I'd like to see the whole of their murderin' lot pushed into the sea!

"Is it any wonder we look down on them? When all's they's good fer is makin babies and murderin'?"

I sensed I'd better move on while his thoughts were occupied with the Irish, and not quids.

He grabbed my shoulder. "What of my quid, Steve? It's two miles to me house, and I got no money on me."

I gently pulled away. "Maybe the walk'll cool you down. Besides," I smiled ever so slightly, "my ancestors were from—"

"Ireland?" He backed off as if I were diseased, then spun about and sulked off, uttering profanities.

I wondered if many other young people in England thought

likewise of the Irish. He hadn't been the first Englishman I'd heard call the Irish lowly, and dumb, and no good. But he'd certainly been the most vehement.

Several hours later I was asleep on the ferry, while it plowed its way across the calm Irish Sea toward Dun Laoghaire, which is about fifteen miles south of Dublin.

The weather when I stepped ashore in Ireland in the dawn was cold—blustery, and spitting rain. Hardly the greeting a tired soul needed. I added a little excitement, though, to the bland setting by riding a double-decker bus to the center of Dublin.

Dublin struck me as a "small big city." There was a heavy mixture of old structures with new ones, none of which was very tall, say over twenty stories. With the usual bumper-to-bumper traffic and crowded buildings, it hardly struck me as a very quaint place. And yet it had something that definitely set it apart from every other town and city I'd seen so far in the British Isles.

It had color. All of the drab conformity of the British was absent. Everyone I saw heading into work was dressed as they pleased and in whatever color and style and degree of orderliness they felt comfortable with.

Dublin was by all appearances a city of individuals, not an institution like London.

But were the people as friendly as I'd always heard them to be?

Swords-Drogheda, Ireland
July 29, 1983

The morning air was chilly and the straw soft and warm, so I stayed snuggled in its depths like some fieldmouse until after nine. I remembered the Irish woman, Flo Warren, I'd met at the birthday party near Pine Plains, New York, and of her advice, "If ever you see an empty barn in Ireland, go and sleep in it without askin' for permission. No one will bother you, that's how friendly they are."

I hoped she was right, because I knew there was lots more hay outside waiting to be brought inside, and the farmer wasn't likely to be much more patient. Not with such an overcast sky above.

Around ten o'clock the farmer and his men helpers caught me. Not in the barn, but outside at a spring-fed watering trough where I was in the middle of shaving.

As he and the tanned, whiskered men grumbled through the gate and drove by in an old Mercedes truck, he cocked his chin to the left and flashed me a look that seemed to say "Ah, life can be tough, can't it?"

I waved and they all waved back cheerfully. Darned if Flo hadn't been right, I chuckled.

Further up the highway, in a tightly-packed little village named Gormanstown, I stopped at a little ice cream and sundry shop which was but two or three feet from the road, and picked up a copy of the *Irish Independent* to see if they'd done a story on me. They had—a nice one with a large photo at the top of page two.

To celebrate, I asked the woman behind the counter for a cone with two scoops of banana-flavored ice cream. While she served it up, I set the paper on top of the counter and read the article.

"Like most Americans, he claims to have Irish ancestors", the writer wrote at one point. They can't even do a news article without a bit of humor, I thought with amusement.

"Is that you in the photo?" the woman behind the counter asked.

"Yes. It's an article about me walking around the world."

She ended up giving me the ice cream for free. "I've no doubt, you'll be the only person I'll meet walking around the world," she remarked quite proudly.

Just north of the village, I passed dozens of delapidated trailer homes parked on the shoulders of the highway on both sides. The trailers were little ones no longer than twenty feet and with only one axle. The tires were still on the wheels, so it looked as if they planned on living beside the highway only temporarily.

Piled outside of the cheap trailers were such things as carpet rolls and auto junk parts for sale. The whole scene was one of a mini ghetto—clothes hanging from bushes and rickety lines, small children running about in soiled clothing and mean looks, and litter and garbage of all sorts lying all about.

Some of the children charged toward me, asking arrogantly for money, usually a two-pence. They were a rough-looking people, and I knew it must be awful trying to cram an entire family into one of those trailers at dinner time, or bedtime.

Since there were no water hook-ups or toilet buildings anywhere, they must have depended upon the hedges and tall weeds of the farms they were camped alongside.

There were some of these nomadic camps, however, where the people looked quite well-off. Their trailers were later models, cleaner, and parked alongside them were new and quite expensive vans and autos.

Just the regular society, though, the "upper class trailers" kept in their own little separate groups from the other "common class" ones.

Later on, I was to learn from several people that the people I had passed living alongside the highway were the "caravan people," or "gypsies" as they were once known. They are a by-product of the Great Potato Famine of the last century.

During the potato crop failure of the 1800's, millions of small farmers who tended their plots on larger, feudal-like farms were uprooted, and forced to give up everything and move on. Some of the rich land barons saw it as a convenient time to shove many of the tenants off their over-populated lands.

The population of Ireland at that time (mid 1800's) was around 9.5 to 10.5 million (depending upon whom you listen to), but after the potato failure was to shrink to just below its present 4.5 million.

Those who emigrated to such areas as the United States were to number around one hundred thousand a year for many years. It is hardly an exaggeration to say that most Irish have relatives in North America. Indeed, nearly every one I was to talk to while in Ireland had someone from their family's past who had moved to Canada or the U.S.

As one retired farmer I talked with, Tom Mills of Belfast, put it so wonderfully, "The families were big, the land small."

Many of this new class of nomads didn't leave the country, however, but chose to stay and remain rootless. They became the gypsies, the forerunners of today's Caravan people. (They are named after the trailers they live out of, which in Europe are known as "caravans," rather than mobile trailers.)

At first, I didn't know what to think when their children came up to me to beg for money. They looked so poor, and yet knowing how children are inclined to waste money on such things as candy, I was able to justify to myself turning away from them.

Yet, they came frequently—frequently enough to be a real nuisance. I was only too glad when I reached the outskirts of the port city of Drogheda and had no more of their camps to walk through.

I stopped at a small grocery store, then sat outside on the street curb to drink a pint of milk and eat some peanut butter sandwiches. No sooner had I taken one bite than yet another beggar approached from an adjoining low-income housing complex. This one, however, was not any child, but a short dark-haired woman of about my age. Tailing her were two little girls, one about eleven pushing a stroller with an infant.

I might have got up and left, except that I had food and things from my pack laying all about.

She came right for me with absolutely no hesitation, like a bee to a flower.

"Good day, dear, kind sir, may the dear Virgin Mary bless ya," she said softly. "Have ya a couple of pounds to give me so's I can feed the young children? They've nothing to eat all day and there's nothing in the house. God bless ya for helping us."

Standing over me in her long, black dress with stains of all sorts on it, and thick white stockings on her thick legs, she knew she had me trapped. When I didn't reply immediately, she pressed harder.

"Just two pounds, sir. God and the Virgin Mary will bless you, and I'll pray for ya."

"Hold it!" I shouted angrily—what upset me the most was not her begging, but the fact that she was practically *demanding* three dollars worth of my money. What ever happened to the "Have you a dime or a quarter to spare, please?"

"Where's your husband at? Isn't he working?" I demanded.

"He left us several months ago. I don't make any money myself, 'cause there's no work. Just a couple of pounds, and I'll pray for ya, dear, kind man."

I looked the children over from the hot pavement. They didn't look the least bit deprived or hungry, and yet how could I really be sure they weren't actually going hungry? Out of the corner of my eye, I noticed the shop keeper looking disgustedly at the beggar woman.

"I tell you what, I'll buy some food for them," I said, with resignation.

She looked a bit disappointed. But only for an instance.

"Yes . . . yes. May holy Mary bless ya."

I had to gather everything back into the pack, throw away my sandwich which was now hard, and carry the whole load back into the store. I got a quart of milk from a rack on the floor (milk is often kept at room temperature in Ireland's stores) and a loaf of bread, and brought them out to her.

She took them without saying so much as a "thank-you" and walked away. I went back in to get something to eat in place of the sandwich.

While I was standing in line at the register counter, I looked outside and saw the beggar woman talking to a carload of caravan people who had just pulled up.

They all laughed heartily at something she said, and then one of the women in the front seat of the Ford Capri stuck a pound note out the window. The beggar woman handed over the food and took the note. She then waved them goodbye, put the note in her pocket, and shooed her children further along the street.

Right then, I decided I'd not give in to any more beggars on the rest of my walk, except perhaps for those who were crippled and obviously unable to work.

I felt incensed and hateful deep inside about all the begging I'd had to face that day. If only a handful of beggars in Ireland could make me feel so upset, what would I be like in countries like India or Bangladesh?

Better to set some sort of iron-clad policy now, rather than risk a violent confrontation later in a more strange, and perhaps more hostile environment. In one sense, I guessed the beggars had been good for me—they'd forced me to face the situation while I was still early into the walk.

A typical country lane in the British Isles lined with stone walls built by feudal serfs.

Ballynahinch, Northern Ireland
August 3, 1983

Dear Folks,

There is absolutely no doubt in my mind from which of my ancestors I inherited my trait of not worrying about the future. Unquestionably it was from my Irish forebears.

I've walked over one hundred miles through the Irish countryside the past week—from Dublin to Ballynahinch, about fifteen miles south of Belfast—and I've yet to meet any likely candidates for an ulcer. Indeed, never have I experienced so much song and laughter and good food and, yes, brew, as I have in my all-too-short hike through the green hills and valleys of this tiny nation.

Surely the national slogan of the 4.5 million Irish who still remain on this largely agricultural island must be something similar to, "What! Me worry?" Beset by enough problems to make any populace moan and groan, the Irish have a seemingly bottomless zest for the pleasures of life.

"Worry is the interest you pay for tomorrow's troubles," Caitlin Chairbre, a feisty mother of six and a pub owner in Drogheda told me one evening. "In Ireland we live from day to day, still believing strongly that everything in good time will be righted by God, or fate, or whatever.

"Aye, it is on our faith that's always made us different, made us strong in spite of all the troubles and peoples who's sought to rule us."

She handed me yet another dark and foamy pint of Guinness that someone in the packed pub had bought for me and continued, "Drink and be merry today, for tomorrow may not come! That's what the average working man here will tell you." Then, with a twinkle in her hazel eyes, she added, "Which makes owning a pub all the much better, you understand."

Caitlin (Irish for Cathleen) so well epitomized the warmth I was to find everywhere in Ireland, be it in the Catholic South or the Protestant North. Somehow, she had heard of me walking north from Dublin and had sent her son, Fiacre, out on the main highway between Dublin and Drogheda to search for me. When he'd found me, he'd left his car beside the busy highway and walked the last two miles into the ancient town on the banks of the Boyne River.

For the next two days I was treated to several sumptuous Irish dinners of locally caught salmon, potatoes, oxen tongue, home-grown peas and tomatoes, freshly-baked bread, gooseberry and custard desserts, and gallons upon gallons of hot tea with milk and sugar. In between the meals and the evening songfests in the pub, we were to take trips to the nearby Irish Sea castles in the surrounding grassy hills.

It was like everything I'd ever seen in picture books and movies—tightly-curved lanes, tall and endless hedges, straw-thatched farmhouses, and lush pastures dotted with what must be the world's most contented-looking dairy cows and sheep.

Even though the car we were packed into—her wildly red-haired daughter Roisin's tiny black Citroen Charleston— was no bigger than a bathtub, the lanes we sped along were barely wide enough for other autos to pass. It certainly made for a lot of wide-eyed gasps on my part as we darted into each blind curve—for the Irish drive as hard and furiously as they drink their stout.

But then one must remember that in Ireland, life is to be lived, and that worrying is for those who've gone and died before they had the chance to make amends. Best to share good times with good company and part with the words, "Zo N-eiri an bozair leaz." (May the road rise with you.)

Steven

Larne, Northern Ireland
August 8, 1983

Dear Folks,

All the way from Newry, on the border between Catholic Ireland and Protestant Northern Ireland, to the city limits of Belfast itself, the people of the North kept emphasizing to me that violence in their province is overplayed by the press.

"You'd not know it even existed, to just walk down the street," I was told by several well-meaning people. But they were wrong. Very wrong.

My first encounter with the tension which exists in the daily lives of these people who consider themselves British, not Irish, was in the rural farming village of Dromara. There I snapped a photo of a policeman coming out of a heavily-fortified police station. In less than one minute, I was surrounded by several armed policemen demanding to know who I was and why I was taking photographs.

In Ireland, I didn't see a single firearm—in Northern Ireland, particularly Belfast, I saw not only firearms in the hands of hundreds of policemen and British soldiers, but also many army helicopters patrolling overhead and dozens of heavily-armored troop carriers constantly darting from street to street. Quite frankly, to me the scene in Belfast during the two days I was there was very much like some war zone!

How a person can claim with a straight face that there are hardly any "troubles" when he or she can't go shopping in the downtown area without first passing through a police check station to be frisked for weapons or bombs is beyond my understanding. Yet, so used to it all have the people of Northern Ireland become, that they are able to believe so.

Perhaps the one incident that epitomized that whole incredible experience was a terrifying, yet at the same time humorous, occurrence that happened to me this morning in the Northern Ireland port of Larne.

I was greeted by the Lord Mayor Thomas Robinson in the elegant, second-story meeting chambers of the city hall. He explained to me his troubles in attracting new industry to his recession-hit area because of the bad image associated with the sectarian violence. Then, just as he was winding up our discussion with a plea for better publicity, the doorman came rushing into the room to tell the mayor that he believed there to be a bomb planted on one of the first floor windowsills.

"It is a package with a wire poking from it. I've telephoned the police, sir," the harried-looking elderly man said.

The mayor motioned for me to be calm. "I'll be right back. I'd best give it a look," he said, rushing off after the old man.

In the meantime, I was anything but calm. Nervously, I stood in a far corner of the huge and long room expecting any minute to be blown out onto the street below.

Suddenly, a disturbing thought came to mind. What had I done with the white plastic sack that I had my dirty laundry in? And didn't it have a plastic drawstring? I had taken it out of my pack when I'd come into Larne intending to wash the clothes before meeting the mayor. But there'd been too little time. So, when I'd stopped at the front of the city hall to adjust my pack and comb my disheveled hair, I'd absent-mindedly set the sack on a windowsill.

I darted downstairs just in time to fetch the "suspected bomb" from the hands of the law. It was an embarrassing situation for all, but luckily Irish humor prevailed.

For all the sectarian troubles and economic woes, the Irish—on both sides—were the most fun-loving and open people I could ever hope to meet. As in most cases of violence, those at the center of the problems are in the minority and are largely shunned by the rest.

"We simply must keep our faith," one tiny, fragile old lady reminded me a moment ago, just before I boarded a ferry for Stranraer, Scotland.

Steven

Newton Stewart, Scotland
August 10, 1983

Dear Folks,

Scotland rose from the eastern horizon of the North Atlantic to enchant me for the first time several evenings ago. Low, softly-wrinkled, and shrouded in the red mist of a melting sun, its gold-tinted humps had lolled on the waves in such a playful manner as to make me think of whales.

With the white plume of a lighthouse spouting from its most forward ridge, one particularly lonely peninsula captured my attention for the longest time. I was fascinated by how the chilly sea breezes swept across its unpopulated hills and dells with total freedom. In the simple unbroken void resting upon its grasses, I sensed a pocket of time and space where the past still weighs very heavily on the second hand of the present. Where, instead of being disrespectfully trampled under, history is simply allowed to crumble away at its own pace, like the ancient Celtic crosses on the emerald Ireland I had sailed away from earlier that day.

As during my first view of this old country, my passage overland on foot these past several days has been steeped in quiet contemplation. Life here in the farmlands of south Scotland strikes me as being so uneventful that even the devil of the Irish, if he will pardon me for saying so, would be hard-pressed to cause much of a commotion among these people on any given day.

Now, lest you think that I am about to let my Irish heritage show through by making jest of the conservatism and the sobriety the Scots are universally labeled with, let me clearly state that such is not to be the case here. You see, there is someone I met three days ago whose experiences with the Scottish mentality will do well enough in illustrating how staid life is in these parts. He is someone of unquestionable integrity and vastly studious of his fellow Scots' moral character, as well as a champion in the garnering of respect. He is, as a matter of fact, a chief constable.

Mister Murray and I met in the village of Glenluce, where for over two decades he has been the only policeman of that quaint highway town's seven hundred or so residents. I had

gone to his station in his home to request an "official signature" from the town for entry into my logbook, my excuse
being that I'd like to get credit for this rather lengthy walk I've
ventured on. Whereupon, he, being duly impressed and all,
instructed his matronly wife to boil us a pot of tea, while he
took the opportunity to learn more about his uniformed peers
on my side of "the waters."

"Is it really like on the American coop showz I watch on
me telly, what where the police goo rooshin' oofter t' roobers
wi' flashin' stroobs ayn lewd sarnz?" he mumbled with traditional aplomb.

I contemplated for a few very interesting seconds what
"flashin' stroobs" and "lewd sarnz" might be, decided with a
bit of disappointment he was talking about flashing strobes
and loud sirens, and finally settled for nodding with my nose
buried in my tea cup. "But t' roobers connear it ayn git 'way!"
he said.

This time I was more polite and nodded with a sugar wafer
poking from between my lips. He rubbed his balding head and
inquired with still more disbelief in his voice, "You mean to
tell me the policemoon really use all them big goonz, too?"
Again, I had to concur with the television dramas.

He shook his head in amazement, saying he had always
thought the policemen in those American shows were too
much like something from another universe to be believable.
What a frightening place to live—or even visit, he said, as
much to his wife as to me. Pointing to a shiny black truncheon
the length of a tall man's forearm, he assured me that that club
was the only weapon he'd ever had in his twenty-six years of
keeping the law in Glenluce. "Ayn not woonce 'ave I 'ad to pool
it froom me belt," he boasted with pride, adding with a laugh,
"Ayn I 'ope I nev'r doo! Cuz I'll a toon a paperwook to fill out
explainin' why I pooled it on soomeone."

I had to laugh, too. Back in the hills of the Ohio Valley
where I was from, the thought of a policeman lasting twenty-six years with only a billy club for protection would have
seemed absolutely preposterous. A policeman without his pistol, his big car, his shotgun, his club and, yes, all those big
flashing "stroobs" would be . . . well, he wouldn't be a *real* cop
in the eyes of most.

By the third cup of tea, I got around to asking the good constable what the most serious crime was he'd ever had to face in Glenluce. Surely like any veteran policeman in the State he'd seen his share of violence. And, from the way his eyes lit up after a brief spell of pondering, I just knew he had come up with a real thriller, one that would prove the Glenlucians were as normal as the rest of us.

The worst thing that had ever happened took place just a few weeks before, he said gravely. The perpetrators had been a handful of the local lads who were having a wake at one of the area's pubs for a buddy killed in an auto accident down in England's way. Came the ten o'clock closing time of all pubs in the British Isles, and the lads seemed a bit reluctant to start for home. So, in strode the large form of Constable Murray to kindly refresh their sense of law and order. At which time a few of the more high-spirited "snook" out a side door, ran around to the street, and carefully lifted—by themselves—the constable's tiny car off the asphalt, only to set it back down a minute later in the same spot—on its roof!

Since those still in the pub were more than willing to "right matters," so to speak, with Constable Murray, all was forgiven within short time. True, an actual crime of a shameless nature had besmirched the streets of Glenluce, but there were more important things to be worrying about, like sleep, than to bother with all that "paperwook."

Steven

Castle Douglas, Scotland
August 12, 1983

The day passed uneventfully, but after dusk all hell broke loose.

First off, I should mention that the day started off like something out of *Watership Down* and ended like something out of Hitchcock's *The Birds.*

I awakened early this morning, having slept in a blanket on a plastic ground-cloth in the middle of a soft, grassy field covered with thick dew. I looked over to my left to see what at first I took to be dozens of weed clumps. Until, that is, they moved!

Rabbits. Huge ones! Everywhere. All around me, too. All peacefully nibbling away in the freshly cut grass of the field I was sleeping in. Never in my life had I seen so many rabbits, and many were the size of jack rabbits.

I stayed still for many moments, completely fascinated with what I was seeing. When I rose, they all scampered off into surrounding hedges. I could actually hear them running off. It was so quiet their every hop sounded as clear as a footstep of a human on a porch floor. With so many big rabbits running wildly every which way for their lives, it sounded as if a cross-country race had just commenced. It looked so funny and so incredible that I had to laugh out loud. Which got me off to a nice start.

I had an easy, flat road with wide shoulders for most of the day. I made excellent mileage and had lots of time to study the countryside daily. (I saw few towns or people in trek through Scotland. A very lonely sort of place.) I marvelled at how lush and bountiful the land of this country was. Birds, livestock, rabbits, pheasants, salmon-filled rivers, streams, thick fields of grain—such a rich land, and so blessed with the space and solitude needed for everything to thrive.

Definitely a paradise at this time of the year, but I shuddered at how cold it must be in the winter with such wide open spaces, and the sea but a handful of miles away.

Towards dusk, the ocean once again came into view on my left. I passed occasional small forests that, as it grew darker, looked thicker and sounded noisier. Such a nice surprise to see the forests after my walk through Ireland, where it had seemed that every foot of land had been put to some farming use. Animals in Scotland seemed so fearless of man, and I saw all sorts of them all day long.

In the evening, gusts of wind started to blow at me. Near midnight, I snuck up to the woods on top of a hill and pitched my tent deep in the tall and thick strand of deciduous trees. It was very dark and very quiet in such thick cover.

I felt safe and serene and lucky I had found such good cover, for a strange wind was coming in from the sea. I started to fall into a nice sleep when I realized that the swaying trees were making an awfully odd sound. Goosebumps rose on my arms. Looking out, I could just barely ascertain that there was something other than leaves on these trees.

Each time the trees swayed far to one side and then far to the other, there'd be a long and mournful kind of sound. Like a sick chicken the size of the Empire State Building, I thought.

Those weren't big leaves up there fluttering in the wind. Those were wings! Millions of them!

What the ___? . . . I stood up outside of the tent and gazed in awe at what must have been thousands of black birds or crows, or maybe ravens, roosting on the tree limbs that were at least thirty to fifty feet above my head.

Now, my whole body was covered with goose bumps. The sound they made was eerie, and in the pitch black I could just imagine bigger—*much bigger*—black and winged *things* staring at me from maybe even just an arm's length away. That was how black it was. With the sky clouded over, the thick tree limbs and leaves, the cover of black-feathered wings, and the night, I might as well have been blind for what little detail I could make out.

I was drowning in blackness—a blackness that moaned so pathetically in the wind. It was like the moaning of a million doomed souls. Aware of all the emptiness around me, I shuddered at the thought of how alone I really was.

I retreated into my tent and even tried sleeping with my head under the blanket to diminish the noise. But it only seemed to grow louder and louder. And my goose bumps were getting bigger and bigger.

It was getting to be too much for me. Too scary, for I thought I sensed more than the birds with me in that forest.

And, so many unanswered questions in my frantic mind. If the birds had been there all along, why hadn't they made any sounds while I was walking through the woods and setting up my tent? After all, the wind had been blowing then, too. And, if they had come after I'd settled into the tent, why hadn't I heard them landing in the trees? Such a huge number of birds could not come or go without making quite a racket.

The more I thought about it, the more I scared myself.

And why were they making such a horrible sound? They did it with such perfect harmony.

Finally, I dressed quickly, grabbed my blanket and plastic ground-cloth, and beat a hasty retreat to the road, leaving everything else to the forest with its moans.

Coming out of the woods into the semi-grayness was such a relief. Little did I know, however, that the frights were not over.

I wrapped the light-colored blanket around me like a poncho to ward off the slightly chilly wind, and headed down the long hillside to cross the highway and sleep on the ground in the heavily-weeded woods on the other side of road.

At the road, I had to climb over a gate in the hedge to get to the road shoulder. I paused on the gate's top board for a few seconds, tottering uneasily in the wind, then leaped down toward empty road. The blanket flared about me like some sort of giant wings.

Just as I hit the gravel shold something big *whooshed* by, let out a frightful shriek, and then made a horrible racket.

"What the bloody 'ell?" a loud voice screamed out more frightened than angered.

I couldn't answer right off, for I was too busy trying to figure out if my heart was still pumping anymore. Whatever or whoever it was that I had scared, had scared me even more. I had felt sure that it had been the *thing* from the woods that had made a pass at me, after letting me think I was "off the hook," so to speak.

What it was, though, was simply an Australian bicyclist—a chap my age named Peter. He was on his way to Shranrier to catch a ferry to Ireland and was hoping to ride all night. When

I'd leaped out of the bushes, the huge ghostlike figure I'd made had frightened him so badly he'd crashed his bicycle. But, luckily not seriously enough to hurt it or him.

"You nearly stopped my heart," he gasped.

When I realized just how terribly I must have scared him I couldn't help but laugh long and hard. I laughed so hard tears came to my eyes. After all the tension of the past hour, it was such a good feeling to have something to laugh about. And, best of all, to have some company.

Scotland was beautiful and big, but of lately was a little too quiet for me anymore. The people in the villages were nice, but to them I was just another passing tourist or someone else on his way somewhere else, and they said little more than the bare number of pleasantries they could get by with.

The Scots I'd met had been reserved and cautious, and perhaps a bit suspicious of me. None had been at all as open and trusting as the Americans or the Irish, and I was finding myself with too much time to myself.

Peter, thank goodness, was a typical, friendly Australian, and for about twenty minutes we shared some of his bisquits and a couple cups of tea he brewed up over a tiny, butane camp stove.

We sat behind the hedge out of the wind, and between us he set in a sitting position a little, stuffed K bear he called Ted.

"My charming travel companion," he laughed. "Without 'em, I'd be a lot lonelier. Never saw such a snobby, say-nothing group of people like the English.

"Wish this wind would push me toward Ireland a little faster. I hear they still know how to laugh."

I hoped he was wrong about the English. I'd had enough of the cold wary manner of the majority of the Scots along A75.

England was a lot longer than either my Irish or Scottish treks, and I certainly didn't fancy the prospect of spending most of my time there staring out at the countryside like I'd had to do here.

Peter was from the Melbourne area, and was spending his "'oliday" bicycling the entire British Isles. He had been totally discouraged by what he had said was a country full of "bored, scared, petty, loud-voiced people whose favorite way to live was to stick their face to a telly screen and think of as many little things as possible to gossip or complain about."

He loved to joke and poke fun at things, and when I told the tall, gangly, blonde-haired Peter why I was jumping out of bushes in the middle of the night scaring people to death, he nearly never stopped laughing.

"You let a bunch of bloomin' birds scare you down 'ere to sleep in the weeds?" he roared. "And *you're* expectin' to walk around the world?"

I should have been embarrassed, but he made it all sound so absurd I had to laugh with him.

"But you would never have believed the sound these birds made. And it was *so* dark in those trees," I mildly protested.

He pushed away his stove and cups and tea bags and biscuits.

"I got to see what it is that could 'ave been so bloody scary," he said, indicating he wanted to go up to the woods.

We climbed over the gate and walked briskly up through the wind toward the trees. When we entered the trees, again there were no sounds of any sort to hint of the birds in the trees. However, it was as dark as ever, and I had a difficult time finding the tent, even though it had a light-blue rain sheet over it.

At the time, I told him to stare up into the limbs for several seconds and he'd begin to see all the birds clustered up near the tops of the trees.

"Have you a flashlight?" he asked a bit increduously.

I didn't—I hadn't had one the entire trip. "You're either a fool, or have bloody good eyes," he murmured, staring upwards.

Sure enough, there the birds were. To my disappointment, though, now they weren't making anymore moaning noise, just an occasional squawk, or flutter of wings. The wind wasn't swaying the trees so much any more, and I figured they didn't feel so apt to be complaining any longer. I explained to Peter that this was nothing at all like I'd experienced.

"Have you a piece of note paper?" he asked.

I crawled into the tent and came back out with a copy of *The Standard*, a Scottish newspaper. He rolled it tightly, then took a lighter from his pocket, set one end of it on fire, and held it high above his head.

The flame flickered and hardly even gave off enough light to illuminate the top of Peter's head, but then, very quietly, it flamed much brighter and cast a bright spooky glow that reached well up into the trees.

What we saw made the both of us gasp.

There were even more birds than I'd thought. Indeed, they seemed thicker than the very leaves. But, it was not that so much that made me gasp, as their size . . . enormous! Blinking, shifting uneasily, staring back at us like beaked, goliath crows. Surely, just like the rabbits I had seen this morning had been the size of small dogs (I mean they could have *eaten* the little cottontails that we have back in Ohio!), these long-beaked crows (were they crows?) were like small eagles in size.

Peter was the quietest I'd heard him since our meeting, and he looked intense, his eyes not leaving the birds, who seemed to be growing more restless by the second. He tipped the roll of newspaper a bit to one side to make it burn even more fully, and the flame flared several more inches.

The birds apparently did not care for the extra light, and from somewhere in our nearly solid ceiling of thick, curved beaks, long talon-like claws, staring beady-black diamond eyes, and rippling cape of feathers, there issued a loud, rasping shriek that nearly made Peter drop the torch.

"Blimey!" he shouted and, like me, started walking backwards when all the other birds started likewise shrieking.

The noise they made was like a million old hags laughing and crying and screaming all at the same time, and added to all that was the rustling of countless feathers, restless, it seemed, to be rid of this intrusion into their domain of black peace.

"Son of a . . ." the remainder of the torch was flung to the grassy forest floor. Peter had been so intent, the flame had reached his fingers and taken a few licks at his skin.

The torch light flared for a few seconds as the paper uncurled and became easier for the flame to devour, but then it was gone and once again we were in darkness— a darkness all the more black now because our eyes had adjusted to the light even as the fire flickered, grew tiny, then whiffed out. The voices and rustling of our winged company grew all the louder and bolder.

Something big *swooshed* so close to my head, I could have

reached out and touched it, and this time, whatever it was, it wasn't a bicyclist, that I was sure of. Peter cursed aloud and stepped into my side as several more of the invisible denizens made close pases at our bodies.

Scenes of Hitchcock's *The Birds*, scenes of the time my best friend and I walked into a swarm of bats, and scenes of talons and sharp beaks as thick as my fingers flashed through my mind.

Involuntarily, I raised my hands toward my eyes, and looking over to Peter, was able to see that he had done likewise.

The din the birds were making by then was also too much for my ears to tolerate. It was as if the whole lot of them had one mind—a mind that had gone totally berserk.

And no longer did it seem to be just us and the birds—but it was like the whole forest was joining in the lunacy.

There was movement everywhere—the air, trees, tent, birds, us—flapping, or screeching, or cursing, one gusting, or prattling, or bellowing, or snapping—this was something out of Poe, or Stephen King!

We dived into the tent, and I zipped the little tongue-shaped nylon door as quickly as I could.

Crouched in the four-foot-high pup-tent like trapped coal-miners, we had to practically shout to hear one another even though we were but inches away.

"The're treatin' me like I's some bug they was goin' to eat!" he shouted with noticable nervousness in his voice.

"Yes!" I shouted back—I'd felt the same. I'd been expecting them to start pecking at my sunburned skin, particularly my eyes, any second.

For many minutes the tent was awash in a stormy sea of wind and screeches, and we were forced, more or less, to sit quietly and marvel at this bizarre tempest swirling all about us.

Then . . . then . . . dead silence. So deathly quiet I thought I could hear my out-of-control heartbeat, and Peter's, also.

Were they gone, were we free at last, or was this some sort of demonic trickery—the silence before the real storm breaks loose?

Apprehensively, I unzipped the door flap and gazed out at the tree limbs above, half expecting a beaked spear to come screaming at my face. Overhead I still saw much fluttering, but only of leaves, and then I saw stars and empty branches.

They were gone just like that. As if it had been one bird—not thousands—they had moved on in total unison.

Paradise had returned. Scotland and the devil were once again back in their respective places.

Peter and I returned to his waiting bicycle, "My ten speed Mercedes," and Ted, "Ah, my dear, you should have seen it . . . the Gods were screaming for your sacrifice, but I wouldn't give in—you're the only true friend I got".

I hated to see him go, but I sent him off down the empty highway with the encouraging knowledge that in Ireland he'd find the laughter and the dreamers he was seeking.

"That's good to know. I thought I was going to have to try somewhere like Harlem," he replied cheerily.

Then it was a couple of handshakes, one for him and one for Ted, who sat latched to the handlebars, and he was gone.

And the silence was back.

He had told me his last name as he was peddling off, and I'd promised not to forget it and to visit him if I made it to Melbourne.

But sometime during the silent night his name stole away, too.

That night, I slept in the weeds.

Shap to Milnthorpe, England
August 16, 1983

Such unexpected and incredible beauty today. From the gray and gloomy little factory village of Shap, where I stopped for half an hour in a steady, cold rain to eat lunch (can of baked beans, pint bottle of milk, tea biscuits) on the steps of a school, to Kendal I was to cross over some of the most hauntingly scenic countryside I've ever seen. Like something out of a *National Geographic* or photo book.

What I found today was exactly the British Isles I'd been expecting all along. Miles upon miles upon miles of thick meticulously and expertly-laid stone walls neatly griding grassy and treeless meadows that contained large, fat sheep and occasional brown Jersey cows with brass bells around some of their necks.

The farms I passed were old and massive and the buildings long and tall and made of thick brown stone and dark slate roofs. Many of the people who lived in this stretch (and there were very, very few) looked to be wealthy sheep and dairy cow farmers whose families had resided here for many hundreds of years.

The land continued to rise all day and at times looked so much like the Wales I'd seen on the bus ride to Holyhead. Although the rain and gray skies never ceased, I actually enjoyed it all the more. For it lent a moodiness and mysteriousness to the land that made it look all the more ancient.

The land itself, as it stretched away for endless miles upon miles of grass, sloped and round-topped mountains, was enough to make me walk very slowly and with awe. The road I was on wound with many tight curves up the sides of these open mountains, and there were few vehicles. At the top of the highest pass the sky's heavy clouds rolled overhead at what seemed to be but an arm's length away, and the wind blew furiously and totally unhindered. There were not even any more of the barbed or stone fences. It was all too easy to think of myself as being on the western American plains or perhaps on a treeless island like the Falklands that I'd seen on the evening news during the recent war between Britain and

Argentina.

Nothing to indicate any other life on this world but some clumps of weeds and a lone, forelorn-looking red telephone booth.

As I wound down the other side of the Cumbrian hills, I saw even less people—only bigger sheep farms and so many miles of the tall stone walls I couldn't help but be amazed.

The walls were around five feet high (some higher than eight or nine feet) and at least eighteen inches thick and built entirely of unmortared gray, rough—shaped flat stone. They looked to have been built hundreds of years ago, and yet they were in such perfect order—hardly a stone out of place, even though each farm must have had dozens of miles worth of the walls boxing the meadows on every bit of land, no matter how steep-sided the sides of the hills and mountains.

On the south side of the range I crossed, there was a sheep farm right beside the road, and I asked for some water. A young, brown-haired farm wife answered the right door of the double home, and in her arms she held a naked young boy of about two that she was so proud of. His name was Steven, too.

She gave me some tea, and then surprised me with a box of cookies and biscuits. I helped myself to a couple, and she had me take a handful more. It was so nice there, I thought, and from the way she smiled and talked and from the sparkle in her eyes each time she looked at Steven, she looked as if she couldn't be any happier with life.

Across the road I sat on a stone wall and watched a muscular sheep farmer and his son below herd sheep into a dipping pen and then drag them through and under the reddish-brown dipping fluid that filled a ten-foot-long slope-bottomed cement trough in the ground. Off to one side in another area, two little black and white sheep collies lay nervously watching the loudly complaining sheep. The work looked to be hard and tedious for the son would grab a sheep by a horn and the rear quarters and dump it into the trough at the deep end, and the father, straddling the two-foot-wide ditch, would hook a metal hook onto each sheep's horns and push it completely beneath the dip solution several times, then let it swim out the other end to join its miserable and baaing fellow companions.

I had to smile and feel frustrated at the same time. The father, just like a true country gent, was dressed in a white shirt and neat cool trousers and a gray gent's driving cap. He almost looked like he belonged in an office, except for the knee-high rubber boots and the sheep passing under his legs. Unfortunately I had no camera film to record him or the scenery.

When they'd dipped perhaps one hundred of the kicking and complaining animals, the father slipped on a spotless wool tweed jacket and called the dogs to attention. They were so eager, they leaped over three walls to be with the sheep the farmer was herding into the adjoining pasture.

I watched the man, the sheep, and the ever-circling and darting dogs move slowly and steadily up the side of the mountain slope, as effortlessly as if the land were flat. The man was at least fifty-five-years-old, I figured, judging from the apparently mature age of his son (who went to work on a tractor), and yet he never looked to be a bit slowed by the sharp steepness of the land. He and the animals moved on, upwards, ever higher.

He will live to be very old and work until that day comes, I thought. For this was the sort of land that only tough people with much patience could ever call home. Here, surrounded by so much space and land and cloud, one had only basics to deal with—none of the innumerable intrusions of others that are a part of living in cities.

Feeding trout off one of the old medieval bridges in northern England.

English Countryside
August 23, 1983

Beautiful lush and grassy hill country. Towns are smaller and very, very old. Many rich stone-walled farms and occasional massive mansions. Quite pastoral and sparsely populated. Liked it very much. Perfect for walking.

Ventured off A6 at one point near Bakewell to walk through countryside on one of the many public footpaths I've seen. A pure treat—crystal clear stream with deep pools and trout (took off my clothes and somehow found the nerve to take a plunge in the ice-cold water to bathe), thickly-grassed dairy cow and sheep meadows, wooden step-ways in the fences, waterfalls and a lake with dozens of wild ducks, many more of the beautiful trout beneath the falls, thick forests on the nearby hills and other side of the lake, and no other people. There was no path as such but just the steps in the fences. With the heavenly scenery and quiet and the soft-gray mistiness, it was (for at least two kilometers) the best I'd seen of England since near Shap. Such an incredibly deep sense of mysticalness I felt when I passed through these short parcels of natural beauty England put forth every so often. There was still magic here, even with all the traffic and row houses and construction.

This evening, at dusk, I became all the more certain that the same spirits that had once inspired writers to use this land for so many tales of magic and heroism still dwelt here.

It was dusk, right before the sky gave up the last vestiges of sunlight, that I looked on a tall hill over Matlock to see what looked to be this ruin of what had once been a large castle. The castle walls looked as black as the soul of the devil himself, and the gray sky seemed to swirl angrily above it, as if part of a large flag of defiance.

Beneath the dark and almost featureless structure still remained the walled hillside plots of what must have been many serfs. As I watched it and it watched Matlock, the sky went from gray-black to all black, and from the valley below the castle rose a ghostly mist, which slowly crept up the hillside plot by plot. How many nights had the mist and the castle and the night sky rendezvoused? How many more of these silent meetings on the hill yet to come?

Yes, the castle was but a decaying relic of men's past, but what of the souls its sight had mesmerized and stirred to contemplation? What of all the souls clothed in mail and silk that had dwelt within that stone edifice, and of those that had toiled to keep its masters satisfied, and of those—like me— who had only watched from afar? Had they all dissipated as completely, as the very mist clawing at the castle must do with the return of the light? I did not know. All I did know was I was not far from them, wherever they were now.

Sheep grazing in lush meadows around Nottingham, England.

Nottingham, England
August 25, 1983

I spent the early morning at the offices of the *Nottingham Evening Post.* After the interview, I was treated to a large breakfast in a guard house by the back lot entrance. Very friendly guards. Much tea and chat. They let me store my pack in their room.

At the breakfast of eggs, sausage, tomato, and tea and toast, I started talking to two upper middle-aged women sitting nearby smoking cigarettes (Marlboros, the most popular brand in England, it seems), and talking and laughing loudly. At the sound of my words they looked at me with surprised looks, then at each other.

"My goodness, Pratty, the purty young t'ng said sumptin' t'us, I do believe," the older said to the other.

"Well, he can't be fr' 'ere then!" the other burst out.

They both cackled delightfully and took quick drags on their cigarettes. Then, with a breath of smoke the first one— who was tall and skinny and heavily wrinkled and dressed in a black blouse and red stretch slacks beneath a head of blond-gray, straight perm hair—said to me, "Where ya from, honey? Lordy, you're too nice to an Englishman. America?"

When I said I was, she cackled and gave the other one, who was shorter, heavy, with gray, curly hair and dressed in a polka-dotted blouse and gray dress and tennis shoes, a friendly little shove.

"Oh, I just knew it!" the other exclaimed. "Them Yankee boys are such dolls! Ohhh, they aren't so high and mighty to talk to us low 'uns," She looked at me, "Are ya?"

They were the morning cleaning ladies, it turned out, and they brought their tea cups and cigarettes over and sat beside me. They both spoke with a very pronounced cockney that at times made it difficult to understand their words. They were as raw as any two women anywhere, and we had an excellent time with all their animated gestures and high mocking voices. Foremost in our discussion was the stratified English social system.

"I was in America once, you know, where's all the bad men

were always gettin' blasted away—"

"Chicago?"

"Yes, that's it. I was there to visit me niece and we went to a funeral and—ohhh my!—I couldn't believe 'ow much the dead woman looked so beautiful. Why the wonders the funeral people in America do. She looked better dead than she'd *ever* looked alive!"

They snorted themselves silly with laughter. "Well, go on ya. Tell 'em the rest," prodded Whissy, the tall one.

Pratty made herself sort of stiff like the corpse, and ran her rough, red-nailed hands down over her dress as she spoke, "And the clothes they 'ad on that woman. Sooo pretty and cute kind'a! Polky dots and frills and silky material. I wanted so much to reach out and feel 'er to see if what I was lookin' at was *real*.

"But that wasn't the half of what I'd seen at the funeral, Stevie. No sir!"

She was really getting into her story now and grew more animated. "'eve, if ya aren't one of them that sits behind a desk all day with a suit and tie and—" she made a face "—a 'oity-toity look on ya face, you aren't to count for nothin'. Ya think in all the morns I've been 'ere to clean the place, one of them reporters ever said 'ello to me?"

"Hah!" Whissy burst out, "I'se be cleanin, right beside 'em, and they'd act like I never existed!"

But at the funeral reception afterwards, Pratty went on to say, there'd been the bosses with the employees, and the rich with the poor, and the congeniality between everyone there had been such that she'd not been able to discern who belonged to what social niche. Not only did everyone dress and talk and act very similar, but they all mingled as if of the same family.

"Everyone has their place 'ere," Whissy sighed. "It's okay to smile and say, 'ello, Mista'—whatever, but if he's got one a 'em fancy, stuck-up noses 'bout all you'll ever get from 'em is a quick view of their back side as they rush past."

Portsmouth, England
September 3, 1983

Dear Folks,

Just a little over one month after arriving in the British Isles, I've reached my final destination here, Portsmouth, on the south-central coastline of England.

Behind me now are some eighteen hundred miles—twelve hundred on American soil, the rest in Ireland, Scotland, and down the entire length of England. Next comes France and then the Basque region of Spain.

First, however, I must take a week in Portsmouth to update my British Isles notes, before going on to Cherbourg, France, by boat. The memories which have built up in my mind and heart these past few weeks are many. And, for the most part, pleasant ones.

I honestly wonder if I'll remember most of what I've seen and heard. Already Scotland and its wide open plains and low mountains seem light years ago. It was in the midwestern-type scenery of southern Scotland and the high, windy, grassy dells of England's Lake District in the northwest that I felt my strongest pangs of homesickness. In those areas, the people were few, the sky and land the largest, and the time for contemplation the longest.

Quickly—too quickly—I was to find myself going from the stone-walled sheep and cattle pastures and pine forests of the north to the more congested central and southern regions of England. Since leaving Nottingham (the friendliest large city so far on my walk), the countryside, like the people in general, has been a bit too "reserved" for my liking. Green and lush, you understand, but also ordinary.

In the north of England where jobs are few and wages their lowest, the people seemed to have more time for a smile and a chat. In the booming south the people seemed more interested in making and spending money. And, more suspicious of strangers who come to their door to ask for a glass of water or directions!

Still, tho, hardly a day goes by when some small incident doesn't occur to remind me of how much love really does exist just below the surface.

Just last night, during one of the only three or four rainshowers I've seen since being here, a retired old man spent a good hour driving all over the countryside trying to find me a hotel room. I didn't ask him to do it, nor even remotely suggested the idea. He just did it out of concern for me. Although he never found a room available, and I ended up sleeping in a horse stable on a floor of straw with the wind screeching madly outside, the night was made all the warmer by his compassion.

Then there was last weekend. The Monday after the weekend was what they call here a "bank holiday." For three days nearly every shop I came upon was closed, which wouldn't have mattered much anyhow because I'd missed the banks on Friday and had only two pounds to last me four days (Friday through Monday). In England, where food prices are terribly high in comparison to the United States, two pounds will hardly buy enough food for one day, let alone four.

I didn't worry, though. I simply knocked on a few more doors than usual and drank a lot more glasses of water (and tea) than usual. In the course of my knocking, a few meals came my way. And, in one instance—from a policeman's club of all places!—a five-pound note.

In all of my walking through the British Isles, there were only two instances when the people I met were less than friendly. One was when I went into London to double-check my plans with some foreign embassies. As usual when one deals with a government agency, there were run-arounds and looks of disinterest.

The second incident was worse, potentially dangerous actually. In the beautiful horse farm countryside to the east of Reading, England, near where the American cruise missles are to be based, a small group of anti-nuclear people happened upon me. I was surrounded and subjected to much verbal abuse. Also, an attempt was made to physically remove the small American flag I have pinned to the back of my pack.

I was able to save the flag and get out in one piece after a brief scuffle, but it was several hours before I could once again begin to enjoy myself. The scars I suffered were not on the outside but on the inside, on my heart. For less than an hour before I was being called a "murderer," I had been visiting with crippled children at a Red Cross hospital—bringing smiles and laughter to their faces.

That evening, after much contemplation, I decided to put the flag back into my pack to avoid any further controversy. I felt afraid, embarrassed.

But my decision was temporary.

As I neared Portsmouth, it occurred to me that the times when I, as an American, will be criticized will probably be plenty—especially as I advance into Third World countries. To start fearing that criticism now would not be wise, I decided. Rather, I should learn how to live with it, not hide from it.

Thus I walked into Portsmouth—with my country's colors showing proudly.

Steven

The walk thus far
162 days
April 1, 1983 - September 9, 1983
1,750 miles walked

FRANCE AND SPAIN

STEVEN'S ROUTE

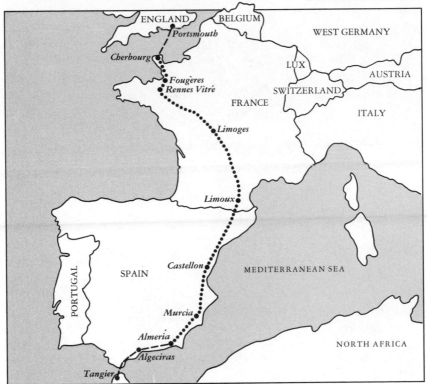

From Portsmouth, England, I took a ferry across The English Channel to the Normandy port of Cherbourg. Wandering like a monk from the past, I found France lush with romance and beauty, almost a heaven on earth, while my walk farther south through Spain often made me feel that I was only a step away from purgatory.

The walk ahead through France and Spain
91 days
September 10, 1983 - December 9, 1983
1,595 miles

**A French peasant woman entering through the side door of one of the
old cathedrals that you find throughout France, to say her daily
prayers. She paused for a second to wish me a good day as I passed by,
and saying that the Lord would be with me, she offered to say a
prayer for me.**

Fougeres, France
September 16, 1983

Dear Folks,

After a week in France, I'm about to fall deeply in love with another country and its people. In this lush republic of rolling hills, moody skies and bright-eyed beautiful people, the essence of romance seems omni-present. Even their language—of which I know pitifully little—flows from their lips and radios like the notes of a sweet love song.

Ah, perhaps it is good I'm walking across this country in the dark, rainy fall and not during the spring. Honestly, I think my heart could never bear to leave if there were sunshine to go with the incredibly beautiful women and scenery.

Strolling south from Cherbourg to Briquebec, St.-Sauveur-le-Vicomte, Lessay, Coutances, Gavray, and St. James to Fougeres has been like floating through a time warp. Sometimes, such as one night when I passed the crumbling towers of an ancient Norman castle in St.-Sauveur-le-Vicomte, I can almost swear I heard the clanking of knights' armor and the hoof beats of their battle-weary horses.

Here in the little gray-stoned villages of the countryside, far from throbbing Paris, life still clings to the past. Most residents live in the same mortar and stone homes that their great-great-great-grandparents were raised in. And their children are being baptized and married in churches that were blessed long before America was born.

There is a calmness, a regularity to life here in Normandy and Brittany, that to this American is almost ethereal, almost naive.

Every farm has its small herd of black-spotted dairy cows, small cornfield, cranky geese, loud dog, overabundant apple trees, and cement-floored, shuttered farm house with attached hay barn.

Each town, whether it be a one-cafe, four-house village or a large city like Fougeres, has a tall-steepled church in the center, on the highest point, with all the shops and homes built around it. Long before I reach a town in this predominantly Catholic country, I usually spy the steeple first, whether the town's built in a valley (like Gavray) or on a tall hill (like St.

James). At times I feel as if I'm merely traveling from church to church, like some wandering monk of the Medieval era.

Caught in the spell of this land of happy faces and sad love songs, I find it difficult to believe that almost forty years ago, tens-of-thousands of soldiers were dying on these very roads I'm walking.

Hardly an hour goes by that I do not pass another high cement crucifix with casualties of World Wars I and II listed on its base. And the most somber reminder—a graveyard of several acres covered with thousands upon thousands of identical white crosses, each one bearing the name of a fellow American who landed on this chubby peninsula on D Day but never made it back home.

As I stood among those crosses near St. James, I realized I am inseparable from the past. Were it not for all of those men who came here to fight, to cry, and to die, I might not be able to enjoy this land today. I might never have known how beautiful a lady France really is.

Suddenly, the Frenchman's strong attachment to his past—as evidenced by the many ruins, the antiquated farmhouses and municipal buildings, the many elders who still help with the farmwork—made a lot of sense to me. So did something else, something that at the time seemed little more than a pleasant surprise but now brought a tear to my eye.

In the little town of Gavray a couple of days before, I had gone into the Marie (the town hall) to get someone to sign my log book. The graying secretary, upon learning I was American, begged me in French to wait for her while she went to get something for me. Excitedly, she led me to a wall hung with old black-and-white photos of a Gavray ruined during the last World War, then she rushed off to do whatever it was she had been jabbering about. As I studied the photos, it became obvious Gavray had suffered terribly at the hands of the Nazis.

When she returned, one hand hidden behind her back, she pointed to the photos and mimicked the Americans coming into the town to fight off the Germans. Marching back and forth across the big room's creaky floor, she stuck out her chest proudly, whistled a familiar American fight song and flashed me the V sign with a big smile and happy shout, "Hooray Americans!"

Then she stopped before my laughing figure and, like a schoolgirl, held out the hand she had kept hidden behind her skirt . . . in it was a candy bar.

I had to come all the way to France, where I don't even speak the language, to realize how proud I should be to be an American.

Steven

The flag always flies at half mast for the 4,410 graves in the American War Cemetery near St. James, France. This photo was taken from the top of the bell tower of the memorial chapel at the cemetery. The cemetery supervisor, Jackie Bell, is Kansas born and raised.

Limoges, France
September 28, 1983

Dear Folks,

You don't rush France . . . and France doesn't rush
you—it's as simple as that. If there's a more complacent spot
on earth, it's likely tucked away on some exotic South Pacific
island. France, like the wines she produces, only gets better
and better with time. Or, in my case, with each kilometer.

The first nine days there were the gray skies, fat dairy
cows, and daily rain showers of Normandy and Brittany. Then,
for about one hundred twenty miles, from near Rennes to the
medieval hill city of Parthenay, the poverty of the villages and
cloudless, hot sky reminded me of Mexico. In that region I
feared that the heat of Africa was already upon me. For four
long days the fruit trees and streams were few, and the lizards,
spiders, and palm trees many. Walking in the middle of the
day was out of the question, and I had to content myself with
napping in the shade like a lazy tomcat.

My clothes needed washing badly and nowhere, so far, in
France was a coin-operated washing machine to be found—not
even in the largest of the cities I passed through! Then, west of
Parthenay, I discovered a beautiful little spring-fed pond, and I
was able to once again enjoy France in comfort.

Here in the south of France toward the Pyrenees, all the
prior aspects of the country settle into a mixture that is
mmmwhaa! How can a land be so blessed?

Walking in the morning is a great joy—looked forward to
all night long. First, one is awakened by the songs of hundreds
of birds. Then—precisely at seven o'clock—the long tolling of
the village church bell. Even the sun knows it's only natural to
be lazy in southern France, and it rises from the cotton-candy
fog ever so slowly. After a few hours, more magic—dew drop-
lets clinging to the vines of fat grapes and leaves of sycamores
lining the roadway sparkle like zillions of finely-cut diamonds.

I can now understand why this region has been the mecca
for artists and writers—there is so much natural beauty here to
rejoice about. The tranquility, beauty, the richness of the land,
come through in the customs of the people. Indeed, at long
last, I have found a people who enjoy lingering for not minutes,

but hours, over a meal. They have not forgotten that the things in life to be enjoyed most, and longest, are most often the simplest of things . . . such as eating.

A dinner I shared with a farm family in tiny, tiny Foufreroux de Souvigne was an excellent example of how the French in the rural regions go about life.

The room in which ten of us ate the late evening meal was a combination living-dining-bedroom. First, a strong before-dinner wine was served. Then a large bowl of tapioca-tomato soup was served with a lighter wine and lots of French bread and pate.

Then, from the same bowl, everyone ate a large salad of fresh garden vegetables. (All homes in France, it seems, have an enormous vegetable garden.) Using the same bowls, we ate a main dish of tomatoes stuffed with beef, pork and onions simmered in a light oil, and more bread and wine in a seemingly endless supply. Finally, the customary after-dinner treats—cheeses of goat and cow milk, yogurts, and cognac-spiked cafe (coffee). Oh, yes, more bread. And grapes, apples, peaches and walnuts, grown right there.

Interwoven throughout the meal were generous laughter and conversation. We sat down at seven-thirty and were not to rise again until ten-thirty, and that was after having enjoyed a two-hour lunch earlier in the day! Now that's a true art.

One young boy (who has had English for seven years at school) perhaps best summed up the Frenchman when he said, "We understand that in America you put money first and love second. Here, we put the love of life first, and then, if there is any, money second."

You know, something tells me my heart will be sad the day I cross the Pyrenees.

Steven

Limoux, France
October 13, 1983

Dear Folks,

When I entered France eight hundred fifty miles ago, I wondered if my unfamiliarity with the language would cause me grief. After all, I had some one thousand miles of foreign soil to cross by foot, and the only word of French I knew was "oui."

It was unsettling to be surrounded by thousands of people making strange sounds with their lips—that first week was not a confidence-bolster!

For starters, upon landing in Cherbourg, I had two pairs of new walking shoes worth a total of $120 that I wanted to mail ahead to Limoges in south France. No one at the *poste* spoke a lick of English, and my clerk was obviously new at her job. She couldn't seem to understand that my sending a package to myself at the post office in Limoges was a perfectly normal thing. I was trying to tell her that I wouldn't arrive in that city for a month and that the poste there would have to hold the package for me. What was ordinarily a two-minute chore turned out to be fifteen minutes of stuttering and pleaful looks. When I left the post office, I honestly doubted I'd ever see those shoes again.

My first five days in France, I met absolutely no one who spoke English. The situation was depressing. "How will I ever learn much about life in France if I can't speak to anyone?" I lamented silently.

Not until I met Jackie Bell, the Kansas-born supervisor of the American war cemetery at St. James, did I speak my first complete sentence in France. Never before had I gone so long without decent conversations, and I relished our long, long chat like a dog might a juicy bone.

After meeting Mr. Bell, it seemed that I could hardly go a day without meeting someone who spoke a little English. Usually it was someone young, in their teens to early thirties, who had learned English in school and then developed an "ear" for it by listening to the highly popular American pop music.

Most songs on the juke boxes in bars are English language rock-and-roll. And in the supermarkets I've shopped in, the background music was often an American pop singer. Even in the open-air markets, many songs piped over the city's loud speakers are in English—from punk rock to country western. Nuns and bereted old farmers with long loaves of bread in their baskets shop to songs they couldn't begin to understand—especially the punk songs!

Since I am traveling almost entirely through small villages and the countryside, I am the first American many of my new French friends have met. Therefore, none have spoken English that much or well, and yet I believe that fact has helped to make our brief meetings all the more special, because we have had to put much effort and thought into both the listening and speaking to each other.

Sure, it has been exhausting at times, but worth every furrowed eyebrow. Language, I have found, is not much of a barrier to those who want to learn.

One can get his thoughts across, even if he must resort to acting them out—something I've had to do many times (which, by the way, can bring a lot of laughter to a conversation). Now I realize those first two weeks I was being timid for no good reason at all.

Now I find myself jabbering away with some French family for hours about everything from politics to food, to sex, even though we probably don't understand three-fourths of what the other is saying. What matters is that we gain something from our meeting, probably a friend.

I have friends now in France, where before I had none. They range from a bright-eyed eleven-year-old schoolboy in St. Hilaire du Harcouet who loves the Dallas Cowboys football team, to a beautiful, dark-haired young poetess in Argentre-du-Plessis, to a gray-bearded ex-third-world rebel near Bourg-St. Bernard who now runs a countryside farm for former drug addicts. In between are many others, perhaps poor in education or money, but worth a million to my heart and mind.

I hope I never again make the mistake of forgetting that much of the time, words are not all that important when I meet someone else I want to know.

Steven

P.S. The shoes? They were there, safe and sound, with a big, bright URGENT stamped on the package.

An ancient fort, Le Chateau, stands in the center of Vitre twenty-two miles east of Rennes). Built in 1530, the fort is still in good shape. The former residence of barons and military men, this castle is overlooking the city of Vitre. Throughout Britany and Central France you'll find usually the highest area of ground in each town or village, and even the cities, occupied by either some sort of fortress or the main cathedral. And often times as I walked across France, I could look off into the distance and tell long before I was coming to the next town how far it was by just simply looking at the tourets on the castle towers, or either the steeple on the cathedral.

Fonollosa, Spain
October 27, 1983

Dear Folks,

Crossing the Spanish Pyrenees ten days ago, near the principality of Andora, left no doubt in my mind that I'd entered the rawest phase of the walk yet.

I spent two bitter-cold days in high mountain passes. There were no villages, and snow and fierce winds pushed me about like some toy. At night, in my thin tent and dressed in all the clothing I have, I shivered hour after hour in below-freezing temperatures.

Then came the sharp, quick descent into the valleys which run to the Mediterranean Sea and a different danger. For nearly two days every breath I took was tainted with the odors of uncontrolled pollution trapped in the narrow, steep-walled corridors leading toward Barcelona. It was the smell of rot . . . rotten buildings, dead animals, and raw sewage.

There were other signs of tension. Machine gun-toting guards patrolled the family dwellings of the national police, factory windows had bullet holes, and on many walls was the hammer-and-sickle emblem of the Communist Party ("PCC" in Spain) with the word "affiliate" violently scrawled beneath.

The fourth day, I turned away from the Mediterranean, with its dust, traffic and cramped cities, to head southwest toward Almeria, on the coast facing Morocco.

At last, on the high brown plains that run parallel to the coast, I found the warm persons I was told filled Spain—persons like thirty-nine-year-old Pep Cruells who lives in the tiny plains village of Calders. A gentle man with a deep laugh and a fiercely independent nature, Pep asked me to be one of his poor family for awhile.

We bumped into one another on one of Calders' narrow sidestreets early in the morning when he was walking to a nearby almond grove to harvest almonds. Short, dark, broad-shouldered, with gray-streaked long black hair, he was dressed in faded denim pants and an old corduroy jacket. He had a straw carrying bag slung over his left shoulder, and in his right hand, a large, dark sickle.

"Are you American?" he asked in flawless English.

"Yes," I answered, surprised. He looked like the last person I'd expect to know English.

"Follow me," he commanded.

We rushed down a tight, shadowed street of joined homes and dusty walks to a building of rough stone and crumbling mortar. Like all the others it was about three stories tall. (Later, Pep told me it was three hundred years old.) It was his home.

I followed him through a dirt-floored cellar of burlap sacks, sleepy-eyed cats, and rusted bicycles. On the first floor, we entered a kitchen that was barely large enough to hold four people. There I met Imma, his younger artist wife. Although it was morning, she was already frying up the lunch that would be served around two o'clock. In Spain, lunch is the main meal of the day, and generally lasts for two to three hours, at which time the entire nation nearly shuts down.

Pep and I then went to the almond grove. All day we shook almonds from trees and put them into burlap sacks, only taking a break when Imma showed up with Pepit, one of their two sons, and the enormous lunch.

Under the bright, hot Mediterranean sun we filled ourselves with a main dish of eggplant, rice, chicken, peppers, carrots, onions, celery, and garlic and side dishes of "Indian Bread" (a flat, gray tortilla), cooked cauliflower, wine and French loaf bread spread with a marmalade.

After we had worked past sunset and collected nearly one thousand pounds of nuts, Pep and I returned to his home of low-ceilinged cramped rooms with walls covered with the artwork of his wife and sons. They have no television, so we sat in front of a roaring fireplace talking of our adventures and dreams. Since I can speak Spanish quite well, the entire family was able to join in, including Pepit and the other son, Pol.

During the day, Pep had questioned me incessantly about the states, particularly California, and I asked him why. He had traveled all over the world he said, except to America, and now had a burning desire to visit that far-away land with all the Spanish-sounding cities.

"I want more than anything to sail around the world and eventually land somewhere like California. That is why I couldn't let you go this morning—not when I had the chance to find out what it is really like from someone who has been there."

As I stared at the fire, I knew how he felt. Like so many others I had met in France and Spain, he had many questions about America, but there had been no one to ask.

The notion that Americans are "everywhere anymore" is not true. Since leaving the states in July, I've met but three Americans. For most people in the rural areas I've traveled through, their only contact with Americans and America has been through the media. Hence, they are not exactly sure of what we are really like.

Much later that night, after a light dinner around nine and presentations of drawings to me by the boys, and a look at Imma's beautiful batiks of dragons and butterflies, Pep showed me one of his prize possessions—a tattered copy of a large book entitled *The Last Whole Earth Catalog*. He handled the five-pound paperback as carefully as one might the family Bible. The book, published in English by a California group, was filled with listings of books dealing with alternative life-styles in everything from natural childbirth to bartering, to Pep's favorite, building your own boats.

"I built a small rowboat from directions last year," he said thoughtfully. Then looking me in the eyes, "It wasn't difficult at all. I know I could build a boat that would make it around the world—I know it! I had no car to take it to any lake, so I had to fill it with water to test it for leaks," he said, rubbing its sides proudly, "She didn't leak at all, not one drop."

Then, to himself more than to me, he added, "Ten years— that is when I will try to sail around the world!"

The next morning, as I was leaving Calders, I heard my name called from somewhere far away. Imma, high atop one of the hills, with a straw carrying bag in one hand, was calling and waving to me. She was, like countless other housewives in Spain that morning, making her daily rounds to the butcher and bakery shops.

"Muchas gracias!" I shouted happily, doubting she could hear me. But she did. For ever so faintly, came the unmistakable reply . . . "Da nada." (You're welcome).

Steven

This is the Cruell family, Pep and Imma, and their son Pepit, with whom I stayed in Calders, Spain. Here we have Imma looking out at me from the front window of their three-hundred-year-old home. Pep shakes an almond tree to knock the almonds onto the burlap sack cloth spread on the ground below. For Pep this is a part-time job to earn money. He's very independent and has always refused to work for another man. He takes on odd jobs like harvesting almonds to make money to support his family. Imma often got up early in the morning and spent two to three hours, at least, fixing the lunch that she brought out to Pep and me in the fields each day.

Castellon, Spain
November 9, 1983

Dear Folks,

After leaving Pep Cruells and his family in Calders, I ventured deeper into a Spain that with each passing kilometer became more rugged, browner and poorer. It was to be a period of bathing from a one-liter bottle under a hot sun, of passing down dark and narrow village streets with eyes peering at me from behind grimy windowpanes and beaded doorways, and of much perplexity and insecurity.

Unlike other countries I'd walked through, I was not to find the interior of Spain to be a gentle region, but one of increasing challenges, both physical and spiritual. So challenging, in fact, that in the end I had to retreat toward the Mediterrannean coastline—or endanger my very sanity.

First, there was the land. Rather than growing lower and warmer, it grew higher and colder by night. Hill after incessant hill, each one adding yet at least a dozen more curves to the rough and steep roads I followed west toward Lerida Leida.

Although there were many terraced hillsides of olive and almond trees, and many dried river bottoms sprouting small vegetable gardens, there were also virtual oceans of sagebrush, rocks, and . . . nothingness. Space, so huge, so immense, that at times I felt as if I'd been set adrift on another planet—a planet where nature controlled destiny, and where man was little more than an insignificant insect.

Then, there were the people—poor, suspicious, as much a part of the dusty terrain as the boulders and scrub pine. In the shops and offices of their dilapidated casa de la villas, their olive-skinned faces could be so smiling, so gentle and ready for a laugh. But in the streets and narrow caminos of the countryside? Another world. A world of fearful, cold stares—of black-garbed figures slinking back into musty doorways when approached, like snakes into a stone wall—of dirt-encrusted dwellings clustered about the tops of ugly hills like some sort of crumbling giant anthills.

Finally, there was the loneliness, and the pervasive sense of isolation that comes from being an obvious stranger in what seems to be such a strange land. For not only were the villages too far and few, so were words and companionship.

On two different occasions when a passing German cyclist stopped to chat with me, I felt as if I'd been visited by some sort of heavenly angel, for miracle of miracles, they *talked*.

After the visits by my two pedaling "angels," I knew it was time for me to seek someplace where there would be more of my own kind, where the valleys were filled with more light and more familiar sounds—like autos and radios, not the screams of pigs being slaughtered. Quite simply, the interior of Spain was too cold at this time of year, too cold in more ways than one.

But my exit to the south was not to be easy. This land that had spawned the restless side of my soul and emotions, that had brought me to the brink of striking out at all those glaring eyes, had to have the last laugh.

The incident of which I speak occurred on the last night of two days that were filled with rain and a bitter cold wind from the west. I was still many dozens of kilometers from the fig trees, palms and flowers of the coast, and I was so weary from all the walking, all the shivering. I needed shelter, warmth, but there was none, only more rock, more black, and more rain. On the crest of a windy mountain, I paused long enough to gaze out into the sea of darkness in which I was drowning. Far, far away were the only signs of life—the tiny glows of villages scattered across the plains below, so tiny did they look—like phosphorescent bacteria colonies clinging precariously to some huge boulder.

So much emptiness between the lights, and between them and me, I thought. We really are so much more fragile and smaller than we'll ever admit.

I pushed on, the sense of isolation growing stronger with the dropping temperature. With everyone else light years away, and my tent and blanket as soaked as the clothes on my back, the night held little promise of comfort.

From around a bend far ahead of me appeared a wobbly globe of light accompanied by the whining of (by now) an all-too-familiar, moped cycle engine. But, rather than droning past me as had all the countless others, this one stopped just short of me and parked, idling, with its lamp beam shining directly into my eyes.

I stopped, my heart pounding. A robber? Surely none of the local people would have the nerve to approach a total stranger on such an isolated stretch of road. Cautiously, and with much suspicion, I watched the shadowy rider dismount and come toward me. To my shock the tiny figure standing before me held neither gun nor knife—only a motorcycle helmet gripped by five very bony, wrinkled fingers. They belonged to an old peasant woman—so old, so bent-over, so fragile, that I wondered if I might not be seeing things. Her black clothes clung soggily to her like weary flesh, her gray hair above furrowed eyes glistened eerily in the mist and weak light. She spoke in a hoarse whisper, and deep inside me something jumped, as if the sound of words from someone else at such a late hour in such an out-of-the-way place was too unusual to accept.

"Do you need a place to sleep?" she asked, unemotionally.

"Si. Estoy m-muy frio," "Yes, I'm very cold," I stammered.

She turned off the road into a grove of bare spindly-limbed trees. Wordlessly I sloshed behind her hobbling figure which stood no higher than my belly.

After about fifty meters she stopped and pointed to the side of a rock cliff. There, its entrance even blacker than the night, was a cave that had been dug out of rock for storing tools used in harvesting almonds.

I thanked her and asked if I could pay her for her help. She only stared, as though she'd not understood the meaning of my words, then returned to her idling cycle without saying another word. I built a little fire from the scraps of reed and lumber strewn about the dirt floor, and huddled beside it most of the night, my blanket wrapped about me like some animal skin, expecting her to return. But, she didn't.

The next morning I left the cave and headed toward a dazzling sun, feeling dirty and raw and tougher—in other words, a bit like Spain herself.

Steven

Almeria, Spain
November 28, 1983

Dear Folks,

We were walking at midnight in Murcia, an ancient and beautiful city of 350,000 in south Spain. Suddenly, my Spanish companion stopped and motioned me to lower my voice. The abrupt fear in his dark eyes perplexed me—in the two days I'd known him, he had never displayed fear. Much of that typically sunny Spanish day, we had climbed sheer-faced mountain cliffs just south of Murcia and not once had he shown a glint of fear. Yet the twenty-seven-year-old mountain climber was suddenly acting as if laughing aloud and walking through the center of Murcia at such a late hour was some sort of crime.

"What was so frightening?" I wondered aloud.

Angel nodded toward a three-story apartment complex across the street. What I saw made the fine hairs on the nape of my neck rise. Standing defiantly on a second-floor balcony was a masked soldier, his brown-fatigued legs spread apart and his thick arms cradling a long automatic rifle, its black muzzle pointing just above our heads. Surely that must be a statue, not real, not in gentle, lovely south Spain, I thought. I stepped into the deserted street to get a closer look at the human-like form.

Suddenly, a deep voice from behind the ten-foot high cement-block wall surrounding the apartment building barked something threatening in Spanish. From behind, I felt Angel's thick arms yanking me back onto the curb. Angrily, he led me around a corner and far away from the Guardia Civil post.

"Why all the caution?" I asked, a bit perturbed. After all, I've visited dozens of Guardia Civil posts in my trek through Spain, mostly to ask directions or have the commanding officer stamp my log book, and never once had they given me any trouble. In fact, I thought the military men who made up Spain's national police force were some of the best policemen anywhere—why, they'd even bought me meals and twice had put me up in a cell on rainy nights!

"Perhaps that's so," Angel cautioned in Spanish, "but still you should not approach them so loudly this late at night." Then waving a finger sternly, he added, "In Franco's day you would have probably been shot trying to get close like that!"

"In Franco's day . . . " How many times had I heard those words in Spain, especially from the young. And, always spoken with a tinge of hatred.

On the long walk back to Angel's sparsely-furnished apartment (which like those of many young Spaniards was but a few doors from his parents' apartment), I thought back to another time I'd heard Franco's name spoken so bitterly. It was in Moia, in north Spain, in the dining room of a twenty-nine-year-old biologist named Jordi.

Tall, bearded, bespectacled, and soft-voiced, the English-speaking government scientist and his pregnant schoolteacher wife had asked me to stay with them one night. Over dinner he had recalled emotionally how he and fellow students at the university in Barcelona had protested against Franco and worked so hard to get a more democratic form of leadership for their beloved Spain.

"Oh, how we danced in the streets and sang with joy when we learned that Franco had finally died!" he exclaimed. Franco's death in November 1975 had allowed them the democracy they had dreamed of for so long. But, almost as an afterthought, he added in a low voice, "Now, however, many of my friends are having second thoughts about whether they really like a democracy form of government." For one thing, their role model, the United States, was involved in so many wars all over the world, he said.

"We are baffled why the United States thinks it must be a policeman for the whole world," he sighed. "It's almost as if America is a modern-day Rome."

I could easily understand his views. After all, I had been reading the same Spanish newspapers and watching the same Spanish national television news programs as he and his friends. And all I had seen or read of America was of soldiers firing rifles in foreign nations, or violent topics such as racial trouble in Miami and crime in New York City. As reported in the media of other countries I had passed through, America hardly seemed a desirable place to live, much less a role model.

Jordi also explained that many of his university friends had no jobs in which to use their education. That, too, has been a theme I have seen in every nation, except perhaps

America—that of too many educated, ambitious young minds and too small a job market for them. He had gone for two years with no work and had landed his present job only because he had made some lucky contacts in the "right places."

With so many restless young, I asked, could there be revolution of any sort in Spain? Could the country even turn Communist? After all, the campaign posters of the Spanish Communist Party had been on buildings in every village, town, and city I'd walked through.

"No," he replied immediately, "even though the Soviets may be closer geographically, in our hearts Spaniards still feel closest to America. Change comes slowly, if ever, in European cultures. We are not like the South American countries."

And the possibility of another dictatorship, another Franco? For Spain did have a history of such leadership, and many older people in Spain are already grumbling that the young have too much say and that life is too unsafe anymore with all the new laxness in social mores.

Jordi smiled. "'Don't count on it,' as you say. In Franco's day, it was like there was a huge weight on our shoulders. At night there was so little of the laughter and happiness you now see all over Spain. We waited too long to be free . . . and every day we have more of a taste of it, the less likely we will ever give it up."

I am now at the end of the Spanish portion of my world trek—from the Pyrenees to Almeria on the south coast—forty three days, 673 miles. The Spain I discovered was one of extremes—sometimes ugly, harsh, mean, and many times kind, beautiful, romantic. But always passionate.

I hope, like Jordi and so many other Spaniards, that Spain is always ruled by her kinder side. For it is a world unto its own—a world that everyone should have the chance to experience.

Now, at long last, Africa. Will the beauty, the compassion, the enchantment continue? Many have told me it ends where Spain meets the Mediterranean. I don't think so. It's time to find out who is right . . . and who is wrong.

Steven

The walk thus far
253 days
April 1, 1983 - December 9, 1983
3,345 miles walked

NORTH AFRICA

STEVEN'S ROUTE

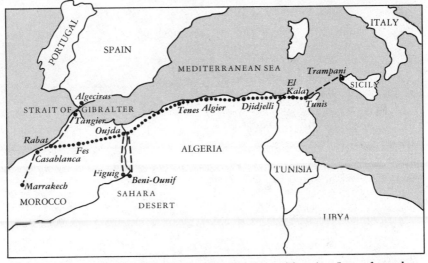

Since there was no ferry from Almeria, Spain, to Tangier, I was forced to hitch a ride to Algeciras, a port near Gibralter. From there, I took a ferry across the Strait of Gibralter to Tangier, ancient gateway to North Africa. After a stormy crossing in the night, I was fearful that Mark Twain's description of Tangier as "a rat's nest of thieves and murderers" would still hold true today. From Tangier, I took a bus south to Marrakech to visit the Jacquiths, an American family living in Merrickech who had read of my walk in *Capper's Weekly* and had invited me to stay with them when I arrived in Morocco. After a month's stay in Marrekech, I took a train north back to Rabat, the starting point for my walk across North Africa.

The walk ahead through North Africa
91 days
December 10, 1983 - March 9, 1984
1,202 miles

Algeria is a rough society and manliness is highly valued and often tested. This boy, although he may look beligerent and already manly at a very early age because of the harshness of life there, really is inside still very much a child I found.

Marrakech, Morocco
December 12, 1983

Dear Folks,

"It's totally insane . . . another world . . . too dangerous for a lone traveler . . . they kept coming at us . . . pawing, reaching . . . ."

The frightened faces, the trembling words, the disgust, the fear, the hate. All day at the port in Algeciras, Spain, three days ago, travelers from Morocco told one horror tale after another.

Alain, a Swiss student, told of two Moroccan men bursting into his motel room and choking him. "I—I cried like a baby. I didn't want to die."

Juan, a Spanish soldier, described a society growing poorer and more desperate each day, especially now that Saudi Arabia had stopped giving the monarchy-ruled northwest Africa nation any more money. "In a car you are half safe. But on foot you'll be robbed in no time," he warned sternly.

Helmut, a German businessman, related how he'd found nothing but greed and open corruption everywhere. "They weren't the least afraid to steal from me. I'll never go back!" He spat.

Even the ticket counter clerk tossed out words of caution. "Never, I repeat, *never* let them know you are American or have any money with you. In Morocco a lone American traveler has no friends, only those who would want your money."

Just one person, an American adventurer named Philip, offered hope. A Steve Canyon look-alike, he had lived, loved, and fought all over the world since leaving an America thirteen years ago that to him was nothing more than "one giant department store."

"The Moroccans know how the tourist mind works, and they prey on it, play on your fears. It's all a mind game to them. Stand up to the jerks. Tell them to go to hell. Inside they're nothing but cowards."

Less than six hours later, in the dead of night on an unlit and narrow street in Tangiers, Morocco, with my life on the line, Philip's advice was to be put to the test.

It was nine-thirty, cold, misty, with policemen all about, when the Moroccan ship I was on finally docked in Tangiers. For three hours the ship had plowed uneasily through storm-tossed seas and I should have been only too glad to finally step into Africa.

But I wasn't. I was scared. Not only from what I'd heard, but also from what I could see awaiting us on the shore. It was like some scene from a bad nightmare, or from *Raiders of the Lost Ark*.

Lining the rotted building and walls about the dockyard were dozens of the men of prey others had told of. Many wore long, dark, sharp-pointed hooded robes that covered all their bodies, except for scarred and hairy faces. They watched our boat as vultures might eye a dying lamb.

Other passengers were allowed to disembark with little trouble, after which they hurried through customs and into waiting taxis. However, I and a young Jewish couple with a baby were stopped by police and made to stay on the ship.

They had read on my entry card that I was a journalist.

"Who," the police asked, "did I work for?"

"I'm independent," I replied.

"Who do you work for?" a policeman demanded impatiently.

"Tell us the name and address."

I was in no mood to argue. I made up a newspaper—*Picadilly Times-Review*, Picadilly, Alaska, U.S.A.

He waved me through. The Jews never did get off, as far as I am aware.

By this time all taxis were gone. After customs checked my pack, I headed into the city on foot. When the Moroccans still watching the dock saw me step from the customs building, they descended upon me like jackals.

I walked straight, looking neither right nor left. I ignored them. Some asked if I wanted drugs, others wanted to be my "friend," others fought among themselves like wild dogs over who would get to me first. Still others offered to protect me from any harm. One, however, wanted to harm me.

He was ugly—no right eye and a long scar across his left cheek—perhaps the same age as I. He blocked my path, pulled a switchblade from beneath his robe and snarled hatefully,

"Say something! You want to die? Talk! Give me some money!"

I was so incensed that anyone would so brazenly threaten me that without thinking, I yelled *"me die!?"* and from my pants I pulled out a long hunting knife I've had the entire walk.

He looked as if he'd seen a ghost and ran off, along with several others. Only three remained with me as I walked directly to the bus station, and they kept a respectable distance, although their mouths never ceased trying to get me to part with some of my dirhams (Moroccan currency).

Not until I was on the bus that would take me to Marrakech, where I hoped to stay with an American couple until after the Christmas holidays, did I feel I was out of immediate danger. Only then did I allow myself to think how close death had passed, and how awfully scared I really was.

When I reflected upon what I'd seen just between the docks and the bus—hundreds of bored young men staring at me, filth on seemingly everything, families in rags hovering around open fires, beggars rushing from gutters and black alleys, women brushing past with every inch of their bodies covered except their eyes, donkey-pulled carts with wooden wheels, wild-looking dogs running loose and fighting over goat heads tossed right into the street by meat merchants, and garbage of all sorts strewn about—my confidence sank to its lowest level of the entire walk.

This time, I thought dejectedly, I've gone *too far.* I was suffering from cultural shock at its worst. No longer was I in just another country—this was another world, another time period, one that I saw no chance of easily surviving.

As the bus pulled away from the station, there was a loud *thump* at my window. Outside, my hooded "friends" were letting me know they were angry I'd not handed over any dirhams. I shuddered. Next time there might not be a bus window between me and their fists.

Steven

Marrakech, Morocco
December 23, 1983

Dear Folks,

It was the Moroccan king's birthday. Most shops in Marrakech, where I'm staying until I start my walk across North Africa in early January, were closed and streets were mostly empty. The quietness of the downtown area was almost unbelievable, for normally a Monday morning in this fabled Arabic city beside the Sahara was a constant clatter of horses' hoofs clomping against asphalt, mo-peds buzzing like gigantic insects, auto horns honking wildly, donkeys braying spitefully at robed owners, and veiled women chattering excitedly like gray, black and white sparrows.

So where was everyone on this day of hot sun and blue sky? After all, wasn't a royal birthday all the more reason for making a commotion?

"Try the souk, the open-air marketplace in the ancient walled area of the city," advised my host, Rina Jaquith. A former Kansas farm girl who now lives in this city of 1.5 million with her doctor husband, Clifford, she had read of my walk in *Capper's Weekly* (which takes four months by boat to reach her) and invited me to stay with them during my visit to Morocco.

So, off I went to the Djemma Elfna at the end of Mohammed V, the city's main drag. Sure enough, there were all our Moslem neighbors, along with sword dancers, snake charmers, mule-pulled carts of produce, and hawkers beseeching all in Arabic or French to "Make price, my friends! Make price!"

But, alas, there were the "leeches" too—the men who attach themselves to every tourist with a ferociousness that is downright criminal. They alone have probably driven more foreigners out of this kingdom than all the wars, pestilences and homesickness combined.

No sooner was my "rich American tourist" blond hair observed than I was rushed like a football quarterback. And since poverty is rampant and money so scarce for the average Moroccan, there was no way these fellows were going to easily surrender my attention. In less than a minute I had everything from human teeth, to curved daggers, to jars filled with dead flies (to be drunk in tea as an aphrodisiac) pushed into my arms and face. Scream as I did "No! No! No!" or "I don't want this!", they only pressed closer and clawed at me more.

I felt as if I were caught in a scratching thorn bush, with a few hundred snakes thrown in for good measure. In desperation I thrust a silvery dirham into a young, innocent-eyed boy's hand and begged him in caveman French to lead me someplace where the market was more than just writhing arms and spitting, hissing heads.

With the bravery of a saint, the wiry little lad grabbed my hand, and pushing aside beggars and foul-breathed camels, pulled me deep into a sunless maze of alleyways that would have confounded Rubik himself. Slowly the leeches lost their grips and dropped away, until there was only the boy, me—and the Devil himself!

"Ohhh! English or American?" crooned the tall, black salesman, flashing a mouth of gold and rubbing fingers as long as dollar bills.

Incredible! Somehow I'd picked the sharpest hustler of the whole bunch and allowed myself to be led into the belly of a souvenir shop that had more expensive junk in one room than Macy's or Sak's Fifth Avenue has in a dozen.

"You can pay in pounds or dollars also, if you wish," the suavely attired salesman kept reminding me as he piled everything I dared even glance at into a large pile. How do you explain to a possessed man that there is no way I'm going to carry four hundred pounds of rugs, ten leather purses, and a wagonload of brass teapots and candlesticks on my back for another twelve thousand miles?

When he tried to drag me *upstairs* to find even more, I dived back out into the marketplace to flee back up Mohammed V. And tagging right alongside were the leeches. With every stride I took, their prices dropped another several dirhams, for now I had dragged them off their turf. One frantic man, for example, was suddenly offering his curved daggers for 40 dirhams ($6) a pair, instead of the 150 dirhams *each* he'd said was such a good buy only half-an-hour earlier.

At last I reached the barbed wire-topped steel gates of the Jaquith residence and was able to shut the leeches out. I collapsed into a kitchen chair, exhausted and suffering combat shock.

"Did you enjoy yourself?" Mrs. Jaquith asked with a knowing smile.

"It was h-hectic," I sighed, "but there were lots of things being sold and I was able to bargain and get some excellent buys." Then, ever so much like a little boy, I heaved my knapsack onto the table and showed her the knives, the teeth, the flies . . . .

Steven

Moroccan city streets like this one were always a whirlwind of activity.

Fes, Morocco
January 9, 1984

Dear Folks,

Last night I sat still for at least forty minutes in the cold darkness of my tent with my head resting heavily upon my arm. Never before had I felt so fatigued and alone after the first week of walking across a new region.

My fatigue is not from difficult terrain or boredom, for the land between Rabat, the capital, and Fes had been one of wide and gently rolling grassy plains. It has been perhaps the easiest terrain I have walked across to date. With the days filled with so much warm sunshine, green earth, and cloudless blue sky, I really could not ask for a more perfect place to be this time of the year. The scenery and weather are much like I would find if I were to walk through eastern Colorado or western Kansas in the early fall.

And my loneliness is not because of lack of conversation or because of meeting few people, as in the interior of Spain. If anything, you are never physically alone in Morocco and the people are hardly shy or unemotional.

Even with all the open plains, there is hardly a kilometer that passes beneath my well-worn shoes that I do not pass two or three dozen rural Moroccans shuffling over farm animal trails in their pointed cloth slippers, bouncing atop tiny floppy-eared donkeys, swaying precariously in horse-pulled carts, or just plain squatting on the ground beside small piles of carrots or mushrooms or tethered chickens for sale.

My problem is simply that of being an American in a land of moochers. All day long, from young children on up to adults, it is a constant, "Give me, give me, give me!" So much so, that on several occasions it has taken every ounce of my willpower to keep from striking out at their demanding hands and faces.

They come at me in dirty town after dirty town, and from one mud farmhouse after another. And because I am on foot, there is no way for me to escape as other travelers can. There is no denying that the vast majority of the Moroccans I pass are dirt poor, that their cities and villages are little more than slums, that jobs are few and the work they do have is of the type that breaks a man before he is forty. Nor can I argue with those who lament that the king is more interested in his own interests than in theirs.

But, does that give them any right to demand money from me immediately upon sight? And to do so in such a rude and incessant manner?

I feel besieged. I feel in danger. There are no others of my own kind to run to, to seek advice from, to hide behind. Even in my most worn clothes with my shoes now torn, and my pack splattered with mud, I still stick out starkly wherever I go.

They can smell an American as easily as I can smell their own unwashed bodies. They come so often I almost feel at times like sitting in the dirt and crying. I like to think of myself as a kind and gentle person, but the Moroccans are forcing me to be a hard and rude person if I am to preserve my sanity. And my *wallet*—for I am not the money tree they seem to consider Americans to be.

"Everyone knows you have money in America. You cannot fool us," one shifty-eyed older man argued yesterday evening. He demanded six dirhams from me simply because I had *talked* with him. And when I refused, he threatened to not let me pass alive.

"You are free to travel, to come to Morocco, to go anywhere you like, to take all this time so far from America," he continued in a nasty tone. "You must have much money to have such freedom."

I did not pay, of course. But then I believe a man *must* have convictions, *must* not be afraid to take charge—two qualities that several Moroccans have told me separate Americans from their own people.

"Look what you have done in only two hundred years. You have become the number one country in all the world. The richest, the *best!*" A university student in political science told me that on the long and crowded train ride from Marrakech to Rabat (during which I had a brand new pair of walking shoes and all my food stolen from my pack). "And then look at us—we are still the same as we were five thousand years ago. Perhaps we do not agree with everything you do, but we must admire your character, the way you Americans stick together and complete what you set out do.

"We expect others to do everything for us . . . and you see

how little we have because of our lack of courage."

He had been especially amazed at how the United States was so united and concerned over one captured American pilot in Syria. That sense of "oneness" was something Arabs in general had never mastered, he observed. And as did so many other Moroccans I've spoken with, he wanted to "escape" to America.

Last night, as I waited wearily in the dark for someone to sneak up on me for some of those "many" dollars I must surely have with me, I, too, was feeling an urge to escape this den of thieves and greedy eyes. Quite frankly, I am too vulnerable.

Morocco is no place for a lone American walker.

Steven

Moroccan nomads, daughter and mother, in everyday dress.

Top; A Moroccan does her family's laundry in typical fashion.
Left; A Worldwalker does his laundry in typical fashion—here in a Moroccan river.

Oujda, Morocco
January 19, 1984

Dear Folks,

How do I even begin to describe these past ten days crossing the sand dunes and desert of east Morocco? So much danger, love, exoticness and mystery have I experienced that it is all I can do to remember I am in the twentieth century, not the tenth or eleventh.

It has been the sort of adventure that even a Marco Polo would have had to admire. So many anecdotes to share, yet so little time and space to write it down. Perhaps the best way to give you some idea of what I've been through is to relate the events of the day I passed through Taza and began my entry into the heart of the desert.

I started the day with a vivid reminder of how fear is still very much a part of life here. In the town of Qued, Amlil, a teacher I had stayed the night with showed me some documents that proclaimed him to be a "Registered Citizen of the World Government of World Citizens." The documents had been issued in America, in Washington, D.C., and also included an official looking (but worthless) passport and a "Universal Declaration of Human Rights."

He pulled the items out from deep in a bureau where he had them hidden, and showed them as if they were made of gold. In a land where so many have told me how much they want to get out, those documents and "passport" were probably the closest he'd ever have to a real passport. And I didn't have the heart not to act impressed.

"If the government knew I had these, I'd be in big trouble and even go to jail," he said as he hid them back under the clothes.

Sad to think that a man could place so much hope, and fear, in something as harmless as papers declaring the right of a man to be free. But then, that is how it usually is under a dictatorial monarchy, as Morocco has.

Next came danger of the kind I'd never have expected in this day and age. I had no sooner entered the large and slum-like city of Taza around noon, than I suddenly found myself directly in the path of a runaway horse team and wagon, charging madly down a steep main street. As I stood petrified, an old man and donkey coming out of an alley were knocked aside like mere toys.

Luckily for me, the horses then became entwined in the chaos, and there was the sickening sound of raw flesh against rough gravel, as the horses and wagon tumbled crazily only inches away.

While I tended to the badly injured man's wounds, others untwisted the donkey's legs and kept all the would-be thieves away from my backpack which I had flung to the road. Incredibly, no one thought to unhitch the horse team, and it and the wagon were soon racing off again to cause more destruction, this time in a packed bus terminal.

Typical of life here, many knew how to help the poor donkey, yet no one else knew the first thing about easing the old man's pains. I shall forever be grateful for the first aid training I received on the oil rigs.

But wait—death was not to leave me alone quite yet. Towards dusk a group of three sickly-looking wild dogs rushed at me from the sand dunes beside the empty highway. As I screamed for dear life, they circled and rushed again and again—their fangs snapping and their minds delirious from hunger, sun and my own panic.

For at least five minutes, I slashed away with my hunting knife and walking stick, while I screamed for *someone* to save me. Were it not for a passing soldier-filled truck, I might not have held out. Three shots from an officer's pistol and the dogs were soon scattered.

However, the most striking memory of that incident will not be of the dogs or the shots, but of three Moroccan women who came out of a nearby adobe house and *laughed* deliriously while I fought off the dogs. To them, I guess, the sight of the dogs and I screaming at each other must have looked quite strange, for what did they ever see but sand, rocks and sheep?

Then came night and the worst-and the best, yet. A strong, freezing wind from the west forced me to keep walking long into the dark vastness. There was no way I could have erected my tent in the gale, and there was nothing larger than boulders to hide behind. Anyhow, my hands were so stiff I doubted I could have unpacked my pack.

On and on I trudged, not a sign of life anywhere—not even a blade of grass. All at once a darkly-robed and hooded figure came running at me from seemingly nowhere. Horrible memories of Tangiers raced through my mind, and I waited for the knife to come out from under his robe. Instead a handshake materialized. It was a young road construction worker who had seen me out on the desert earlier in the day. He immediately led me to the camp he shared with several other workers. Their dwellings were nothing more than plyboard and tin shacks with only cots and kerosene lamps for furnishings, but to me they were mansions. Although unheated, they provided me with needed relief from the continuous wind.

Through one of the older men who spoke Spanish, we communicated mostly about jobs and money in America for the next several hours, all the time drinking one glass after another of mint tea, "Moroccan whiskey." (In a Moslem society, real whiskey is forbidden.) Toward midnight, I fell asleep under a ton of blankets and with a stomach full of bread soaked in olive oil and sardines (two Moroccan staples).

It had been another typically tiring day of living on the edge of death in Morocco.

Steven

This is a good example of the unreal, harsh desert setting of East Morocco.

Tenes, Algeria
January 31, 1984

Dear Folks,

Of all the countries on my walk, the one I knew least about was Algieria. To me, it was a big question mark. All the travel books I had read before my journey had simply ignored this huge North African nation as if it didn't exist.

Basically all I knew of Algeria by the time I reached its border at Oujda, Morocco, was what I had heard from second-hand sources, and it was hardly encouraging.

Their embassy in Washington had told me I *might* be allowed to cross over from Morocco (with whom they are at odds), but most certainly not to let anyone at their visa offices know I am a journalist.

An aristocratic French couple in Revel, France, who had lived in Algeria before the Algerians gained their independence from France in 1962, had described the Arabs of Algeria as now being reckless, militaristic, and largely insensitive.

The American embassy's consular officials in Rabat, Morocco, seemed to know even less than I, except that I would have to purchase 1,000 Algerian dinars as soon as I entered their country and, again, not to let anyone know I was a journalist—and that I might get in . . . and I might not. And, as for the Moroccans, they described their neighbors as racist, stupid, and just plain crazy and belligerent.

All of the above, together with what I did know of Algeria—that it's government is socialist, that tourism or visits by outsiders (except to work) is not exactly encouraged, and that most of the geography is desert or semi-desert, was hardly encouraging.

Ever since day one of my walk I'd worried the Algerian border might be the end of my walk across North Africa. And as events developed, I could hardly have been blamed for switching my walk route to southern Europe.

At the grimy Algerian consular offices in Oujda I was told I could cross into Ageria, but only if I went four hundred kilometers *south* into the Sahara Desert to Figuig, Morocco, and *then* walk across the "Frontier" (as the borders are called here) to the tiny Algerian village of Beni-Ounif. Even though

Algeria was but fourteen kilometers from Oujda, I could not cross there, not even in a bus. The only persons allowed across at Oujda were those who had their own vehicles or who worked or lived in Algeria.

Tempted as I was to get away from the incredible pettiness and arrogance I had found in all my dealings with the Arab governmental services, I nevertheless went ahead, got my visa, and took the long, bumpy and dusty bus ride to Figuig.

Quite truthfully, when I stepped off that bus in the middle of the night in bitter cold Figuig during a fierce sandstorm, with nowhere to sleep but in a dilapidated, cement-walled, spider-infested place on a dark alleyway called the "Motel Sahara," all I was thinking of was how quickly I could *run* to Tunis and get back to the European continent and civilization. But first I had to get past border officials of both countries. That turned out to be most nerve-racking.

First Morocco police, then their military, checked every bit of my gear and filled out paperwork on me. I made it through them though, and my last sight of Morocco, as I walked across the barren "no man's land" between the two countries, was of four large canvas army tents billowing beside a palm trees-ringed oasis.

At the Algerian post, not only my gear but I, too, was searched, inch-by-inch for drugs, weapons, alcohol (forbidden in an Islamic society), etc. Since I had listed my profession on their form as an "artist," I had hidden all papers I had with me that identified me as a journalist. To my relief I picked the one place to hide those papers that they didn't search—my English-language dictionary.

To my horror, however, they found a personal, sealed letter in my jacket pocket from someone I'd met in Morocco to a friend of his in Oran, Algeria. With no hesitation, the officials tore it open and read the letter. In it the Moroccan identified me as an American journalist. My heart sank as the senior officer looked me in the eye and asked if I was a journalist.

I was an artist, I said firmly, the Moroccan was mistaken. Perhaps because my photographic art work sometimes appeared in journals, he had thought I was a journalist.

They huddled and talked among themselves in low voices while I sweated. To my shock the senior officer finally looked at me and said, "Sofee," (Arabic for "that's all"). I could go. But the letter couldn't. That, they put carefully into a desk drawer.

Steven

A mother and daughter coming back into an Algerian village from a day of gathering firewood to use at home and to sell. It's very much a harsh reality for them each day.

Jijel (Djidjelli), Algeria
February 17, 1984

Dear Folks,

Monkeys screeching from dark grottos high atop red cliffs .
. . . snarling long-tusked boars charging angrily through deep
snow . . . deserted stretches of jagged coast littered with
wrecked ships . . . what an adventure the scenery alone in
Algeria has turned out to be! More and more as I weave further
east along this nation's serpentine-shaped coastline, I traverse
natural settings that won't allow my imagination to rest . . .
gnarled bare-limbed forests of fire-blackened trees reaching for
a painfully blue Mediterranean . . . panoramic quilts of breeze-
kissed meadows of clover and yellow flowers, sunny skies, and
misty, snow-capped mountains flaunting skirts of long eucalyptus trees . . . .

Does the beauty ever stop? One day I'm dipping in and out
of lush fairy-tale forests of tall thundering waterfalls and
cone-covered pines—the next, I'm shivering myself over Hima-
layan-like peaks. Or perhaps I might even be cautiously step
ping my way along some cliff-hugging road that drops away on
one side to a thundering surf of boulders and foam hundreds of
feet below.

. . . dilapidated seaside resort hotels full of roughly-chiseled
faces whose eyes hint at evil thoughts . . . lonely old French
cemeteries with large clumps of unmarked graves and not a
gravestone left intact, testimony to a past when the Algerians
and the French became bitter foes . . . tiny villages of mud,
barefooted children crowded around water wells, stooped wom-
en with everything from babies to firewood on their backs, and
dark-faced men whose twitching eyes speak of the unspent
energy burning inside them . . . .

I couldn't have picked a longer and more rugged way to
cross north Algeria than its coastline. I know my body has
suffered greatly because of the times I have been burnt, frozen
and soaked these past twenty-six days and 550 miles in Algeria. But I don't really care so much about all that—for this is
the stuff of which *real* adventure is made.

This is learning in the best way, in a classroom that knows
no limits save those of my imagination. Unlike the coastlines

of America and Spain, the Algerian coast is virtually undeveloped and sparsely populated. Here, nature still rules mighty, and the twisting narrow roads I have followed have led me—at one time or another—through the likes of Nepal, the Pacific Northwest, Norway, China, Central America, and even Ireland. All that on just a tiny piece of African coast! Just think of how many other natural jewels must exist on this continent. I suspect there are more than enough to fill any explorer's treasure chest.And any writer's or dreamer's soul, too. For me the lands of Homer's *Ulysses*, Robert Louis Stevenson's *Robinson Crusoe*, Frederick Forsyth's soldier mercenaries, and James Michener's hero-warriors are no longer fiction, but a part of my everyday life. They have gone from being words in a book to being the very dirt under my nails, the rain soaked into my sleeping bag, and the reason for the blisters on my toes and the cold in my sinuses.

. . . spooky, vine-covered mansions of rich Europeans who tried, but failed, to exploit the fertile valleys and lowlands tucked between sandy beaches and sudden mountain ranges. Those former fortresses of stone and silk are now but the playgrounds of snakes and migratory songbirds . . . long-haired billy goats scampering up steep hills, their little girl herders scolding those that can't resist taking an extra nibble . . . the moanful wailing of the *Koran* over the loudspeaker of some far, faraway mosque in the cold darkness of a clouded dawn . . . .

What a shame, in my opinion, that so many people will settle for a world of words or video images, rather than take the time and effort to see and *feel* the real thing.

Exploring North Africa has been anything but a picnic. In fact, it's been one daily challenge after another. Everything here is so *different*. It's taken me nearly this long to adjust to the land and the people. But the bags under my eyes, my peeling nose, the rips and dirt in my gear and clothing have been worth it. For isn't anything that's *really* worth having usually gotten only after much effort? Africa is proving that the pursuit of firsthand knowledge isn't the easiest thing in the world . . . but when you do find it, it is usually worth every sacrifice that had to be made.

Steven

El Kala, Algeria
February 28, 1984

Dear Folks,

Once past the suspicious border post officers in the Algerian Sahara, my nerves were able to relax—for a minute. Then the confoundedness that is Africa came roaring back in enough shapes and sizes to drive any man short of a sadist into a fidgety wreck. For starters, another sandstorm blew along. Then I couldn't connect with any buses heading back to the north, where I plan to resume walking on this side of the border post that had originally turned me back. And, after two days of digging out from under sand drifts to chase after tootling buses that had no intention of stopping in the first place, I decided to brave the heat and hitchhike north, only to have a merciful bus driver be the first person to pull over.

By the time I was back to the coastline area and finally finished with the 800-kilometer-long detour, I was not only ready to get on my way as quickly as possible, but to be over and done with any and every North African, hopefully for the rest of my life. Certainly, if ever a people lived that could get a man's senses more twisted than a pretzel, it would be these Arabs of the Mediterranean. Their lives are such a tumbled mixture of contrasts that I am never really quite sure if at any given moment I am safe or in danger. Take, for instance, the unusual experience I had this time a week ago in a rotting former French resort town beside the sea.

I had already set up camp in the forest near the city of Cherchell, when, under the threat of a rainstorm, I walked into its buzzing open market area to buy a broiled chicken and some vegetables for dinner. As was so often the case in the towns I've passed through these past two and one-half weeks, the crumbling cement row houses and old colonial-style lamp posts were watching me with every step I took. Plastered all over them were the stern, white-haired faces of this socialist nation's "President for Life," Chadli, with his dark eyes that followed you everywhere. There had been an election a few weeks before, one shopkeeper had explained with a slight roll of his own eyes. Chadli had been a candidate—the only candidate.

A little further on, however, there was a very different sort of face watching my approach. Set atop a grimy brown trench-coat in the doorway of a seedy hotel, this face had a horrible slash scar across its left cheek and the conniving look of a hungry fox in its deep eyes. To my dismay, it came toward me in a cloud of cigarette smoke. It asked in French if I was from France.

It would have been so nice to have answered a quick, "No," and moved on. But such curtness in the circumstances I find myself in here in Algeria would not be in my best interest, I fear. Since I am so different-looking, and foreigners, especially Americans, so infrequent in the areas I travel, I am under constant scrutiny by the hordes of idle men and boys that seem to hang around the fronts of every tea house and cafe. Though they never try to harm me and ask nothing of me except answers to their questions about America, the fact that there are so many hundreds of their hard eyes staring directly into my own, when I pass down each main street, is unnerving beyond description. Where my eyes move, their eyes move—as if even my very thoughts are exposed for all to see.

So, I knew I could not let my fear of the scar-faced stranger show, for that might cause me to lose respect in the others' eyes. And, rightly or wrongly, I have always felt it is the respect they feel towards me that has been my best amulet against harm being allowed to befall me. Therefore, I took the time not only to talk to the stranger, but also to accept his invitation for a steak dinner inside the hotel, whose manager he seemed to know quite well.

My guard relaxed considerably as the first steak turned into a second one embellished with a couple bottles of locally-grown wines that should have been well on their way to France, since drinking alcohol is normally taboo for Moslems. It returned, though, just slightly at the sight of the fist-sized lump of dinar bills he pulled from his pockets to pay for the meals. But still not enough to discourage me from being talked into following him through the dusk and entwining alleyways to what he promised would be a very interesting "private club."

Oh, but if I had only known then what I know now . . . . The private club turned out to be a speakeasy that was enterable only after a certain code was rapped out on the

planks of its crude door. Inside its sunken hole of a room was
the stench of enough whiskey, tobacco, sweat and intrigue to
choke even the steeliest of adventurers. Lit only by smoking oil
lamps set on the wall ends of some of the long wooden tables,
the pit held a small army of shouting ruffians with dark faces,
all glistening with spittle and the grease of the broiled chicken
I had never gotten around to buying. Just behind my rib cage
there returned a very sinking feeling—I had about as much
business being in such a place after dark as a mouse does in a
den of cobras. How would I ever get out of this one alive!

All too quickly I was rousted out of the doorway by a lively
mob of half-drunken soldiers, and made the guest of honor at
their table. Scarface, much to his obvious displeasure, had to
work his way to the other side of the room where the only
other place to sit was visible. Even through all the shadows
and haze, his glare could be seen as clearly as the gold teeth of
some of the soldiers closing in on me every second.

"Are you with that man?" asked a stern voice to my left. It
belonged to a sergeant built like a pit bull, and the worried look
in his bulging eyes left no doubts that I was in far more trouble
than I had the courage to admit to myself. "He is no good—a
very bad person!" he cautioned in a low sputter. Then, in a
lower tone yet, "We have heard that maybe in the years before,
he has killed two or three people from other countries with
light hair like you. You know—tourists."

Death flashed before my eyes—the unusually big wad of
money, the scarred face, the wine, his friendliness with the
hotel staff, the stare, the knife he'd used on his steak. What
chance did I have, so deeply buried in such strange settings?

The sergeant decided he and his men would work their way
in a friendly manner to the other side of the room and block
the killer's view. I was then to bolt for the door.

At the door I paused just long enough to make sure the
killer's eyes hadn't caught my flight. They didn't. I dashed off
into a driving rain that tore at me in the night's black like
thousands of icy claws.

I did not doubt that the killer would quickly scent the
soldiers' gambit, and his knife's blade would rapidly be closing
in on my throat. Soaked and frightened by all the strange
forms leaping at me with each explosion of lightning, I eventu-

ally ducked into the cold dampness of a dimly-lit tea house. As always, the men quickly crowded about my seated figure.

Just then, in the brilliance of a streak of lightning, the scarred face thrust its burning eyes through the doorway. In the pitch black that followed, a sharp *Crack!* resounded through the heavens, like that of some giant's spine being savagely snapped in half. My nails dug into the table's boards, my heart pounded—surely the killer had spied my pale face between the others' bodies. Surely his leer would be joining the others' smiles.

It never did. And eventually I found inside myself enough courage to push on through the rain and dark to my hidden tent, still expecting to meet my foe once more. But, of course, I never did.

Thank God.

Steven

Heading east along the main highway of Algeria coastline. To my great pleasure I found that the Algerian coastline road was still largely undeveloped and sparsely populated, which allowed me a lot of time and peace just to soak up the wonderfully rugged scenery along what I was to think was the most spectacular stretch of coastline I would follow anywhere in the world.

Tunis, Tunisia
March 8, 1984

Dear Folks,

In eastern Algeria I was to discover unwittingly that police surveillance is very much a part of life in Third World socialist societies. Twice my camera landed me in the police station for questioning by the "inspector." (Every police inspector I met in North Africa looked to be from the same mold—thin, trench-coated, mustachioed, and always holding a cigarette with a cocked wrist. They reminded me of a bad Hollywood film, and I might have laughed, except they also had a grumpy disposition.)

The first incident was in Azzaba. While eating lunch, I snapped two photographs of a mosque that had originally been a Catholic church. Within minutes, plainclothesmen and a uniformed officer were escorting me to the police station. After about forty-five minutes of questioning, I was told to hand over the roll of film. However, I somehow convinced the inspector I'd been photographing children in front of the mosque, not the building itself.

The second incident was in El Kala. Very naively I photographed a harbor that had two small military patrol boats in it. The plainclothesman who had me follow him to the inspector had been chatting with me only minutes before. He'd said he was a "hotel manager."

My frequent brushes with the ever-present (and ever-suspicious) Algerian police authorities also had their lighter moments.

Some would ask to see my "national indentity card" in addition to my passport. When I'd explain that, unlike in Algeria, we didn't have such a thing in America, they'd often look at me doubtfully. So to satisfy the more skeptical, I'd "sheepishly" pull out my Ohio driver's license. Since they couldn't read English, the license was the card they'd been so sure I had to have.

The most unusual incident was in El Kala. Inside the post office a policeman, who had followed me in, stood beside me and insisted I tell him what I was writing and to whom. It was all I could do not to smile. I was writing my notes of El Kala,

111

and the topic just then was *police surveillance*!

At the Tunisian border area later that day, the Algerian customs officials nearly flipped when they found sixty rolls of film in my backpack. I was asked to turn over the roll I'd shot in El Kala—which I did. The film was then taken to a back room where the officials talked with someone behind a closed door. After a few minutes they returned and, surprisingly, handed me the film. It will be interesting to see if it was tampered with.

After all the dangers of Morocco and the perplexities of unforgettable Algeria, Tunisia was to seem like a playground. The tiny nation of windswept meadows and pine-covered hills allowed me some peace in the eight days I took to cross it.

While also poor, it nevertheless was much cleaner, quieter, and modern than the other two countries. Only when I reached Tunis, the capital, on March 8, did I again find stark poverty.

Even though the Tunisians were perhaps the most westernized of the northwest Africa Arabs I met, they were the harshest critics of America I had yet met on the walk. Most of the young who came up to me didn't want so much to ask questions as to preach Islam. All thought of the United States as a racist country currently on some anti-Arab, anti-Islam campaign.

There was a sort of "fundamentalist" tone to their exhortations. The "pro-Islam, anti-American society" theme was voiced by all of the many Tunisians I had long talks with— from the old caretaker of one British war cemetery, whom I shared a pot of tea with, to the schoolchildren who followed me about.

In each of the four homes I stayed in, I was constantly told of how holy Islam is and how evil a society like America's is. The young were anxious to know my feelings about the Islamic upheaval in Iran. Curiously, none of the families had a television, even though they were upper class.

Still, there was that unmistakable fascination with the American. As in Morocco and Algeria, I sensed a desire to be close to the American people, but they just couldn't quite bring themselves to trust such a "liberal" society.

In many ways their questions revealed the sort of things they have, unfortunately, been told of our nation. Questions like: Is Chicago still constant Al Capone-style Mafia gangster shoot-outs? How many bottles of whiskey did I drink every day? Did we believe in God? Why is the government so intent on killing all the Indians? Were we trying to make Lebanon into a colony? Was it true poor people in America were starving to death? Why were we so racist?

Perhaps an experience I had near the village of Tebaba sums up the feeling I found the northwest Africa Arab to have toward us—and for that matter, perhaps it sums up the Africa walk, too.

Kaled, a bright and curious eleven-year-old boy, took me by the hand and led me from the "Garde Nationale" post to the enormous farm of his grandfather, in whose house his family also lived.

The squat concrete house sat atop a hill, on the sides of which were crowded the smoky, cavelike stick and rock shacks of the farms' serfs (yes, serfdom is still practiced in Africa). As it turned out, Grandfather was not only a large land holder but also a member of the National Assembly and quite powerful politically. His name was Abdelaziz El Bahri.

Like dozens of other times in Africa, I was led to a household, completely unannounced, by a child. The large family immediately welcomed me inside and treated me as an equal. All that rainy day and into the evening I was fed and entertained. I was even allowed to sit in on a fascinating Koran prayer chant session done in loud and rapid voices by four Muslim holy men.

However, the next morning, as I heaved my gift-heavy pack to my back, one of the men relatives came to me and handed me my hunting knife. The others watched, smiling. I hadn't even realized it had been taken out of my backpack the day before. As each one of the family stepped up to plant a customary kiss on my cheeks, the message of the knife flashed all too clearly through my mind . . . as close as they and I and other North Africans had tried to be during the past three months, there was no denying our pasts lie in totally different worlds.

Steven

Aboard an Arab ship on the Mediterranean Sea
March 10, 1984

Dear Folks,

In some ways it was a blessing that the current animosities between the United States and Libya prevented me from continuing the walk across North Africa. Though the North African Arabs had on a person-to-person basis been perhaps the gentlest people yet, the prevalent poverty and oppressiveness of their society in general had been so disheartening. There was an instability to their militaristic governments that both offended my democratic ideals and left me wondering if any minute I might be swept up in another of their frequent violent revolutions.

Even as I boarded the ship that was to take me back to Europe, the images of soldiers and guns were still dominating my thoughts of what I had learned in the 1,202 miles I walked there. The city I was sailing from, Tunis, had hundreds-of-thousands of the homeless Palestinian refugees living in shocking squalor on its edges. Only a week before my arrival, the city had been ablaze with anti-American riots, while just a few hundred miles away our own navy had been bombarding Beruit at the same time. How utterly mad I would have looked to any of my own, had they seen my lone, vulnerable figure coursing its way so calmly through the chaos of those last miles in Africa.

As I leaned my elbows onto the railing of the ship's stern and stared at the Dark Continent sinking into the froth of a stormy Mediterranean, I felt all those dark eyes of Africa were still burning into my mind, especially those of a grim-faced soldier I'd passed on the way to the docks. Standing guard before a large shed marked Grain Storage, the intensity in his eyes and the firm grip on his automatic rifle left no doubt danger was very much a part of his life. And lurking throughout all the confusion of ugliness and hospitality that is Africa, there are always the beasts of desperation and frustration waiting to spring at those who are foolish enough to show their hidden fears.

Such a heavenly paradise North Africa could be, if only another race of beings—ones who didn't know war, or jealousy, or religion-had settled it. So blessed by nature with its sun and fertile soil, that part of our world should by all rights be the perfect bride for man's soul, not his latest Hell. What a crime, indeed, to find amongst all that scenic treasure such monsters as a former French Catholic cemetery desecrated beyond repair and, on the other hand, an ex-freedom fighter in Algeria still twenty years later wearing the torture marks of his French captors.

Yet nature, too, has her own bogeymen. In a setting as rugged as that of Africa's, it was not all that uncommon to have her testing my heart as unexpectedly as man could. Take, for instance, the wild dog attack in Morocco, or the monkeys that beaned me on the head with a rock when I was walking along some sea cliffs one evening. Or the time I was dreaming of some fair maiden kissing my mustache, only to awaken eyeballs to eyeballs with a spider as large and shaggy as a humpbacked tomcat drooling over the *nice* caterpillar that it evidently thought it had found napping between my nose and upper lip!

However, as big and fanged and ornery as that eight-legged cousin to the tarantula may have been, it still would have had to grow a few more feet and pounds to try playing in the bristles of the thirteen wild boars that chased me through the snow on an Algeria mountain pass many nights ago. As long as my own legs are, it was all I could do to stay just out of reach of their tusks and scramble up onto a tree limb. In a country where the Moslem religion prohibits the eating or touching of pork, those oversized swine evidently had forgotten that I would have just as soon had them for breakfast rather than play monkey just above their backs.

Fortunately, pigs are not particularly well-mannered, and in time they became too occupied with arguing over who should have first chomping rights to pay much attention to me. Around sunrise, it occurred to some that perhaps the service might be better elsewhere, and off the gang waddled in a black horde of bristles, snouts, fangs and grumpy grunts. From my perch, my tired eyes gladly watched them disappear into the forest, to wherever it is that real bogeymen go to wait for night's darkness to return.

I dropped to the snow with enough stiffness in my frozen

joints to qualify for old age benefits. But at least I was still in one piece, which was all the incentive I needed to shuffle onward to the next adventure.

Now that adventure is the Italian island of Sicily, where I am far away and safe from the dangers of Africa—though not necessarily from its spell.

Steven

The walk thus far
344 days
April 1, 1983 - March 9, 1984
4,547 miles walked

ITALY
STEVEN'S ROUTE

Of all the countries I walked through in my journey around the world, Italy was the only one in which I liked every single village and town and city through which I passed. As I walked across Sicily and up "the boot" of Europe, I couldn't help but delight in this land of surprises and high spirited people.

The walk ahead through Italy
91 days
March 10, 1984 - June 8, 1984
1,050 miles

One of the heaven's majestic lords looks over one of earth's subjects in front of a church, sweeping away the dust of another day of history.

Nicastro, Italy
April 3, 1984

Dear Folks,

Imagine Yonkers, Southern California, and the casts of about one hundred bad Hollywood films thrown together into one small area of terraced brown mountains and gray old towns, and you'll have a good idea of what my ten days of walking across Sicily were like. If I had any notion that I was going to stroll across some quiet Mediterranean island of vineyards and sleepy fishing villages, that was quickly dispelled in Palermo, my first large city after the port of Trapani.

First on my agenda, upon entering, Palermo was to be a quick stop at the post office. What it turned out to be was like a scene from a bizarre play and a good hint at what lay in store for me on that 220-mile-long Italian island. At the door of the post office, a short, balding, middle-aged man, screaming rapidly at me in Italian and laughing hysterically, lunged at me. If that and his clutching at my neck weren't enough to give me a mild heart attack, you can be sure his bloody mouth and glossy wide eyes did the trick. Try as I might to squeeze myself, my huge pack, and the raving lunatic clinging to my neck through the narrow *Posta* doorway, it couldn't be done. I had no choice but, after casting a look of helplessness at the staring passers-by, to take a deep breath, grab him by the neck, and heave him a good ten feet down the walk.

Even at that, I still barely tumbled into the lobby before he was back at the door screaming deliriously. Several persons in the lobby expressed a sign unmistakable in any culture—the finger pointed to the head. I nodded and set my backpack against the wall, thinking naively that life was back to normal.

Wrong. In Italy that was just the opening act. Just then through the door burst two quite young national policemen, "carabinieri," their long hair ruffled and hatless and their smooth boyish faces red with excitement. Swinging from their hands, their fingers pressed against the triggers, were short military-style machine guns. They waved the guns through the air like half-drunken cowboys.

I crouched as I handed the clerk my letters. If either gun had had a hair trigger, that would certainly have been my last trip to any post office.

Incredibly, others in the post office barely took notice of the two shouting gestapo-like figures. My heart was beating wildly, my common sense was telling me to lie on the floor, but everyone else was calmly haggling over postage. Could they be that accustomed to such utter recklessness and open thuggery from their uninformed civil *servants*? I felt sure that had any police officials in America acted in that way, outcries would have been immediate.

However, as I nervously awaited my change from the clerk, something happened that made me realize there were still some on that sun-soaked resort island who knew when things were a bit too abnormal.

One of the older women clerks, a tiny lady with gray-streaked red hair, listened patiently to the policemen for about one minute, then decided she'd had all she could take of their rudeness. Rising calmly from her stool behind the counter, she marched out into the lobby and stared tight-lipped at the still-shouting men.

When they continued to shout orders at the other clerks, waving the weapons about like toys, the older clerk put her left hand on her hip and with her right hand pushed the first husky man back into a disbelieving second one. At last, the lobby grew quiet—but only for a second. For then, the clerk began to scold the two men as a mother might scold a pair of unruly children. With her sharp, stern voice rising higher and higher, she continued to push against the dark blue uniform of the wide-eyed policeman. Slowly, and red faced, the two carabinieri backed clumsily toward the entrance.

I could not understand a word, but it was quite obvious she was letting the young men know she'd had about all she could take of guns, rudeness, and others treating her as less than an intelligent being. Embarrassed, the men finally apologized in kinder voices, while her finger waved accusingly in their faces. But she was not satisfied until they had turned and retreated onto the congested, noisy street outside. As they left, I almost expected her to reach up and "tweak" their ears for good measure. From the others in the lobby came applause. I clapped too.

Since entering Spain last fall, it seems that machine guns

and uniforms have become a part of daily life. How wonderful it was to see someone—yes, even a little old lady!—show the "establishment" that armed intimidation and uniforms did not have to be forced onto anyone and everyone.

The rest of the walk along Sicily's north coastline of rich beachfront villas and auto-congested towns of cement buildings and innumerable small businesses, was not to reach such a state of craziness again. But still, I was to meet more than enough drunkards, braggarts, and strange-acting people to keep me on my toes. And, of course, as always in any place where tourism is heavy, the usual petty thieves and bungling con men.

Italy, it appears, is going to be anything but ordinary. Indeed, a sort of circus at times, if Sicily was any indication. It's enough, I guess you could say, to kind of make me wish I had a little, old, red-haired lady along for protection.

Steven

Cantinella, Italy
April 7, 1984

Dear Folks,

Some wore rags, some dressed in silk. Some talked my sunburnt ears silly, others could only gesture timidly with their eyes and dark hands. Yet there was something all of them— American, Anglo-Saxon, French, Spanish, Arab, and Italian— shared in common, no matter how awkward our speech.

That "something" was *motherly care and compassion*, perhaps one of the greatest morale boosters any one kid far from home could wish for.

Mom, you and I have been unable, for over one year, to share any time together. Believe me, it hasn't been the same without your sparkling eyes, encouraging words, and endless smile. Being so far from home, and all alone at that, has been one of the most painful sacrifices I've had to make for the sake of this trek.

Luckily, though, my days have been blessed with the compassion of so many other mothers, who somehow found yet more love in their overworked hearts for one more gangly kid with a big stomach and a sore body and spirit. Of course, it's not quite the same as you, Mom, but still I don't think I'd have made it these first five thousand miles without all the fussing and care of my "Moms away from Mom."

I don't know why I've been blessed with so much love and warmth every time the walk reached its roughest stages. Maybe I'm just luckier than I give myself credit for, or maybe they've seen something in me of their own children who've long since grown into adults and parted to other regions to live their lives.

I've become certain of one thing, though, as a result of all the kindness shown me by my new moms—without mothers and their seemingly depthless reservoirs of love, this world would be much less beautiful.

How can I ever forget, or even begin to thank, all the moms of the world walk? Moms like Ella, the very first, who treated me to a huge home-cooked steak dinner even though she'd been laid off from her Cincinnati auto assembly job for over a year and was nearly broke. Or Linda, who had to heat my bath water in a big pail on the wood stove in her Appalachian cabin? Or Estaline who with her bright blue eyes and tiny frame *made* me sit down on the porch of her Virginia house and eat breakfast because she thought *perhaps* I was an angel sent by God to test her charitableness. She wasn't about to let me pass and blow her chance at heaven!

Or what of Jodie, who didn't think her elegant, large Washington, D.C. home too fancy for my hobo figure to stay a week? Or Caitlin, with her firey Irish temper and always-crowed pub on the docks of the River Boyne? Or seventy-eight-year-old Connie and her gut-stuffin Northern Ireland soda bread and potato cakes? Or Therese and Danielle, two mothers of huge French Catholic farm families who found room for yet one more hungry lad in their tiny poor homes? Or Rina and her American hospitality and Bible lectures deep in a hostile Morocco? Or Fatima, who insisted on feeding me the Algerian specialty "couscous," even though it meant squatting on a dirt floor for hours to grind and mix the wheat grains by hand?

So many loving moms on this big planet, so many along my solitary path.

Perhaps the best way I can think of to tell them—and you, too, Mom—how much they have meant to the success of the first one-third of my world walk, is to say those three simple words I suspect many never heard enough of in their laboring motherhood years—I love you.

Thanks, Moms. May each of you have a very special Mother's Day.

Steven

Matera, Italy
April 17, 1984

Dear Folks,

There are some aspects of my life before the world walk I used to consider so mundane that I would go out of my way to avoid them if at all possible. One such thing was what I often referred to as "kitchen table chatter." You know what I mean—Dad moaning about the grass turning brown, the brother-in-law telling for the umpteenth time of the pipes freezing last winter, or Sis jealously rambling on about the other girls in her high school class.

I remember so vividly how I'd sit squirmishly at the kitchen table during breakfast or dinner and try my best, as the "wiser older brother," to let it all go in one ear and out the other. All the while, of course, I'd smile or nod at appropriate intervals, and always there'd be a tiny voice somewhere in the back of my mind, groaning, "How boring! The world's on the verge of all-out destruction, and we're slipping into another great depression, and all they can talk about is *that*?"

Ah, but now? Now, I'd give anything to be seated again at that wobbly, old, wooden table listening to such golden words. Yes, that's right, golden.

Golden because I now realize those oftentimes silly bits of chit-chat are the "language" of family, relatives, and close friends—persons I haven't laid eyes, or ears, on for over a year now.

Oh, I've had many conversations around many kitchen tables since departing home, but it's not quite the same "quality" of drivel. For one thing, their relatives have weird names like "Franco" and "Fatima" and are too unknown to me to appreciate their eccentricities. And, most of the time, the others at the table want to do all the talking, for it was their curiosity of America that initially attracted them into inviting me into their homes.

Or worse yet, because I'm a journalist, they seem to think that I'd prefer not to discuss anything below the level of genetic science, or nuclear proliferation, or political elections.

If only they knew how much I don't want to hear another word about cruise missiles and inflationary economies. It's all I can do to keep from asking them, *begging them*, to tell me about something more homey, like how the neighbor's wife filed for divorce again, or how little Bruno's school marks unquestionably hint at the great genius he is destined to be.

Oh, for a big bowl of cornflakes, a steaming cup of coffee, and an earful of good, old, dumb gossip! For, you see, if there is one thing all my observations of various families in this world is teaching me, it's that life is mostly a succession of little and seemingly insignificant events. And those who don't learn to find such tiny events interesting and enjoyable, and instead live only for the "important things," are denying themselves an awful lot of joy.

Luckily, every so often I manage to meet someone on this side of the globe who comes darn close to being a worthy kitchen table chatterer. The basic requirement, of course, is that he must be a fellow American—and some of the best "down home" chats I have had recently were with such people as the American couple in Marrakech, and the U.S. Marine guards at our embassy in Algiers. A super bunch, the six Marines shared their rambling old house with me for two days and nights, while I haggled with Algerian officials over why I needed a one-month visa extension. (Compared to all the other places I stayed in Africa, the Marines' residence was like a palace in a fantasy novel—a happy-go-lucky Scot cook whose brownies could have gotten him elected President, recently video-taped American sitcoms and movies on a large color television, cupboards and a *refrigerator* stuffed with food, and, best of all, a *hot shower*—as it turned out, the only one I was to have the entire twelve hundred miles I walked across North Africa.)

But, perhaps the best yet was a Navy cook from Lawrence, Kansas , I met while visiting Rome last week to pick up more money and my waiting mail. Nearly the same age as I, Brian McCanon and his Wichita-raised wife, Brenda, had me stay overnight at their modern apartment before I headed back to Matera, just about where the heel of the Italy boot is joined to the sole.

Like myself, Brian had also been a restless wanderer in his teens and early twenties, and had frequently taken to hitchhiking all over the great Midwest with usually no more than pennies in his pockets. As a result, we quickly discovered that we had had many of the same types of adventures.

We chatted away for hours in the kitchen, just like old buddies, laughing delightedly at our "the time I got stuck with all the weirdoes in Austin, Texas" stories, and other similarly nearly-forgotten tales that probably wouldn't have meant much to a non-hitchhiker.

In other words—nonsensical chit-chat. The same sort of talk that used to make me groan was now providing me some of my best moments of my life. I couldn't help thinking that not only do the best things in life come in little packages, as the familiar saying goes, but in little stories, too.

The next morning as Brian drove me to the train station I asked him what he missed the most in the seven years he and Brenda had been living away from America. He parked the old Alfa Romeo and thought for a moment.

"I miss not being able to just jump in the car and drive over to one of the family's or a friend's house to talk," he replied slowly. "Phone calls here are too expensive, and I'm not much of a letter writer," he sighed . "Yep, I guess that'd be the biggest complaint I got—not being able to just start talking with the family when I feel like I need to."

I stared silently out at the waiting train.

Steven

An abandoned seaside castle on the southern Adriatic coast of Italy whose very walls seemed to sprout from the rocks of the cliff upon which it was built, and in whose eerie presence I camped for one very mystical night.

Pescara, Italy
April 29, 1984

Dear Folks,

After 5,200 miles and thirteen months of this journey, I'm beginning to suspect that I'm not directing the walk's course so much as it is directing me. In a way it's uncanny, as if the trip has taken on a mind of its own.

Normally, I'm not inclined to be led by "another," yet perhaps this is one time I might be wiser to be the quiet follower. Oftentimes, my best adventures and learning experiences come in places I had never intended to visit in the first place.

Thus, I now find myself in Italy ambling about the rolling grassy countryside and aged village streets with the devil-may-care freedom of King Hobo himself. One hour I will be firmly in control and well on my way toward Yugoslavia, still several hundred kilometers away—then the next hour I'm wandering about aimlessly as if hopelessly absent-minded. That's when I know the walk's "doing it again to me," and it's best to keep my knobby olive branch walking stick tapping onward, for surely some enchanting surprise must be awaiting me.

And oh, what delightful treats I have sampled these past few weeks in the haunting tranquility of southeast Italy's sparsely-populated region—again, a place I hadn't originally intended to walk through. I had wanted to head up the quick, warm Mediterranean side of Italy to Rome and the north, but along the way my feet couldn't resist probing the wispy mountain range always off to the right. So up, up, up I went, for over twenty-five kilometers, completely undisturbed save for the sweet notes of innumerable songbirds and spring-fed brooks, and one old hermit who waved me into his animal-filled cabin for a couple of hours of homemade wine and hunter's sausage.

Then, much to my surprise, but not to the spirit of the walk, my size twelve feet were to go down, down, down the other side of the mountains, never to turn back to the honking traffic and peeling sterile condominiums of the road to Rome. What I descended into was the Italy I'd been searching for all along—a kindly, peaceful land of gray, stone-walled olive groves, breeze-kissed meadows of margarine-colored daisies and blood-red poppies, oceans of deep, wavy grass, and misty-cool rock beaches.

Thanks to the greater wisdom of the walk, I now had something far better, something called *magic*. How else can I describe the excitement that rushed through me one gray afternoon when I came upon the cliff-top shell of a lonesome castle ruin guarding an abandoned earthquake-shattered sea-side lane? Or later that evening when I huddled very close to a driftwood campfire on the tiny beach hugging the castle's tall rock foundation, sure that more than enchantment was peering out at me from the blackening hulk towering overhead.

Several nights later there was to be the "sassi" (rock), the decrepit old city area of Matera. When I first gazed, wide-eyed, down into the enormous spotlighted bowl of low hills containing the crumbling sassi, I could not believe what I was seeing. Surely, I thought, this is as if gazing into Time's window itself. For glaring back at me were the ashen-faced walls and hollow-eyed windows of not one ruin, but an entire city! I could only stare over the wall at the mortared ghosts like a mesmerized Huck Finn, then impatiently await Dawn's sanctifying light with which to explore the five-hundred-year-old relics.

Next to bewitch my senses was the Adriatic Sea. Across one vineyard, then another, I walked to reach the distant beach where I had seen groups of fishermen spreading long nets into the surf. What mysterious creatures could they be trapping, I wondered eagerly? To me, the sea is a thing of ceaseless fascination. Coming from cornfields and maple forests, I can't help marveling child-like at all the squiggly, scaly, saucer-eyed things that liquid universe continually divvies up.

When at long last, after several minutes of grunts and straining muscles, the nets were pulled back onto the pebbles and their cords peeled apart, a pile of the most fragile glass-and-diamond-like figurines I'd ever beheld was revealed.

"What are these?" I asked the smiling red faces above the shimmering finger-length jewels.

"Sardines!" one exclaimed scooping several into his mouth, then offering me a handful. They looked far too precious to eat, yet the adventurous side of me couldn't resist the temptation. Three or four passed my lips. A warm smile creased my face. Like everything else in southeast Italy meant for the stomach, or the soul, they tasted . . . heavenly.

Steven

Regina, a tiny, sleepy, hilltop Italian village, catches the new day's sun.

Cesano, Italy
May 16, 1984

Dear Folks,

Gone are the wind-brushed fields, the darting lizards, and the sun-splashed towns of south Italy. In their places, I now have fog-shrouded forests, fat snails, misty breaths and rain.

And more rain. And so much so that the Adriatic Sea I've been camped beside the past nine days no longer whispers, but roars.

It's a good time to be shut inside and let nature get over its growing pains alone. And, in my case, away from all the howling eighteen-wheeled hurricanes splooshing to and from the factories in Florence and Bologna.

Thus, I have found myself conversing with the villagers in nearby Cesano primarily over countertops and with cursory glances from puddled sidewalks to dripping panes. Or, when not chasing down more "via aerea" envelopes or a loaf of "pane," I've been in my tent whittling down my usual backlog of tardy correspondence.

This railroad, track-hugging, resort town, with its merchants staring wistfully toward winter-weary Germany, and my little poplar forest with its woundup cuckoo birds, have been perfect places to coax the thoughts from my head, to the pen, to the paper. While the front pages of the *La Republica* and the *Corriere Adriattco* (one doesn't read just one newspaper on days like these) report Rome torn by soccer fans rioting, the closest I've seen to a dispute here was a portly housewife correcting a grocer's tabulation.

He thought her small plastic sack of groceries worth 15,000 lire. She thought 14,840 more accurate—a difference of ten cents in our tongue. She, of course, was right, and he had little choice but to go back to watching the northern horizon.

Lest you think I've been lonely, with little more than tent fabric and empty beaches to look at, may I remind you of my writing chores? Much of it has been updates of the first one-third of the walk for several newspapers in the states. Therefore, I've been revisiting many of the walk's personalities, during which time I've had to laugh aloud, or shake my head and marvel at the types and number of faces answering my mental "knock." There were many whom I haven't shared with you in these letters.

Some I had considered perhaps a little too odd, like "Baldy," an extremely meditative monk on Boston's Commonwealth Avenue, whom my meeting was to lead to a temple room in London's Soho District filled with wildly gyrating Krishna worshipers, glaze-eyed street bums, blue-coated bobbies chasing a burglar, and a mental institution escapee who ate flower petals off the floor.

Others were perhaps a bit too sweet, like dear Mrs. Heasley, a seventy-eight-year-old oasis of roses, hot water bottles, and quilted bedspreads in the midst of a warring Belfast.

A few too mysterious, like the aging millionairess, who materialized from the Nottingham fog in a long Rolls Royce to tearfully share her realization that beauty is as temporal for the rich as for the rest of us.

Many, too young, like Xavier, the eleven-year-old French schoolboy with an intensely deep curiosity about that faraway land of behemoth sports gladiators and dazzling technology called America, whose passion for exploring life helped me overcome my language difficulties.

A handful too idealistic, like Guy and Isabelle, with whom I spent several days in their rambling south France home that reverberated with the energies of their three small children, and ten young men successfully overcoming past drug addictions.

One or two may have been a little too sad, like Rosa, a beginning Spanish schoolteacher, whose class I helped learn the words to the "Fame" song. On her own, in a cliff-hugging fishing village with a tragic past and elders who scorned individualism and new ideas, the pretty, dark-eyed English teacher was learning the hard way, how ignorance of the past can still reach out to blind the innocent.

And then there was Ricky, a lame and long-bearded recluse I stumbled onto one rainy afternoon in a cavish tunnel beneath a roadway line with millionaires' condos overlooking Spain's south coast. All his possessions I could count on both hands, including the ragged, Middle Ages Europe Economics textbook he'd re-read so many times in the three years he's been hiding from a society he no longer understood. As his first "guest" in all that time, I was to be honored with his favorite meal—rice-and-mayonnaise stew served in a crusty soot-blackened tin can—and an evening of conversation beside a crackling wood fire that would put most fiction to shame.

So much diversity. So much love. So much wisdom unwittingly imparted to me.

Now, if I could only figure how to use that wisdom to make this rain stop before I go . . . *cuckoo!*

Steven

My only cooking utensil on the entire walk was this soot-blackened ravioli can with a wire handle. For the four months that I walked along the Adriatic coastline of Italy I cooked many a good dinner of spaghetti or macaroni in this can using the salty water dipped right out of the sea.

Venice, Italy
June 2, 1984

Dear Folks,

May 31 was my second birthday on the walk, my thirtieth overall. It's my habit not to pay much attention to such occasions, but still I couldn't help contemplating how eventless the day looked to be.

In Italy, a land where not one native family had invited me to stay overnight in their home, I had hoped to treat myself to Venice's gondolas, arched passages, and fading canals on this transition into my fourth decade. But, by noon, I had to admit that the fabled Venice was still another day's distance.

A little forlornly, I surrendered to the shade of a sycamore towering over an abandoned lane of weeds and crickets. No friends, only myself . . . not much of a birthday at all, I mused, as I settled down to a long afternoon of writing and waiting for what I wasn't sure.

Many hours later, in that period when dusk is born, a mass of panting fur and saliva startled me from my thoughts. I looked up to find a collie with its boy master only a few tail lengths away.

"Are you in need of anything?" the conservatively-dressed lad asked in a soft and refind manner.

I was thirsty and out of water, I replied, still confused as to where he'd come from. He had me take my goatskin water bag and follow him and Yudda into a nearby forest.

Hidden deep in the trees was an ancient barn that had surely been used by a race of Goliath farmers. The barn was set into a massive, tall wall, like some guard tower built into the stone wall of a fortified city. It took all the strength Guiseppe's teenaged arms could muster to slide open the twenty-foot-high doors of thick planks and bolts. We passed beneath one yawning archway, then another, to step into a football-field-size courtyard of sculptured shrubbery and manicured grass, so emerald in color that it hurt my eyes.

I stood as mesmerized as the statues about us. Stretching far to our right was an immense home, dressed in wrought iron frills and white hems on yellow, that rivaled the roses in cheerfulness.

From the house emerged a man with faded jeans, sun-reddened cheeks, and a strong handshake. His smiling eyes met mine on the same plane, a rarity in this long nation of short people.

"How many live here?" I asked, at the same time guessing perhaps a few dozen.

Romeo, Guiseppe's father laughed. "Sempre, uno famiglia," he said merrily.

"Hey! Anyone for some coffee?" a blonde-haired bundle of energy shouted from a crystal-paned window.

We shared a pot, poured into cups of warm milk and sugar. And then, the customary replenishing glasses of wine. Besides raising sugar beets and corn, Romeo was also a grower of grapes. Time passed unnoticed and soon the walk's stories had captured yet another audience of crossed legs and chins on palms.

Eventually, someone remembered to yawn, and Francesca poked her bright head out into the night. It came back with a "tsk" and the offer of a spare bedroom. It was beginning to rain, she said, in the peculiar melancholy tone all Italian women use whenever the world about them is not in perfect order.

Flashlight in hand, I dashed to retrieve my moist notes, Yudda all the time keeping any lingering spirits of old at a distance. Like a goddess, Francesca hailed my return with more hot milk and a plate of thick crusty bread and sweet sausage slices.

"We've a surprise for you," she teased, glancing at Romeo, still keeping the kitchen fireplace hearth occupied.

Taking more flashlights from a drawer, the trio directed me across the front antechamber, past the grand piano, and through a low doorway set in a wallpapered wall. What my flashlight's beam reflected made me gasp. Deep inside of me tiny muscles and nerves tingled. I was gazing at treasures, indeed.

"They are as old as the house, over five hundred years," whispered Romeo, as I touched the faded wall fresco with a reverence I had felt around a painting only one other time. Then, I had been on Mount Washington, in western Massachusetts, in the cabin of a very shy minister who'd shown me an original Norman Rockwell presented to the man of God as a gift by the famous painter.

Now before me were four cool walls of maidens harvesting grain, of Neptune guarding his watery home, of an armless Grecian statue, and of benignly smiling cherubs. So, there had been dozens in the house, after all. Only some were of paint and imagination.

In this room, no longer in use, were antiquities some would pay thousands to travel the world over to look at through museum cases of glass with "hands off" signs. Yet, there I was touching and smelling the frescos as intimately as I might flowers in a mountain meadow.

Back in the antechamber, Romeo showed me several bits and pieces of Roman statue anatomy he had plowed back into the world. The past, particularly so close to a place like Venice, was never far away, from all the evidence he showed me.

That night, I found myself smiling as contentedly as the cherubs downstairs. It had been a heck of a surprise-filled birthday after all.

Steven

These are the parking spaces and avenues of Venice where the roads are not of asphalt—but are all of water. Venice was the most romantic city I would spend any time in, in all the world. I spent four days there immersed in the romance and the beauty in what I thought was the crown jewel of Italy.

Trieste, Italy
June 7, 1984

Dear Folks,

Since this letter will be reaching you around the Fourth of July, I would like to share a story from the walk concerning others' struggles for freedom. In this special story, which still haunts me even now as I am completing my very pleasant walk through Italy, we journey mentally back to Africa, to meet someone very young who reminded me how lucky I am to have a free nation like America as my birthplace.

Fourteen-year-old Luc, a Polish boy I met in Boudouaou, Algeria, last February, knows all too well what it's like living in a nation whose people are controlled by an outside power.

At the time we met, Luc "Skywalker" and his parents, professors of mechanical engineering at a university in Algeria, were also staying with the same Polish priest in whose home I was a guest. The boy and I shared the same bedroom, and as the evening wore on, I couldn't help thinking he was the brightest lad his age I'd ever met. Besides speaking six languages, including English, he could discuss just about any subject with complete comfort. To my delight, he even picked an entire album of tunes for me on a banjo, ranging from Beatles to bluegrass.

With such intelligence, his future should be very promising, I told him. His smile disappeared, and he silently set the banjo on the bed beside him. In the weak glow of the overhead light bulb, his expression seemed to age twenty years. His eyes ceased to sparkle, and his voice grew deeper with much thought behind each sentence.

"In America, I believe what you say would be true. There, I could do what I wanted. You have much work and, for me, I could pick many professions. Or—" he glanced fondly at the banjo,"—if I wanted to only be a musician in a little band all my life, I could do that, too.

"In Poland, though, I do not think I have any future." His voice went from resignation to bitterness—the sort of bitterness that has been burning inside for a long time. "We are a very poor country, and we have no way to escape our poverty.

"The Russians have too many soldiers watching us for the

Polish people to try to be free."

He stood and paced nervously. "Everywhere in Poland, everyone you meet on the streets will tell you how much they hate the Russians.

"How can we ever grow when we must do only what they want us to do? They keep us poor, so we can't fight them and be rid of them. They have too many soldiers. They are too strong. We have nothing to fight with.

"The Polish people can only hope that someday they will have to go away, or someone stronger will defeat them."

He suddenly plopped down on the bed beside me. "Did you read about the American cosmonaut who was able to leave the Columbia a few days ago, without any rope attached to the Columbia?"

I hadn't. I asked him if he meant the astronaut had been using some sort of manually controlled propulsion unit.

"Yes!" he replied. "I was so happy to read that. Do you know what that means?"

"It meant that repairing satellites and building stations in space itself was now possible," I answered.

He nodded approvingly. "That means the Russians will be very nervous. Now, they will feel they have to do the same as the Americans. It will be necessary for them to take more money from the military to spend on their space program.

"Every time the Polish people hear about the Americans doing such things, we are so happy, for we think maybe the Russians will have to spend so much money that they will not be able to keep so many soldiers watching over us."

He said no more about the Russians. He had left no doubt of the frustrations the situation there was causing his people.

"We could be proud, if we could only live like you do," was all he added.

Luc is one of the many examples I've found on my journey, of how detrimental it is when a nation is controlled by another. In those nations where other powers ruled the inhabitants for a long time (like Morocco, Algeria, Tunisia), I found a society that had not been allowed to grow at the rate it could have. Life in these countries was decades behind, in terms of technology and standard of living, even though the people are as intelligent and energetic as people of nations which have progressed.

The temptation to exploit another nation's energies and resources has, in every case, proven too irresistible to the ruling country and its men of power.

Although, increasingly, America is viewed abroad as a sort of imperialistic nation, particularly after Grenada and with Beruit, there still remains a sense of awe at our nation's rapid growth, and freedoms allowed its citizenry. Take, for example, the nearly one hundred names and addresses I came away from northwest Africa with, of young men who hoped I correspond with them, so they could use that as a device to convince their government to let them visit America (where they then hoped to work and live).

America is still unquestionably viewed as the land of opportunity and as a role model by a large proportion of the world's peoples.

Our nation's founders were very wise indeed to have struggled early on for freedom. They realized, as I'm now learning, that true growth, prosperity, and happiness are not fully possible when others hold the strings of freedom.

When I see firsthand how the French kept the North Africans purposefully poor and dependent, and how the Russians are now doing likewise in Poland, I have no doubt the same would have occurred in America, had not a small and vastly under-equipped, but highly heroic group of colonists, taken their own destinies into their own hands.

We should be thankful they did so when they did, while it was still possible. Now, especially in the Polish case, these dreams of freedom may have to remain only dreams.

Steven

The walk thus far
435 days
April 1, 1983 - June 8, 1984
5,597 miles walked

YUGOSLAVIA, GREECE AND TURKEY

STEVEN'S ROUTE

Through the mountains of communist Yugoslavia, to the cradle of Western Civilization, Greece, I finally came to Istanbul. It was with great anticipation that I handed a boatsman a coin and he rowed me across the Bosporus Strait from western to eastern Istanbul, taking me in one short boat ride from Europe to Asia. After walking across Turkey to the Iran border, I was forced by the politics of war to backtrack to Greece, hitching rides all the way back to Athens, where I flew via Moscow to the next leg of my journey.

The walk ahead through Yugoslavia,
Greece and Turkey
126 days
June 9, 1984 - October 12, 1984
2,254 miles

The daughter of a Turkish village chieftan watches the sun set on the communal baking oven and a load of freshly baked bread in a setting still very much like that of a thousand years ago.

Sibenik, Yugoslavia ✓
June 18, 1984

Dear Folks,

I continue to be astounded at the great difference existing between the European societies, even though their borders are as compacted as those of our own states. Italy and Yugoslavia provide the perfect examples.

Italy was money and frivolousness, oftentimes carried to their most absurd levels. Venice, the "crown jewel" of my three-month-long walk in that nation, was perhaps an excellent microcosm of that country's character.

There I found a breathtakingly beautiful city of culture and history and, too, a conglomeration of religious architecture so splendidly huge and richly adorned that no modern-day government could afford to recreate such a fairy tale island. Yet at the same time, Venice was as much a carnival, a "historic Disneyland," as it was the sophisticated kingdom it likes to portray itself as. Side by side with its ecstasy and Peggy Gugenheim art pieces were what seemed to be innumerable vendors or just about anything plastic or sweet imaginable— from "made in Japan" gondola lamps to what is undoubtedly the most scrumptious ice cream this side of the real heaven.

As in most of Italy, the number of visitors (mainly German and American) this time of year seemed to make the Italians look like an "endangered species." During the four days I explored Venice's maelstrom of big-headed deities, clanging bells, flapping pigeons, delighted laughter, and clicking cameras, I honestly believe I met more twangy-voiced Texans and Okies than I'd ever met at any one time in Oklahoma City or San Antonio.

But if it's basics one wishes to explore, then perhaps the "Socialist Federal Republic of Yugoslavia" would be more appropriate. It is a nation that is "officially" not a nation, but instead, six nations—Serbs, Croats, Slovenes, Macedonians, Montenegrins, and Moslems (although eight percent of the populace is of that faith, in this case "Moslem" does not have anything to do with the religion.) Largely because of the disagreements created as a result of combining so many "independent" states, the general poverty of what is mostly a rural lifestyle, and a long history of invasions by its more powerful neighbors, the Slavs have remained about as basic and simple in make-up as the Italians have advanced financially and technologically.

With the typical Yugoslav rural family, for instance, a major home improvement project might be a fresh coat of paint on a pair of old, wood window shutters. In Italy it would have been new, brass-ringed storm windows and aluminum shutters for every door and window.

On a broader scale, the number of semi trucks has dwindled to a negligible level, and rather than rushing about to replace dwindling stocks of potato chips and panty hose, trucks in Yugoslavia groan mostly under such loads as fuel, firewood, cement, and chemicals.

The Slavs themselves, men and women, are as rugged, long-limbed, and strongly built as the mountains that tower over their communal farms of potatoes, corn, wheat, and, of course, grapes. Their daily lives are hard, physical, tedious, and with few luxuries such as leisure time. Every day at sunrise the villagers (which is what Yugoslavia is mainly composed of) go, many in horse-drawn wagons, to the fields to stay bent over for much of the day. For most, I have observed, a long-handled sickle and hoe are their primary work tools, and the same horse that brings them to and from the fields must also pull a plow for a good part of the day. The machinery I do see is never more advanced than small tractors. More often they are hand-pushed gasoline engine-powered tillers.

All times I am around such people, hardly a day passes that I'm not invited to join in a hot meal around the kitchen table. The diet of the average family is simple—often potatoes, pork, watered-down wine, and coarse brown bread with nothing to put on it.

As for houses, they are often bare cement blocks with the yards being virtual zoos of goats, fowl, sheep and peacocks.

Persons my age are an uncommon sight, as most have sought to escape such a life by living in the cities or staying longer than necessary in the schools. Each tiny village I pass through is heavily populated with black-garbed elders, still as strong as ever and with craggy faces that leave me wondering if they were closer to 110 years in age or to 80.

Yugoslavia is my second socialist-run country. If I thought its lifestyle might be different than Algeria's because of its European heritage, I now know better.

As in Algeria, the grocery stores are pathetically barren. The choice of brands and foods is virtually a bad joke, and as for fresh produce—forget it. Many rural stores (what few there are) have less than half their shelf space stocked. Apparently, army rations are a big seller, if their availability in stores is any indication.

I bought a tinned army meal to see just what their soldiers march on. The contents left me wondering if maybe the poor fellows don't do more crawling than highstepping. What I found was a strip of virtual lard one inch thick and five inches long packed in very bitter sauerkraut.

Again, such things as nightclubs, cinemas, and libraries are found only in the largest cities and towns. They are of such poor quality and run-down condition that the fact anyone at all attends them attests to what the human will endure to seek entertainment. The music in what are supposedly night clubs for the young is an odd mixture of Frank Sinatra, old Motown, Bavarian polka, and pre-Woodstock acid rock.

Even more perplexing, if that is possible, are the films. As in Algeria, they are usually shown in old gymnasiums with male audiences, which is probably why the local film censor can get away with showing mostly grade-B, American-made sex films.

But most disturbing of all has to be the reappearance of the ever-suspicious authorities. Once again I find that walking alone, away from any tourist routes, and talking to the citizens are viewed by those in uniform as something of a criminal act. For the third time in a socialist country (versus no time in non-socialist countries), I have been forced to undergo a tiring and humiliating interrogation for doing something I thought perfectly innocent.

The incident took place two days ago in the state of Croatia in Benkovac. This time my questioners were not the police but, worse, the military. What had begun as a friendly chat and exchange of gifts with two new army privates was to end in my being made to get into an unmarked auto, ride into the army base compound, and undergo a three-hour interrogation that eventually broke into a shouting match when I refused to give the names and addresses of every Yugoslavian I'd met since entering this republic June 9.

In my next letter, I will explain why my revealing those I'd met with since crossing from Italy could have turned the whole ugly affair into a nightmare of headaches and possible expulsion.

Steven

A typical city scene in Yugoslavia, with sterile-looking new buildings, and farm horses and tractors meeting in the streets.

Titograd, Yugoslavia
July 7, 1984

Dear Folks,

One of the longest continuing debates in discussions on international politics is whether this nation of twenty-four million is Communist or not. To listen to its leaders and media, one would say it is, or at least, fervent socialism.

Yet, to listen to man and woman on the street, the government is no such thing. Indeed, they can't seem to come to any consensus as to what it is, other than it's not worth their breath praising.

"Communism is brute!" spat one old Slovenian farmer, while sharing the customary large white tin cup of homemade wine with me. "We are not like the damned Russians. We are socialist . . . I think."

"Socialism? Hah! Only on the front pages of the newspaper every morning," a village merchant scoffed. His wife, who, like her husband, had worked most of her adult life outside of the country, nodded firmly.

When I met the merchant and his wife, it was late evening. After a long hard day working in their tiny store, they were on their way to work their small farm plots until it was too dark. It was something they had to do, they said, if they expected to eat and live a decent standard of life.

"In Yugoslavia the people work only to pay taxes, social security, and hopefully have enough left over to get drunk," the merchant joked with a touch of seriousness.

Their combined take-home wages each month totaled around $400, which actually wasn't bad compared to the lawyer who told me his state-controlled wage was $200 a month, or to the fifty-three-year-old doctor who revealed to me that his salary was $5,000 a year.

"It's a Mafioso which controls everything," a senior construction engineer said sadly, as we walked back to his small inner-city apartment after a swim in the cold Adriatic near Split. "The best of everything goes to a few families that run each of the region's governments. What is left, which is very little in such a poor country, goes first to their friends, and then the people."

An example of the above, he said, was in the availability of apartments. Those who knew the right people could get one within a couple year's time. Others, such as himself, would have to bide their time on lengthy waiting lists. In his case he'd had his firm search for a place for himself, his wife and three daughters to live. After ten years he finally got one, even though it was in a neighborhood like the Bronx in appearance.

The facts are that Yugoslavia's Communist Party has been the dominant political force since the 1940's, but that its control over the diverse nationalities of Yugoslavian Federation has never been allowed to become as stoic as that of Russia's.

Here, there are few state or collective farms—agriculture is mostly small private holdings. Individuals may own businesses but can't employ more than five persons. While most businesses are managed by councils elected by the workers, those same workers have been known to go on strike. And, too, the borders are open to the citizens, who can come and go as they please.

"After all," remarked one Yugoslavian waiting on spare parts being smuggled in from Italy for his fishing boat, "encouraging the people to work abroad eliminates what would certainly be much unemployment here."

So, is this nation Communist or not? Perhaps the best way to tell is to let its leaders speak for themselves. Following are quotes taken from a tape recording I made of a three-hour-long interrogation I underwent as a result of talking with two army privates in Benkovac, in Central Croatia. In my opinion, their message and political slant are all too clear.

The words are those of a young army translator who told me in English what the army captain said as he questioned me:

"Why are you walking in this area? No tourists come through here. You cannot walk in this part of the country—there are things you are not to see.

"You must tell us the names and addresses of everyone you have spoken to since you entered Yugoslavia."

At that, an assisting policeman, officially a part of the military here, tried to take my log book. In it are the names and addresses of all I've met while walking. A shouting match ensued—I grabbed it back and refused to hand it over. I saw no reason to have them question (and frighten) innocent people who had done nothing but help me. Also, one of the Yugoslavians named in the book was a former pilot for the C.I.A. He had flown supplies during the Vietnam War to the Loation anti-communist fighters. His past was known by the Yugoslavs who also tried to recruit him for their secret service. Now an American citizen, he was visiting his sick mother when I stayed at his boyhood home on Pag Island, off Yugoslavia's coast.

"In Yugoslavia, everyone is a policeman," the translator half-whispered to me near the end of the questioning, as his captain busily scribbled down my last reply. His words were like something from Alexander Solzhenitsen's *Gulag Archipelago*, and I asked him to repeat, sure I must have mis-heard him.

"In Yugoslavia we are all policeman," he repeated. "You cannot talk about anything you want with everyone you meet. It will be best for you to remember that—believe me."

I believed him . . . and more so, the deeper I travel into this nation.

Steven

Tito's influence is still very much apparent in Yugoslavia. Photos of him are everywhere —you see them hanging on the walls or in the windows of most shops, homes, and public buildings.

Top; Every morning the housewives can be seen watering and sweeping off the streets in front of their homes. *Bottom;* An old man and his wife drink from a pump in the market area of a Yugosalvian town

Titov Veles, Yugoslavia
July 18, 1984

Dear Folks,

Nearly every Yugoslavian home, business, and public building I've been inside has had a framed photo of the deceased Marshal Tito on one of its walls. Also, it's common to find the crisply-uniformed Tito parading proudly on the windshields of buses and semi-trucks.

Much to the chagrin of the present Communist collective leadership, which, according to a journalist I spoke with, wants to phase out Tito's influence and get the country moving forward, the spirit of the former paternalistic "president for life" continues to be strong, even though he has been dead for over four years. As is common in eastern Europe, changes among the common people are sure to be extremely slow and arduous.

But while all this "backwardness of the common people," as one Eastern Bloc leader recently termed their clinging to the habits and beliefs of the past, may be proving to be a headache to some, for me it has provided a wealth of wonderment. Without turning to my imagination, I've been able to go back decades and live in a world where the horse is still a necessity, where gypsies wander from smoking and seclusive camps to dusty villages to sell tin pots and firewood strapped to the backs of donkeys—where religion, be it of church or mosque, invokes a great sense of devotion and mysticism.

This has been especially true these past two weeks, as I've slowly worked my way around the forbidden and mysterious Communist police state of Albania, which protrudes from the Adriatic into Yugoslavia like some ulcerous scab, and which is off limits even to Yugoslavians. My journey around its mine fields and soldier-patrolled perimeter has taken me through the hearts of two of eastern Europe's poorest and most orthodox regions—the Republic of Montenegro and the Serbian Muslim Province of Kosovo.

In Montenegro, thick forests of pine, beech, and cool shade replaced the harsh sun and semi-arid rockiness of Croatia, as did endless mountain peaks from which springs spilled water so cold it hurt to drink it.

As in Slovenja Republic, I again found myself zigzagging down dirt lanes along leftover snow fields and lush steep meadows of white-petaled daisies. Bathing in brightly-bouldered rivers of liquid snow left me wondering if I would ever again be warm.

Herders of goats or sure-footed cattle, rather than farmers as in Slovenja or Croatia, the Montenegrins were tall, lean and finely featured, unlike the short, thick Croatians. Still exhibiting many of the features of the dark-skinned and dark-eyed Turks who ruled over the area for over seven hundred years, the people were as eye-catchingly beautiful as the land.

For the first time since America, I found homes built of wood, although not American-looking with their tall, steep roofs, wood slab exteriors and tiny shuttered windows. Sometimes, as I came upon their stick-fenced dirt yards of farm animals, wood piles, open wells, and women cooking over open fires, I thought of Africa or the Middle Ages.

Like so many times on this walk, the terrain could have been very exhausting, but the sights which greeted me were so fascinating, so different from anything I've ever known, that the kilometers of sharp switchbacks and steep mountain passes passed by almost too rapidly.

In Kosovo, the society was as colorful, rugged and jumbled as the scenery of Montenegro. Its mosqued villages were as close to being like North Africa as anything I've seen in Europe—only instead of a strictly Arab populace, the people were a swirling mixture of Turks, Albanians, Slavs and Gypsies.

Many warned me not to walk through Kosovo. Or, at least, not to sleep in the open there. Apparently the dark-skinned Muslim men with their white skullcaps, their shaven-headed sons, and their thickly-clothed and subservient women, are still too unusual for most Slavs, even after one hundred years. And, too, there are the Albanians, of whom it is said more live illegally outside of Albania than live legally inside that nation.

More than any other region, Kosovo has been the most troublesome for the Yugoslav government. After Tito's death in January 1980, the Muslims, partly inspired by Khomeini's actions in Iran, began to demand more independence from the central government. Two years of harsh police action and much interracial violence took place. Also, many Albanians feel that part of Yugoslavia should belong to Albania.

I found none of the dangerous characters of whom I had been warned, only continued warmth and deep hospitality and curiosity about my American background. I could easily understand the other's concerns. As in all Muslim-dominated societies I've ventured through, the living conditions in the towns were extremely poor, primitive, and dirty, and the men are totally unused to the idea of privacy. In almost a repeat of Africa, I had large groups of ragged-clothed boys and men crowding and grabbing at me.

The littered and crumbling streets of every city or village in this also mountainous region knew more hooves and bare feet than tires, and from the shadows of the dilapidated shops were always the staring eyes. In public, good manners seemed to be mostly non-existent. Yet, whenever I was brought into a home, I would inevitably find myself receiving the best of their food and attentions. While the children and wife quietly attended to any need, the men and I sat in our stocking feet on low cushions around a table set with thimble cups of ferociously hot Turkish coffee and plates of goat's milk curds and cheese and rough dark bread smeared with honey and plum butter. Overhead would be the usual tapestries of Arab desert scenes and the holy shrine in Mecca soaking up our laughter and excited conversation in broken English or French.

Since I spent so little time in the cities, which seemed to be nothing more than the usual socialist-created slums, I found in Kosovo more enthrallment than worry or disappointment. The notion that "the country folk are a gentle folk" was as true here as in any other country I've visited. For example, I watched the gypsies scrounge through garbage in the cities for food to eat and for cloth from which to make clothes, while in the mountains they held their jeweled heads as high as any man's. In the countryside there were no handouts—every man found himself, along with all the others, making the trip each morning to the fields to dig or harvest, or to the town to sell his produce or wares.

In both Montenegro and Kosovo, most were too poor to make each morning's journey except by horseback or horse-pulled wagon. But from the almost haughty posture of their work-chiseled figures, you'd have thought they were in Cadillacs.

Steven

A farmer's gaily painted cart and his horse patiently waiting his return from working in the fields.

Kauala, Greece
August 7, 1984

Dear Folks,

It was circus time in Kauala, a popular vacation town along Greece's northeast shoreline. Time to set aside one night to visit the striped Hoffman London Circus tent, and *ooh* and *aah* with chapped lips at all the twirling leotards, prancing hooves, and glittering spangles.

Like most of the audience, I was to spend a good bit of time gripping seat edges and applauding. Then, when all that remained in the ring was sawdust, I found myself secretly wishing for still more bedazzlements. So, perhaps it shouldn't be any surprise that when the others filed out the front, I ventured out the back curtains to seek the fulfillment of a fantasy those with the heart of a child will always carry—that of living with a circus.

As has happened so often when I've sought to feed my curiosity, I was to find my wishes granted through the kindness of total strangers who, like myself, find life too full of wonderment to not be shared with others. My newest adoptees were to be Brenda, a fifty-three-year-old English widow with a circus career dating back forty years, and her son Mario, twenty-four years old, and as handsome and thickly-muscled as his Swiss father had been. Through their invitation to stay with them in their little trailer, I was able, during the circus's last four days and nights, to intimately observe the behind-the-scenes life of a circus. And to even be one of its performers, even if it was only shoveling after Mario's four trained elephants!

The world I was to be a part of turned out to be every bit as rewarding as I had always imagined it would be. I often found the most tense dramas and best thrills to be nowhere near the ring, but in the private lives of the performers themselves. Take the "Great Karah Kauak" and his monstrous alligators and boa constrictors, for example.

In the arena the reptiles were so obedient to their German master's "hypnotic" commands. But come dinnertime? Hoboy! Then it was a case of everyone for himself, as jaws snapped and the reptiles lunged viciously at Karah's heavily-scarred hands and forearms.

Then, there were the Moroccan acrobats. Late one night, as the rest of our group ringed the flashing dance floor to wildly cheer them on, they gleefully demonstrated to the discotheque's unsuspecting patrons the right way to boogie. Oh, what fun to watch the Greeks' faces, as the Africans somersaulted, spun, and leapt in ways that made a mockery of gravity!

However, the best insights into the daily world of the Big Top were provided by perhaps the least visible person of the entire troupe—Brenda.

Petite, blonde, an endless reservoir of energy and kindness, she had for a long time been a star herself in the English circus world, first with her husband's Wild West act and later, after his death, on her own with riding horses and trained elephants. Now, though, she was considered too old for the ring, and for the most part the glare of the crowd were things of the past.

Although every night she was able for a few moments to don a feathered cap and bright gown and assist Mario in the ring with the elephants, her time was mostly spent doing all the side chores—sewing costumes, selling refreshments, grooming animals, etc.—that everyone must help do to keep the circus's cost down and make some semblance of profit and paychecks possible. It was a schedule that kept her going full tilt from early morning till past midnight, after which she'd drop to sleep on her bed, one of the kitchen table's cushioned bench seats.

I thought her present workload too much for someone her age. Very late one night, after Mario had literally passed out from exhaustion, I let her know my thoughts. She merely smiled tiredly, rose from her bench seat, and reached for some thick photo albums on a shelf. She handed them to me and slowly turned the pages as I studied the large photographs. Most showed an extremely cheery man with huge sideburns dressed in a fancy cowboy outfit, complete with pearl-handled pistols and an extra wide-brimmed cowboy hat. Usually at his side was one of the most beautiful tan-colored stallions I'd ever seen. Maybe I'm nuts, but the horse, too, looked to be always smiling and full of enthusiasm.

The man, of course, was her husband. The horse was his

lead show animal, Trigger, a horse all others had dismissed as being too dumb to be trainable.

"I've too many happy memories with the circus to give it all up," she said softly. "Because of the circus, I had my husband and Trigger, and they showed me for so many years how happy life can be when you don't think only of yourself, but are always wanting to make others feel good."

Unlike many trainers who look upon their animals as dumb and responsive only to fear, her husband used only patience and gentleness in teaching his show's horses. As a result, Trigger showed responsiveness to her husband, whereas others had found only stubbornness. While other horse-riding performers needed whips, or loud voice commands, or even a swift kick to get their horses to heel, her husband needed but a subtle hand signal, or a whisper in the horse's ear, to make it perform.

On Trigger, her husband and the horse seemed as one. They were to become enormously popular, both in and out of the ring. He and Trigger were a perfect example of how love and patience could bring out the best in everything, she said. While he was alive, the days seemed to go so quickly and effortlessly, no matter how grueling the travel schedule and number of chores.

But then, in 1971, the dream stopped. In the middle of a Wild West performance, Trigger, as always, reared high and with nobility. Her husband's hand, however, never made it as far as his big cowboy hat. Instead, it went to his heart. Too overcome with grief, Brenda retired to her home in Southport, only to be coaxed back to the circus later by her son's own aspirations. She had her husband buried in his cowboy suit.

For her life has since become one of chores, memories, and helping others live their dreams.

On the morning I was to continue on my way to Turkey, and the circus to the other side of Greece and eventually back to England, she went into Mario's bedroom and came back out with a large plastic bag. Inside it was something obviously big and light. She handed the bag to me. I opened it. Inside was her husband's cowboy hat. I was nearly at a loss for words.

"I can't take this," I protested. "It means too much to you."

She brushed aside my words and had me try it on. It fit perfectly.

"I'd be proud knowing his hat went around the world with you," she said with an approving look. "For thirteen years, it's only been catching dust. How nice it'd be to think my husband is still helping others in some way."

When it came time to finally part, I was wearing the hat. After a minute or so of walking, I turned and gave Brenda and Mario my customary big final wave. Gripped in my hand was the hat. I swung it as wide and high and grandly as I possibly could—much in the same manner I imagined its former owner would have done.

From her trailer door, Brenda waved back, then wiped something from her eye.

Steven

Brenda's all "spruced up" for one of her acts—serving hot dogs. She is on her way to the circus tent with a tray of some of her fried onion rings and hot water for warming the hot dogs.

158

Istanbul, Turkey
August 23, 1984

Dear Folks,

As the geographical and cultural meeting point of West and East, Turkey will provide many of the best adventures yet on the walk. With Istanbul as the door into Asia, it seems fitting that the journey's halfway mark is only five hundred miles further.

I must confess that this nation of forty-five million was not on my walk route originally. It was only with the greatest reluctance and anxiety that I decided to cross its windswept plains and rugged mountain passes. When I was in Morocco, I realized I would reach this area of the world in the hottest part of the year. I would have to forfeit my original target of Egypt and, instead, cross the northern, cooler land mass of Turkish Asia Minor.

At the time of my decision, I felt as if I was trading a diamond for a dull, filthy dagger. Egypt is so well-known internationally for its warmth and kindness to visitors, while on the other end, all I'd ever heard of Turkish society was of police and military brutality, corruption, and poverty. The fact that over three million Turkish men work in Germany convinced me that in Turkey I'd again find the terrible poverty I found and suffered through in Morocco. A nation that must send such a large percentage of its males so far to find work must be a desperate place indeed, I worried.

As a result of negative publicity from newspaper accounts of Turkey's ruling military's harsh, oftentimes deadly, crackdowns on public demonstrations, and the highly popular Hollywood film, *Midnight Express,* which depicts a true account of a young American's horrendous experience in Turkish jails, I felt a great fear of being alone and on foot in Turkey's remoteness.

In militaristic and Moslem Morocco, I had my own nightmare experiences. And long before that, a bad incident at the Turkish Embassy in Washington, D.C., back in February 1983, during my pre-walk visit to all the embassies.

Late one afternoon in Washington, D.C., I had gone to the heavily-guarded Turkish Embassy with my briefcase, searching for their consulate offices. When I located the consulate's thick steel door, it was locked. A sign on the door directly below a bulletproof peek-window listed the work hours as being during morning hours. I set my briefcase down beside the door to fish out a pen and notebook, when suddenly a gruff voice from behind commanded me to raise my arms or I was a dead man. I reached for the clouds, and spun about to find one of the biggest, meanest-looking D.C. law officers I'd ever seen. Expertly gripped in her hands was a cloth-covered machine gun, and the look on her face left no doubt I was in the wrong place at the wrong time.

After much loud and brusque questioning, I was allowed to leave. I tiredly snapped that it wouldn't hurt her personality to try being a little nicer.

"I don't get paid to be nice!" she growled.

That evening I decided I would most definitely go to Egypt after Greece. Guns, fear, and armor-plated doors had no place on my agenda.

Now, after all the new Turkish friends I've made in crossing the 160 miles of this country's European portion, I feel a bit embarrassed at how easily I had prejudged a people I'd never even met. That policewoman was an American, not even an embassy employee. Her roughness toward me had not been personal, but no doubt occurred because only a few days before, in California, a Turkish diplomat had been killed by an Armenian assassin. Could she be blamed for fearing I had a bomb in the briefcase, especially when I'd set it against the door?

As for the film, *Midnight Express,* I should know that Hollywood is not always close to reality. Now I realize I was most wrong in thinking that all Moslem societies must be alike. Not so, I've discovered. Just as a society's overall character can't be based simply upon the skin color of its people, so it is with that society's religion. Each Moslem nation has been as vastly different from the other as, say, Catholic Ireland, France, and Italy are from one another.

In fact, long before I left Africa, the thought of visiting Moslem Turkey had become intriguing. In contrast to Morocco, Algeria's hospitality bordered on the fairy tale. There, in village after village, I was surrounded by dozens, sometimes hundreds, of curious people wanting so much to know who I was, where I was from, and why—for the sake of Allah!—was I in their corner of the world on foot and alone. They wanted nothing from me, other than stories of my own homeland (which they receive so little of in their tightly-controlled media). The Moslem Algerians wanted to give and give and give—so much so, that many days I had to continue walking well past nightfall, lest the local people discover where I was camped, and come to my tent to merrily drag me away to their homes to stuff my agonized insides with yet another meal of couscous, mint tea and goat milk.

In many towns I had to stride through with my eyes riveted to the asphalt, pretending not to hear the shouts of welcome from cafes and tea houses. Being befriended by a Moslem nearly always means several big meals, constant entertainment, and unquestionably a bed for the night, complete with a tucking into the covers (always done by the men, which, as with all the handholding and kissing of the men with each other among Moslems, took me quite a while to get used to).

Had I not learned to be "rude" to all the Moslem benefactors constantly coming to me in Algeria and Tunisia, I might still be in Africa living the life of a blessed tramp. To illustrate the warmth I am finding throughout the Moslem cultures, in Algeria I had to spend only 200 of the 1,000 dinars I was made to purchase upon entering that country, even though it took me forty days to cross to Tunisia.

And now, in Turkey, I find the thought that these same people once plundered alongside the likes of Genghis Khan and Attila the Hun an almost preposterous idea. The past twelve days their warmth has been a stark contrast to all the cold, high stone fortifications I've passed throughout south Europe, built long ago to keep out the Turk's warring ancestors.

"I think you will find yourself spending more days in Turkey 'resting' than walking," laughed a carpet dealer from Istanbul who, like many others, had invited me off the street to the family's meal table.

I guess India will have to be a bit more patient, if my "evil" Turks have their way. Unless, of course, I learn to be more "rude."

Steven

Top; A kindly old gentleman stops for his photo on his way home with his daily bread. *Bottom;* A gypsy family outside Tosya in Turkey who shared their campsite with me. I found their nomadic lifestyle and their close clinging to the earth like something from the imagination of a John Steinbeck. Their poverty and hard lives, as well as their warm, sincere faces oftentimes made me think of the Okies of the 1930's here in America.

Tosya, Turkey
September 5, 1984

Dear Folks,

Like some endless procession of long, rectangular and angry elephants, they rumble through the bottleneck entryway into Asia Minor as if the dusty brown hills still hold the bandits of centuries past. With air horns trumpeting loudly and with insides fuming, the eighteen-wheelers of Europe charge to and from warring and material-starved Iran and Iraq in numbers that seem insane.

As it has probably been since the time of Alexander the Great, Allah's Turks hold the overland keys to the Near and Middle East. And like the banner-draped caravans of long ago, today's cargo haulers still wear the distinctive color of their place of origin upon their canvas coverings.

The covered semi-trailers of communist regimes, for example, are always uniformly sharp, taut, of spotless military gray or blue, and marked with nothing more than efficiently-stenciled block letters spelling the nation's name. on the other hand, those of "capitalist" societies, such as the very rich West Germany, boldly fly the colorful badges of their entrepreneur lords.

However, the most exciting members of this parade of growling, gnashing work beasts are the much smaller Dodge, Fargo, and DeSoto vehicles of the Turks themselves. Darting recklessly in and out of the paths of the more arrogant and high-riding Volvos and Mercedes-Benz trucks, the Turks' ten-wheelers are driven with an intensity once reserved for their Allah-directed battle horses! Gaily adorned with silk tassels, rainbow-colored beads, tinsel, and hand-painted frills, flowers, and scenes of mountain homes and big-eyed children, their vehicles are wonderfully wacky misfits in the conservative world of commerce and trade. As I have found the people themselves to be, their trucks seem to take a mischievous delight in not conforming to the rules of a modern society.

Combine all these would-be vehicular warriors with the incessant curiosity and hospitality of the masses packed along the road shoulders, and you will have some idea of the maelstrom of human energy and encounters I was immersed in during the first 150 kilometers east of the Bosporus Strait.

Let's take a look at just three of probably a dozen different persons who managed to wave me off my feet during one day in a stretch between the cities of Adapazari and Bolu.

First to shout "Gel! Gel!" (Come here!) at my passing figure was tassle-haired thirty-four-year-old Acip. As did most Turks, he mistook me for a German, but was all the more excited to find I was of a much less common species—American. He is what is jokingly referred to here as a "Turk-Deutsch." As have millions of Turkish men, he has spent most of his adulthood working in Germany and has thus begun to look and act more Western than Eastern.

In our stocking feet and over the usual Turkish breakfast of pickled black olives, hard boiled eggs, heavily-sugared tea in tulip-shaped glasses, honey, bread, and bitter yogurt mixed in cold water, he revealed that we were in his father's home where he had returned for a brief visit. Although he, his wife, and three children were now able to live a modern lifestyle, as a result of his employment in faraway "Deutschland," they were hardly able to enjoy it because of homesickness. The cold and rains of Hamburg only added to his and his wife's sense of isolation. Like it or not, he knew that his aging "Baba" (father), "Anne" (mother), and "Turkiye" (Turkey), would never be fully his again, for his children had been born in Germany, and it would be all too foolish to ever leave behind the privileges of the little ones' German citizenship.

Lunch, and my next insight into this society, were in the town of Duzce, in the insurance offices of twenty-one-year-old Birol's father. Between heaping plates of rice topped with fried goat kidneys, mutton meatballs stewed in peppers, and honey-covered apricots, the soft-spoken Birol described how last year, as a university student, he had been imprisoned for six months for passing out socialist literature. In addition to giving up any hope of a college degree, he was still under police surveillance. Also, he had been beaten with a whip during his imprisonment.

Later, as I packed my notes to leave, a co-worker asked to see my notepad. He scratched out the word "Lenin" that Birol had written while emphasizing some point. It would be "hayir guzel" (no good) for me if the military or police found such words on my person, he warned.

My dinner "host" for the day was to ride up from behind in the dark on a big old bicycle to invite me to tea in the tire repair shack where he worked the night shift alone. Thickly mustachioed, wide-chested, and handsomely iron-jawed, twenty-year-old Aydin was the fiercely proud son of Russian parents who had fled the communists when he was a small boy.

At one point, while stuffing ourselves with cantaloupe and a rough, flat bread smeared with red-rose-petal-flavored honey and goat milk curds, he pointed to a poster of fur-capped Russians with curved swords leaping high above pony-tailed maidens, and making a fist, he shouted that he would love nothing more than to be a free and fighting Cossack of his Caucasus homeland. Reaching into a desk drawer, he pulled out a grease-smeared harmonica, wiped it across his leather vest, and blew through it a Russian dance tune that would have had the maidens leaping, too.

When the harmonica at last became silent and the floor stopped shaking from the pounding of heels, Aydin invited me to give up the road for the night and try sleeping on a cot in the back of the shack. I accepted. It hardly seemed sensible to turn down three offers of bed and shelter in one day. And besides, the world could do without one more misfit for at least a few hours.

Steven

Top; Aydi, my generous and jovial host, stands proudly with his rice paddies behind and below him in the valley. *Left;* The stairs leading to Aydi's veranda. Notice the jumble of sandals and shoes left at the bottom. Typical of most countries in the world that I was to walk across, the shoes come off before one goes into the house, which I think is a very sensible and hygenic thing to do.

Koyulhisar, Turkey
September 17, 1984

Dear Folks,

His face was ugly enough to scare away the meanest grizzly, his hands thick enough to be roots of the mountains guarding his golden rice paddies. In a more primitive setting, say central Africa, his strength and seventy-three years would have made him the village chief. To the one hundred or so inhabitants of Guney, Koyu, however, most of whom worked in his rice fields in the valley far below or were related to him through his four previous wives, Aydi Bekir was simply the boss, grandfather or father.

My path across north central Turkey to his mud-walled domain had taken me through a land whose character changed quickly and erratically. One day I might be staggering over terrain as barren as a lunar plain, while the next day would be spent floating through a deep river valley as lush and green and filled with children's laughter as a postcard from Katmandu.

About the only consistencies I could count upon in this jumbled region were the rising of the land, the lowering of the lifestyles, and much to my weariness at times, the incessant large crowds of curious menfolk in each distant village. And so it was to be in tightly cloistered Guney Koyu, too, when I climbed its dirt footpaths to photograph some housewives I'd spied baking bread in an outdoor stone oven.

At first I was tempted to politely refuse Aydi's offer of tea. Already that long day I'd consumed twenty-two teas and two colas in the previous village of Hacihamza (Ha-gee-hom-sa), where I'd allowed myself to be enticed into several waiting crowds of men and boys dressed in crudely patched cloth. But when the smiling giant quickly added a bed and dinner to the tea, I motioned him to lead on.

The hospitality ritual which followed was typical of treatment a guest receives in Turkish rural homes. In many ways it is still largely unchanged from those described in Marco Polo's own journals. Like then, the guest is made to feel that he, not the host, is the most important person present under that particular roof.

At the bottom of the stairs leading up to Aydi's home

above a grain storage barn, my shoes joined at least ten pairs
of thin rubber sandals. Atop the wooden steps was a veranda of
bamboo shades, intricately patterned wool rugs, rough wood
benches, and one low hard sofa piled with long and heavy
flowery pillows, upon which I was made to recline. Very
quickly, the usual huge round tray of tea and food was placed
before me by his sons, and the benches and rugs were filled
with males of the village, come to satisfy their curiosity and
show their respect to another of their kind.

As is normal in a Muslim household, the females stayed out
of sight, their presence made known only through the comforts
obediently served by the sons and, rarely, from a fleeting
glimpse of a scarved head stealing a peek through an open
door.

This particular day happened to be the first, and most
important, day of the four-day-long Muslim "Bayram Kurban," or feast of the sacrifice. All through the Islamic world on
this day, all who could had killed and butchered a ram for
Allah, with one-third of the meat going to the owner, one-third
to his neighbors and the remaining to the poor. Thus, besides
the normal bowls of yogurt, spicy vegetable soup and whole
freshly-picked tomatoes and peppers, there was a generous
heap of the sacrificial animal, diced and covered in its simmer-
ing greases, on my tray.

Five times, once every hour, one of the young boys sitting
silently off to the side rose and poured perfumed water into
each man's cupped hands. Then for several seconds the air was
filled with the fragrance of lemon and the sounds of palms
rubbing together against forearms and stubble, instead of
coarse voices grumbling or boasting.

The Turkish language has been one of the easiest I've tried
learning. So I was able, even if only in Tarzan fashion, to add
my fair share of manly chatter during the evening. We joked
about how I would become a "Bayram Kurban" if I dared to
cross into Iran and how it seemed everyone but me in the room
was related to Aydi. Trying to figure just exactly how many
grandchildren he did have provided plenty of argumentation.

Late that night, after the village men had returned to what
must surely be some of the world's most patient wives, I was
buried beneath a ton of blankets on that same sofa. A beaming

Aydi sat beside me dressed in striped pajamas and stocking cap, looking as if he wanted to do one more bit of goodness for me before retiring.

I hinted that a glass of water might be nice. He rose from his chair and dashed into the house as if every second meant the difference between life and death. He strode back to my side several minutes later with the water and a plate of more kurban. Not until I'd finished every morsel and he'd had the pleasure of fetching me one more glass of water did he go off to the wife I was never to meet.

For a while longer sleep remained as elusive as the stars shining between the mountain peaks now forming my bedroom walls. On my arms were goosebumps that I knew came not from the chilly air or the muffled thunder of the Kizi-lirmak River far below. Rather, they were caused by the realization that my walking was doing exactly as I'd hoped it would—placing a question mark in the minds of those I passed and impelling them to invite me into their homes, their hearts and their minds.

Now, only a handful of days from being halfway around the world, I've already seen so much it almost frightens me to stop and dwell upon all the new scenes added to my life the past eighteen months. During the past week alone, I've camped with three gypsy families, bathed in a lavish seven hundred-year-old village bathhouse and marveled at the beauty I'd found inside a mosque a caretaker had silently waved me into.

I shudder. Supposedly the most exotic still lies hidden over the horizon.

Steven

Erzurum, Turkey
September 29, 1984

Dear Folks,

Just before the one-quarter mark of my journey, I wrote the following from Spain to a friend:

"The World Walk continues to provide me with more romance, excitement, beauty, and wonderment than I'd ever have imagined possible. So much has happened to me that at times I am moved to tears by the impact of all that I have seen and learned.

"What an incredible planet we live upon. How will I ever be able to properly share with others even a tiny fraction of all the new things I have become aware of? Indeed, these past months since departing from my Ohio hometown of Bethel have seemed more like fiction than reality.

Can life really be this magical? I've asked myself so many times. Let no man tell you that he is bored or that life is dull—for there can be no excuse for such feelings on such a paradise of activity as Earth. And, likewise, let no one convince you there is not heaven, for it is all about us."

Now, the halfway mark itself—7,500 miles—has become another ingredient in my memory's caldron. Those words I penned in south Spain ten months ago remain true. Still, with all the obvious benefits that have come my way through the walk, the question of why I'm doing it remains strong in the minds of many who've learned of my journey.

The whole thing began innocently enough as a nine-year-old's whim to someday grow up and explore the entire universe. My inspiration was (and still is) that old killer of cats—curiosity. Growing up with the awareness that there's a whole wide world of strange things out there waiting to assault my senses was all I needed to keep my itch alive. It was to be one fantasy which refused to go away in the sobriety of growing up.

Still, the dream might have slowly passed away if not for the disturbing words of an eighty-year-old woman who wore the world's firmest smile, though her own legs were too weak to support her anymore.

"Whatever your dream is, do it while the urge is strong.

Don't put off the dream until a 'better day,' because life never gets any better than when you're struggling to see your dreams come true," she said softly during one of our frequent evening chats.

At the time of my grandmother's advice I was twenty-three and more tempted than not to follow the secure course of a nine-to-five journalist. But the more I contemplated her words, the more sense my boyish fantasy made, as opposed to what seemed the "normal and reasonable" route to take.

Taking the extra time and effort to explore in detail the world about me just seemed to fit. I loved learning, meeting people, exploring and traveling. So, why not?

Traveling on foot, strange as it may sound, even made sense journalistically—when you're walking an area you are exposed to everything. Little misses your senses. Plus, I would be able to collect enough interesting personalities, settings and stories to satisfy my writing needs for a lifetime times ten.

I also felt there had to be more goodness in the world than the stories coming across the news wires were telling me. I disagreed strongly with my journalistic peers' pessimistic views of the world and its future.

I knew from hitchhiking across the United States several times during my teens that, more than anything else, people love to help others. Many times they couldn't seem to do enough.

Thus, all the more reason to travel on foot with only a backpack. In that manner I would be purposefully depending on the everyday common people to help me around the world. In a sense I wanted to test mankind, and if it responded as I thought it would, I might even, in my own small way, help to break down the popular conception that this is mostly a cruel, cold, selfish world.

Depending on others forces me to meet many day in and day out. So, in my own subtle way, I was forcing myself to experience far more human encounters than the average traveler can ever have. And a greater variety, too.

There seems to be a mystique about the young lone traveler with a pack on his back. It's as old as history. In the Middle Ages monks and people of the church used to go on long pilgrimages alone. For thousands of miles they would walk and

people always took care of them. And it's still true. People—
you and I—still feel an inner compassion for the lone traveler
seeking nothing more than knowledge and friendship.

All of which, as you might guess, suits this particular
knobby-kneed pilgrim just fine.

Steven

Like in some surrealistic Salvador Dali painting the farmhouses and
the cow-dung cones nearly jump out of the scenery from the barren
landscape of eastern Turkey.

Athens, Greece
October 15, 1984

Dear Folks,

Turkey, in the remaining miles to the Iranian border area, was as desolate as my own boots. Dirt turned into restless dust, then into rock, then finally into lava, cooled and battered into grotesque forms by centuries of Russia-bred winds. Objects like farmhouses and grazing livestock, normally barely noticed in passing, stuck out from the earth's baldness as starkly as the subjects in a Salvador Dali painting.

The people themselves often took on the raggedness and ugliness of those in a Charles Dickens' slum. From the hairy lips of many of the men there no longer came forth offers of tea and food but, rather, fanatical exhortations to the greatness of Allah and bitter grumblings about their deepening poverty.

When the tractors turned into oxen and the stacks of firewood into high cone-shaped piles of cow dung, an uneasiness grew inside me. The villages had decayed into settlements nearly as primitive as those Genghis Khan's arrows had once targeted, and the dirty faces that stared at me from inside the smoking mud-walled homes had an intensity I'd not seen since Africa.

There are many who say the devil himself presently reigns in neighboring Iran, a beautiful and exotic land once known as Persia. Perhaps there is more truth to that than the rational mind is willing to give credit. Certainly from the amount of war-related material moving in that direction and the deteriorating state of nature and man as I drew closer to its borders, I was left with a strong impression that beneath the curtain currently draped over the Iranian society there are few rays of laughter and song.

A young English-speaking and fanatically devoted Muslim police commandant whom I was brought before in Eleskirt, a military-ringed town twenty miles from the end of my Turkish journey, may have provided a glimpse of what would have awaited me in the present Iran, had I gained permission to cross it. At the very least he was a good example of the condition a man's soul can take when he refuses to learn about others firsthand but, instead, relies only on his own emotions and on what others tell him—a situation very much in effect in Iran now, according to most of those I've talked with who have been there lately.

The commandant's Gestapo-like subordinates found me in a dark tea house on a side street choked with horse-pulled buckboards and shouting schoolboys in dark suits and ties. I was busily working on my notes at the time, which apparently gave them the excuse they needed to raise their voices and show how intimidating they could be. While the others in the room slunk past the grimy windows and back out into the street, the officers fired away with questions like: "Why are you here? Why aren't you in a part of Turkey where the tourists go? What have you seen? What are you writing? Whom have you spoken to?"

My explanation that I was walking around the world and their town simply happened to be along my route seemed to fall upon deaf ears. Even my clippings, journals and signature book failed to make an impression. I was perplexed. Why didn't they want to believe me, or even listen to me for that matter?

At the police station their commander's words and actions provided me the answer. To my embarrassment, I was brought to his office with a policeman close on either side of me, as if I were a criminal. Before I could sit, his first question was hurled at me.

"You (Americans) think you are first class citizens?" he asked loudly in a mocking tone.

When I answered yes, he flung my passport at me and spat, "I think you are fourth class citizens!"

He continued with much disgust, "Everyday I read in the newspapers how your country is all homosexuals and drugs. You are perverts—you think only of money and sex!" A sick laugh came from his muscular chest and he snarled with much delight, "And I think your President Regan is the biggest pervert of them all."

So that was why his men had refused to listen to me in the tea house. Like their commander, they hated Americans, and relished the thought of having a chance to bully one for awhile. In all likelihood I was the only American to have stopped in their little domain in years, certainly the most vulnerable and accessible one. My fears became all the more certain, the more the commander spoke.

"Where is your permission from our government to write about us and take photographs?" he asked.

Of course, I had no such papers, something I hated to admit because he knew I was a journalist.

He smiled arrogantly and tapped my journals, saying, "I think I will lock you up for a few weeks. How do I know you are not a spy?"

What he was saying was not only obviously absurd but also potentially embarrassing to both him and his government, I said with more shock than anything in my voice. He laughed all the louder.

"Everyday people write bad things about Turkey—what is one more bad story?" he said angrily. "If I want to I will lock you in prison for years and not tell anyone! This is Turkey. You are under my power now."

No, I thought sadly to myself, this is not Turkey, not the warm and gentle country of smiles and new friends I'd been walking through the past two months. This was something else, an extension of Khomeini's hell perhaps, but no, not Turkey.

The rest of his profanities and mockeries seemed to be aimed at provoking me into some angry response or action that would give him a real excuse to toss this "enemy of his beliefs" into a cell to rot. But I remained calm. I had seen for myself, both growing up and in my walking, what my own society was like, and it was nothing like what he had so foolishly let others convince him it was.

I became very much alarmed when the commandant placed me under house arrest, and realized things were getting seriously out-of-hand when his two armed guards marched me off to a separate building. There they left me alone in the empty, darkened house, with one machine-gun-toting guard remaining stationed outside the front door.

Later that night, when I found to my amazement that the rear door was open and left unguarded, I took it upon myself to make my escape. I wondered if it was just a "set-up," whether they were out there just waiting for me so they could shoot "an American spy trying to escape." I decided that I must take my chances and stepped out into the night. Under the cover of darkness I crawled on my hands and knees away from the jail, and made my way out of town.

I walked all night, carefully avoiding the roads, and arrived at Agri, twenty miles away, under the grayest clouds I'd seen in my fifty-five days of walking through Turkey. I was exhausted and feeling sick, but I was happy. I'd escaped what I felt was certain death at the hands of that madman, and to make it all the better, I was now at the end of my walk through Turkey, and halfway back to home.

Steven

The walk thus far
561 days
April 1, 1983 - October 12, 1984
7,851 miles walked

PAKISTAN AND INDIA

STEVEN'S ROUTE

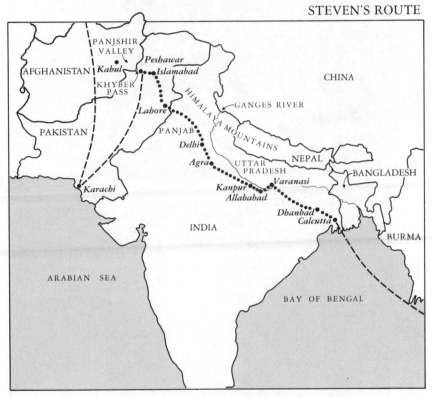

Because   the wars prevented me from walking across Iran and Afghanistan, I flew from Athens, Greece, via Moscow, to Karachi, Pakistan.
Having planned to start my walk across Pakistan from the Afghanistan
border at Khyber Pass, I had to take a train from Karachi north to
Peshawar, where I continued my walk at the foot of the Himilayas.

The walk ahead through Pakistan and India
114 days
November 2, 1984 - February 23, 1985
1,347 miles

It's off to school with big smiles and sparkling eyes for this young Indian sister and her brother even if it means that one of them must go barefoot like some present day Huckleberry Finn.

Peshawar, Pakistan
November 7, 1984

Dear Folks,

After three weeks in Athens, Greece, resting after crossing Turkey, and preparing for the second half of the World Walk, I flew onward to Pakistan. On the long flight aboard the Russian Aeroflot jet, first to a freezing Moscow and then to a steaming Karachi, bouts of frustration gripped at my insides from time to time.

I was mulling over my failure to gain the permission I'd needed to cross Iran on foot from Turkey to Pakistan. I had visited the Iranian consulate in Istanbul, Turkey, before my return to Greece, in the faint hope of finding a way to cross its interior on foot, but, alas, the results were as disheartening as ever. I was told I must wait up to eight weeks for a visa, and then I could only visit (not on foot) certain areas for a very short period. Any way I looked at the conditions offered, it amounted to a waste of my time and energies.

Perhaps it is as well that I had to go around that nation, for while inside the consulate I studied a map which showed that much of Iran's western area, even up near the U.S.S.R., had suffered attacks by the Iraqi army or air force. Also, there were posters and blown-up photos on the walls—dozens of them, all screaming of death and the glory of spilling blood.

It was so saddening to think the once beautiful Persia had aged into something so wretched and devoid of smiles. Had she no more compassion or love or humbleness? If she has, they hid themselves well from my eyes.

Iran now lies behind, the first missing link in the walk's growing chain. The empty pages that should have held her stories now must serve to remind me of how vulnerable learning is to tyranny.

In Karachi I bid the hefty stewardesses of the world's largest airline good-bye and descended onto the opposite side of our world. Now it is Pakistan—a nation that, from what I have seen these past several days, still simmers in a heat and a humanity as stifling as when it was known as the Western Province of India.

As before, the beggars still defy the imagination in their

contorted frames and variety of afflictions. Also in their numbers, as one is never far from their reaching arms. And, too, there is the endless crowd of loosely-garbed humans still rushing and buzzing as if possessed with the energy and mindlessness of insects.

Such commotion I have never witnessed. There is the temptation to conclude that here man has lost all control of society, that somewhere in the past he suddenly went mad and is becoming all the more so with each minute. This is the land that many who should know of such things have said the walk's final chapter will be written. So frightening have their views of my chances been, that I have come to wonder if by coming here I, too, have lost my mind.

In the walk's dawn there were those like Pakistan's own embassy officials in Washington: "You will not walk there!" the consulate director had shouted, angrily flinging his eyeglasses to his desk top. "There are too many thieves—you will be killed, of that I am certain. You must take a train or a bus."

Then later, many like Phillip, a seasoned traveler who had been to that still distant nation: "In Africa you stand a chance because the bandits have only knives. But in Pakistan," his eyes narrowed, "they carry rifles. Life there has no value. They'll shoot you for less than your shirt."

And now, just a little over two weeks ago, a warning from my own nation's embassy in Athens: ". . . a high incidence of nighttime robbery by bandits. Visitors should be certain to reach their destination before dark. Bandits have been engaged in robbery, abductions and shootings directed against road travelers in daylight hours . . . " the State Department's computer printout warned of several areas in Pakistan.

As I write these words to you, I am being mercilessly rocked about in the dusty carriage of a train taking me to the Khyber Pass on Afghanistan's northeast border with Pakistan. The land rushing past my window has, for the most part, been flat and hazy with dust being kicked up by camels, oxen and the sandaled feet of what has seemed like a million fragile brown-skinned figures. Today the world has shown her age and her weariness in trying to support so many for so long without any sleep.

Yet, I am not worried about her. Soon she will be young

again—soon, in only a few hundred kilometers, nature will once again sing and man will be reveling, not suffering. Where I am going, it is said, the snow on the distant peaks rivals the sun in brightness, the fields are full of fruit and the perfume of rare flowers, and the people so fiercely independent they have never been conquered by any army, from Alexander the Great's to those of the British colonizers.

It is the land of the Pathans I dream of—the largest tribal society in the world. It is beneath their turbaned heads and handmade guns that pass the most famous routes from the Middle East and Central Asia to the Indian sub-continent. So great is their determination to live as they wish, that the military rulers of this young nation (formed in 1947 for India's Moslems) have not dared to wrest from those men their many guns.

Perhaps some may think me a fool for entrusting myself during the first part of my walk across Pakistan to so much pride and cold steel, but I think it is my safest option in a nation filled with lawlessness. It has been my experience on this journey that those peoples whom others speak of with much awe and reverence are always societies in which law and order dominate, where there is a heightened sense of what is right and what is wrong.

And, especially important in my case, such esteemed peoples generally are all too aware of the painful consequences to be suffered by any of their own who dare to act dishonorably.

Steven

Wah Village, Pakistan
November 15, 1984

Dear Folks,

The road explodes into dust with each step. Every morning my tent is frosted with brown. Winter's rains have yet to venture down from their Himalayan nests. Each leaf is thirsty, each face needs a bath.

The towns are flash floods of faces, colors, sound and movement. Mankind has become like an ant colony, always moving and going somewhere. Nothing rests, not even the invisible. Never would I have thought the air able to bear the weight of so many smells and sounds. Surely I am fallen into the orchestra pit of the very universe itself. And with an orchestra conducted by not one, but a million mad conductors!

These musicians don't play violins or clarinets. Rather, they toot auto horns, buzz scooter engines, ting-ting-ting bicycle bells, clang hammers against glowing iron, crack horse whips, bubble curry over crackling wood fires and thump bare soles over packed dirt and garbage. They are the music of life overflowing, of too many proclaiming to the very reaches of the universe the energies burning inside them.

And what of the dance floor? Pakistan is a land decorated in the ugliest poverty but also with more color than a thousand springtime mountain meadows. Then, too, there are the singers, wailing the Koran from lotus-shaped mosque towers, chanting from overcrowded schools and harping of their gold, silk or rotting fruit from inside seedy closet-sized shops.

Finally, there are the dancers themselves. As numerous as atoms they twist, roll, squirm, bob and side-step from one spot to another with all the quickness of untiring sprinters. Most are dressed in turbans and mustaches. Many are young. A few peer over veils with eyes as seductively beautiful as those with which earlier civilizations graced their goddesses. Nearly all seem happy to be swirling with life's forces.

How is it possible one tiny planet, let alone one nation, could be such a paradise of life? Everywhere there is a throbbing, a dashing and clashing and mashing of man and beast that won't allow the heart to slow. Even time must race to stay ahead—no sooner anymore am I shaking off the chill of dawn than dusk has again returned and I am crawling back into canvas and down, to avoid bumping into those who prefer the darkness rather than the flames of twigs or kerosene.

The warm smiles, the limp handshakes, the humble bowing of heads leave no doubt I am among friends—perhaps the gentlest yet. Still, my eyes dart about like caged animals. With so much energy loosed, one must be constantly attentive, or suffer the inevitable collisions with everything from bicycles to hand-pushed carts to arrogant camels. Five minutes in the market district of any town or city brings with it more speeding objects than a "Star Wars" battle scene. Unlike the western societies where technology and strictly enforced laws have managed to direct each day's rushing masses into some semblance of channels, here man, beast and machine are always challenging the other for the right-of-way.

Half a dozen civilizations have flourished here along the banks of the Indus River. It's tempting, with all the exotic foods and architecture and people, to think that none of those of the earlier societies have left. Yet the millions of graves and the tired soil say otherwise. Historically, this land is one of the most ancient cradles of society. Cities thrived here before Babylon's first bricks were laid, and the inhabitants of those cities were supposedly practicing citizenship before the Greeks knew of such principles.

"Love is life." So goes a popular saying in this almost exclusively Moslem nation of over eighty million. If that is so, then here love is greatly manifested. Certainly there is no doubting their love of life. Nearly three out of four people still farm the land. Even in the cities the side streets are more like barnyards than roadways, while in the markets the caged chickens, pigeons, canaries and parrots for sale add their squawking to the din.

Though the present culture is Moslem, the vestiges of the prior one of the Hindus are everywhere. Not only is there the love of the soil and of nature in general, the temple-shaped mosques, the spicy rice and curry dishes, the long shirts and baggy, drawstring, pajama-like trousers and sari wrappings, but there is also a love of color that borders on obsession. The most ordinary buses and trucks, with their skirts of wind chimes and their streamers and hand-painted panels of peacocks, jet planes, roses, tigers and nature scenes make it appear as if everyone is rushing off to a Mardi Gras parade.

Indeed, I'm still waiting to be served my first bowl of rainbow rice!

Steven

Farmers with their camels come from outlying districts to the market at Lala Musa, Pakistan, each day to sell their produce. An incredibly exotic scene, like something from the pages of *Ali Baba and the Forty Thieves*, one will never see so much confusion as that of a narrow market square jammed full of cursing truck drivers, shouting merchants and cantankerous camels. Lala Musa, a city of 75,000, is in northeastern Pakistan.

A farmboy beside a haystack whose big smile made me forget, at least for a few moments, the pandomonium and the cacophony of the traffic along the royal route (the G.T. Highway) I followed across Pakistan.

Top; I was surprised to find that the people in Pakistan, despite the dusty and grimy conditions that they had to live in, still made an effort to keep their clothes so clean and pressed, even though it meant for many using an iron that was better suited for the last century. *Bottom;* A barber's entire set of tools on a roadside stand in Pakistan. They may look crude but they did the job. Oftentimes I paid little more than twenty-five cents to have my hair cut with these rusty, old-looking implements.

Lala Musa, Pakistan
November 25, 1984

Dear Folks,

The words of a stranger. How often I hear those, and yet how few I can still recall by day's end. Most are of the simple and ordinary things in life, like how the weather is, or praise for someone's work. While other times those words from an unfamiliar voice are too important to ignore, and to forget them, to not pass on their message, may mean all the difference between living and dying for others.

A lot of tragedy, oppression, and need reaches the ears of one willing to listen earnestly to the voices of the public. This is especially true when, as I sometimes do, you let the others know you are an actual journalist searching for *their* view on life. So, how do I decide which of those stories or messages is retained and shared with others in my writing, and which are to be condemned to silence? It's never an easy choice. Sometimes, something as innocuous as the look in the other's eyes, when they tell me their words, can be the key to my taking any action after we have parted and gone on to new distractions.

For almost two weeks now, I have had just such a pair of eyes tormenting the back of my mind. Ironically, they belonged to another journalist about the same age as I am. He was an Australian, and when I met him in Peshawar he had just returned from one month with the mujahadeen (freedom fighters) in Afghanistan's battle-blackened Panjshir ("Five Lions") Valley, just north of that occupied nation's capital city, Kabul.

Peshawar, where journalist Anthony Davis and I met in the dining room of the Green's Hotel, has always been more than just another town. Built at the spot where the infamous Khyber Pass spills down from the barren ranges of Afghanistan's Hindu Kush, Peshawar was directly on the path of most of the trading caravans, nomads and conquering armies that swept down from the vast expanses of central Asia to the Indian subcontinent. As in the past, the greatest riches to pass through its shadowy narrow streets of hashish smoke and overhanging balconies are its people—especially the hardy, enterprising Pathans, the ever-changing tiny crowd of adventurous foreigners, and lately, the steady stream of refugees from the war in Afghanistan.

It is the plight of those three million refugees that have crossed into Pakistan since Moscow's December 1979 invasion which Tony loves to cover the most. A Bangkok-based correspondent for the highly-regarded newsmagazine *Asiaweek* and *The Washington Post*, the short and stocky writer speaks the Afghans' language fluently and is well-known to the mujahadeen's leaders. Three times he has risked his life to illegally cross the closed Pakistan-Afghanistan border and travel firsthand with the guerrillas to get the complete story of the fighting there. This latest trip was prompted by reports of a massive Soviet offensive on the Panjshir valley last April, the seventh of eight offensives since 1979.

"We wanted to see just what was left," he said.

Very much a "people's journalist," rather than one who just stays in an office and gets everything over the telephone or from bureaucratic spokespersons, Tony can truly feel for common, everyday people whose lives are affected by the wars he covers. Which is why he found the latest scene awaiting him inside Afghanistan to be "thoroughly depressing." As well as why he believes sharing their plight so important that he risks his own life.

The destruction in the Valley, now deserted by its former one hundred thousand inhabitants, was total, he said. Its villages stood as empty blackened shells. The once lush farm fields were reduced to scorched earth, torn apart by tank tracks. What had once been picturesque orchards and dirt cart lanes were little more than junkyards for destroyed tanks and armored personnel carriers. Where in the past there had stood grazing goats and sheep, there now lay endless spent cartridge cases and craters.

The one-hundred-kilometer-long valley's tranquility was but a memory, he added sadly. To more easily control the people, their rural livelihood had been taken away so they would have to move to the city to survive. Crowded together like sheep in a pen, the Afghans could then be kept in order by fewer of their Russian masters. Anymore, the Valley was a killing field populated by the fighters of both sides. The songs of birds and the voices of children had turned to the screeching of shells, into the explosions of bombs. Or worse, screams.

About the only ray of hope in the Valley was the estimated seven thousand to eight thousand freedom fighters. In spite of having mostly old carbines for weapons and horses for transportation, the mujahadeen still controlled most of the area. The Soviet led force of over twenty thousand, with its hundreds of tanks and helicopter gunships, still hadn't figured out how to win that confounding Valley.

"It was the lesson of Vietnam all over again," Tony had said in a soft voice.

Evidently the lessons of war do not seem as apparent to many others, as they do to persons like Tony. I haven't crossed a nation yet that hasn't had its share of such bloody lessons spilt onto its soil and streets, only to see them repeated again and again.

If only more strangers would let their words be heard, perhaps those lessons would come fewer and further apart. At least Tony can say he tried.

Steven

This city street, a scene of life overflowing, of utter mayhem, is typical of urban Pakistan and India.

Lahore, Pakistan
December 4, 1984

Dear Folks,

As long ago as the fourteenth century B.C. the road along which I'm walking from Peshawar, Pakistan, to Calcutta, India, was known as the Royal Route. It was for thousands of years the principal route over which many of the Indian subcontinent's dynasty-makers directed their armies, and perhaps even their worshipers. Millions of pilgrims trekked over its congested potholes to pray at the sites where the Buddha had dwelt during his many reincarnations.

Today the former imperial roadway is simply known as the G.T. (Grand Trunk) Road. Yet, while the royalty and mystics, together with nearly every one of their hundreds of forts and monasteries, have crumbled back into the earth, there remains, as vibrant as ever, the masses. Rudyard Kipling, in his story *Kim*, perhaps best summed up that throbbing, ever growing vestige when he described this west-to-east artery of energy as a "a river of moving life, such as does not exist in any part of the world."

Since continuing my journey eastward from Islammabad over two weeks ago, I have entered into a fertile plains region known to some as "the land of five rivers." Here I have found very true the words of the many who've told me that everything I see and experience will greatly multiply the deeper I progress toward Calcutta, the very womb itself. As the land grows more productive, so too shall mankind and all its trappings, good and bad.

It is in this same area, what is now east Pakistan, that the Chinese pilgrim Hsuan Tsang wrote in 630 A.D. of one of the rivers, "The Sin-tu (Indus) is extremely clear and rapid. Poisonous dragons and evil spirits dwell beneath this river in great numbers. Those who embark carrying rare gems or celebrated flowers find their boats suddenly overwhelmed by waves."

Hsuan Tsang spoke from experience. On his return journey the Indus claimed fifty of his manuscripts and all the seeds of exotic flowers he hoped to grow in China. The pilgrim, however, was spared. He crossed over on an elephant.

Toward the end of these past thirty days I've spent crossing Pakistan, I wished often that, like Hsuan Tsang, I had some sort of indomitable beast of my own to ride upon and keep me from the deepening poverty I am traveling through. At times like these, walking can be a curse in that it brings me too close, for too long a time, to the elements of a lifestyle that is anything but healthy. Anymore, the dragon of overpopulation has reared amongst its litter so many things totally contrary to what my American mind considers civilized, or even sane, that I can't help feeling trepidation and much anger at times.

Accepted practices, like having the homeless old and the crippled begging on the streets for money to survive on, the overlooking of flagrant corruption among the police and civil servants, the government not providing even such basics as garbage collection and sewage facilities, the right of men to have several wives at the same time (resulting in incredibly enormous households), the division of persons into caste rankings and the widely practiced marrying of one's cousins (to keep the family's holdings intact) make absolutely no sense to me. Yet here they are as much a part of daily life as the crows scavenging through the garbage dumped unashamedly upon the streets and walks.

As I stare incredulously at the uncontrolled pollution, the animal corpses, millions of flies swarming over uncovered food and the people, who take no notice, I worry about my own health. There comes a point at which a society's clinging to the practices of the past goes from being exotic to being decadent and dangerous. Such has happened here.

By nature I look for the goodness in people, and I completely dislike writing of ugliness. But when the ugly has become of such magnitude as to swamp all of my senses, I can no longer remain silent. Furthermore, there has reappeared the most consistent and maddening aspect of all that I've found in every underdeveloped nation I've crossed—the continual military presence. True to form, the soldiers, their rumbling convoys and their weapons are everywhere. Many mornings I awake to the pounding of drums and soldiers' boots marching crisply to the beat, their voices drifting to my ears from some nearby compound. Then for much of the day there is the dust choking me from all the passing trucks and jeeps piled high with battle-ready figures and various implements of death. It has struck me that there are a lot of persons roaming about in search of a war.

The main culprits, or "evil" spirits as Hsuan Tsang might have said, have been the same in Pakistan as in the many third world nations I've journeyed through—overpopulation, illiteracy and just plain not thinking past one's own interests. I have noticed on my walk that one unmistakable characteristic of an advanced and mature nation is that its members, from the common man to the government, are always thinking ahead, always planning and building and researching, not so much for themselves as for their children and the unborn for centuries to come. That is why the controlling of such things as nuclear weapons and pollution of the environment has become so important in the policies of the developed societies.

Some of the men here have told me that if they practice restraint, or purposefully have fewer babies, Allah would be greatly displeased, might even deny them entry into paradise (where, for sure, they will have several wives!). These men's thoughts are reflective of perhaps most of the others on the streets. They are of the opinion that any changes in their lives are totally up to fate. As I look about and see the very, very poor quality of life their way of thinking has brought them and their children, I wonder if perhaps Allah hasn't already passed judgment.

What, I wonder, is to become of such societies as Pakistan's, which is a mirror image of the majority of the world's nations. Why do most still refuse to stand up and face directly the complexities of the twentieth century? Surely part of the reason behind their fear is a lack of the necessary education. Here the illiteracy rate is a shocking 70-75 percent. And yet the government, which is headed by the military, continues to allocate less than a handful of percentage points of the national budget to education, while over half goes to armaments. Even worse, General Mohammed Zia, the president since 1977 when he assumed power through a coup, is trying hard to gain ownership of a force even more unpredictable than his own subjects—nuclear weapons.

Bad governments, poverty and overpopulation are nothing new, of course. Undoubtedly these faults of mankind will always be around, for as we are imperfect so must be our societies. Still, I can't quite understand why in some parts of the world those things are allowed such free rein. I suppose some things are never meant to be solved entirely.

Sometime ago, a housewife from deep in the Midwest wrote to me to tell me that the more I saw of the rest of the world, the greater my appreciation of being born in America would become. You know, I think she knew life pretty darn well.

Steven

A line of village women head down a foot path to begin another long day of working in the fields.

Delhi, India
December 20, 1984

Dear Folks,

The temple stood in a slight patch of eucalyptus and mango trees, just on the edge of a small lake that reflected a blue sky and several white hump-backed sacred cows. It stood on its own and looked out over a broad spread of dormant rice paddies. Not a remarkable temple in any sense—squattish, peeling, made of cement blocks, and with a veranda wrapped around a thick, steeple-like center.

Yet, it was its utter simplicity that probably drew me away from the slow-motion bicycle riders, hopelessly lazy buffalos and shade of the Grand Trunk Road in the first place. Places of worship, I've discovered, can be very much like cities and towns. In enormous cathedrals, like in cities, those one meets are often fidgety, rushing around with a great air of significance, their minds seemingly preoccupied more with tasks than people. In the simpler homes of God, as in little towns and villages, there is usually someone around only too willing to sit down to a cup of hot liquid and an earful of questions.

In the small courtyard around the temple, I timidly kept my distance and intently observed the strange new scene that greeted me. Several beautiful young village women, barefoot and in plain cotton pants and dresses, were taking turns pouring water over the small statue of a resting cow at the temple's entrance. During this they also bowed three or four times to the statue, then circled the temple itself, sprinkling water on its sides and on the floor of the veranda. All the while, a very frail old man sat nearby on the temple's steps, in the warmth of the morning sun's rays, deeply absorbed in a book.

Quietly, I shed my pack, sat beside it, and shook my head. Inside of me a part of my soul wanted to burst into delighted laughter. The India I'd spent the past week crossing was not at all the India I'd been expecting, or perhaps I should say "worrying about." The increasing filth and crudeness I'd passed through in eastern Pakistan had seemed to promise a continuation of the same across the border in poorer India. And even less encouraging had been all the scenes of ugliness placed in my imagination by other travelers.

My route across northern India, through Delhi to Calcutta, is along the plains of the Ganges River, the world's most populated region. So much squalor did I envision to be packed along the eleven hundred miles of the route, that it was fully my intention to walk its length quickly and sternly and to avoid much close contact with the people, and certainly not to risk my health by eating the food any of the poor should offer me.

The manner in which I'd had to cross India's first state, the Punjab, had done little to dispel my anxieties. Though closed to foreigners ever since the turmoil following Indira Gandhi's assassination, it is now possible to cross the Sikh-dominated Punjab overland on only three days each month, and then only by riding in a convoy escorted by heavily armed policemen. To prevent any close look at the situation in that military-controlled region, the convoy departs from the Pakistan border area at dusk and speeds through the supposedly dangerous no man's land in the blackness of night.

It is, of course, quite against the rules to disembark from the convoy before it reaches the next state of Haryana. To do so would be quite risky to one's peace of mind, assured the convoy's potbellied sheriff, who had thrown back his star-studded shoulders and given his over-sized turban a sharp tug for added effect.

But as the old saying goes, rules are made to be broken. Thus, it was the American missionary with whom I hitched a ride across the Pakistan-India border who "inadvertently" deposited me onto Indian soil fifty kilometers shy of the Haryana welcome sign.

What transpired during the one hundred fifty kilometers, between the next morning's tentative first steps and the stroll up the dirt lane leading to the little temple, was not at all what everyone had me expecting. Rather than danger and tension, I found a great tranquility and natural beauty. For the first time since France, I felt a deep and real sense of spiritualism, of being in an almost ethereal world of holy spirits and dwellings. There was an almost uncanny manner in the way the people lived, so at peace with each other, the land and the many wild and domestic animals, which they believe to contain the reincarnated souls of former persons.

Because so many of the people depend entirely upon the animals and the land for everything they have, including the mud and reeds for many of their homes, they have a profound respect for their surroundings. So little was allowed to go to waste. Just as the forests were completely clean of any dead brush and branches, no cow or buffalo dung lay untouched for more than a few hours, or in some cases more than a few seconds. For many women and girls, the collection and making, by hand, of dung into patties for heating and cooking fuel was a fulltime chore.

A sudden, dull *clang* from inside the temple snapped me from the laziness into which I had been lulled by the warm sun and the fragrance of incense and roses. From the temple's dark interior emerged an older woman walking slowly backwards and bowing toward the temple door. On the side of her nose facing me gleamed a tiny gold pendant connected by a gold chain to a hairpin of gold shaped like a fan. Around her ankles, thick bangles in the shapes of snakes crowded together like the folds of droopy silver-colored sock tops. Fine steel and brass or copper bracelets covered much of her forearms. After a final reverent bow to the cow statue, she turned and approached me. Her cupped hands extended out and down to my surprised figure. Nestled inside them were some tiny sugar candy balls. I was at a loss for what to do. Part of me wanted nothing to do with that icky mess she was offering me.

"Please to accept her prasada?" came a kindly voice from off to the side. I turned to face a wrinkled, stick-like figure wrapped in coarse cloth and propped up by an ancient walking stick. It was the old man. I'd not seen him move from his spot in the sunlight.

"She has offered the treats to our God, Bhagawan, and now wishes to share them with all she meets. Such food blessed by God we call 'prasada'," he explained softly, a look in his eyes hinting that it would be most unkind to turn down such an offering.

I tried my best to look quite honored and let her push several of the sticky things onto my right palm. She grinned broadly and gave the rest to the old man, who promptly passed them on to me.

"Please, you drink tea," he asked me.

I followed him to a two-room, cinder block hut that was his home. On the way he paused long enough to show me the inside of the temple. In its unlit, closet-like room stood, simply, a plain pedestal in the center. Set on top of it was a paint-streaked rock in a large bowl of flower petals and smoking incense. On the walls were several old calendars topped by faded posters of the flute-playing Hindu god Krishna and other deities, some sprouting many arms and one, an elephant trunk where his nose should have been. Resting peacefully at their sides were many of the animals familiar to India, particularly the cobra and the cow. Suspended from the ceiling, at the end of a long rope, was a small bell. The old man gave it a nudge—it made the same dull *clang* I'd heard earlier.

"It is for calling down God," he said, with what I'd have sworn was a touch of jest.

As it turned out, he was a monk and the religious caretaker of the temple. Hunched on the dirt floor of his hut over a tin pan of boiling tea and buffalo milk, he explained much of his lonely lifestyle. He was paid nothing to be a holy man, he said, adjusting the twigs flaming beneath the tea. He subsisted entirely on the charity of the temple's worshipers. Like monks thousands of years ago, he still spent each morning wandering from village home to village home knocking on doors and asking for food with which to prepare that day's meals.

His knowledge of English came from the thirty-seven years he'd served in the army, from which he received a small, almost negligible, pension.

"You please stay for lunch," he asked. "It is our duty to feed and give rest for free to any monks who pass by our temple."

"But I am no monk," I replied.

He rose and placed a cup of sweet, milky tea on the bench beside me.

"Ah, but I think you are," he replied with an odd grin.

He sounded as if he'd been reading some part of my inner soul, of which even I was unaware. I stole a glance over the rim of the teacup. He was smiling more than ever.

"You can throw them into the fields if you want," he said with a nod toward my right hand, which was clenched tightly.

"The prasada," groaned a voice inside me. I stared down at the sweaty lump stuck to my fingers. Now it was my turn to smile, even if it was an embarrassed one.

"What's for lunch?" I asked quickly. "Maybe more prasada?"

He laughed. "The families today had much buffalo milk to give away." He paused, as if to think that over, then added with a sigh, "As usual. . ."

The thought of so much raw buffalo milk made me a bit hesitant, too. But just then, as if a sort of omen, the bell inside the temple rang unusually loud and sharp. I involuntarily sat up straighter.

"When do we eat?" I asked without further delay. Then, I cast aside all my foolish worries and sat back to enjoy the sweetness of the meal's first entree—the poor woman's sugar candy.

Steven

A woman sits resting in a dry river bed under the arch of a bridge in Vindraban, an ancient city of "five thousand" temples which I found extraordinarily beautiful and peaceful.

Delhi, India
December 26, 1984

Dear Folks,

Someone struck a match and an oil lamp's wick flickered to life. Monstrous shadows leaped and loomed with the unsteady flame. I hugged myself. Hideous alien shapes seemed to throng about me. The cold air was thick with dampness and musty smells that settled deep into the lungs.

I stared, as if mesmerized, through the diffused glow at the darkly stained mud brick walls and dirt floor. My mind momentarily hesitated to believe I was still in the twentieth century, let alone on the same planet. Several hump-backed, horned beasts tethered to iron rings set in the wall upon which the lamp glowed made me think all the more of the Middle Ages.

A tall, narrow figure wrapped in a ragged blanket pointed a long finger at me, then at five hempcord cots lined against a far wall of the stable. A dozen other similarly shaped and clothed figures clustered beside the cots, anxiously waiting for my shivering body to join their company. I sat down slowly on the middle cot. Their forms closed around me like the fingers of a giant hand.

"It is a great problem for us these days," murmured one.

I leaned forward to more closely study Ajad's angular face. His voice had struck me as suddenly sounding much older than that of the young farmer who'd talked me away from the Grand Trunk Road two nights before, to this little farm village called Jhattipuri.

"The electricity going off, you mean?" I asked, vaguely recollecting that, as we were weaving down the dirt road to Jhattipuri on his old bicycle, Ajad had seemed especially proud that his village of fifteen hundred had four street lamps and four televisions.

Ajad nodded. He lamented that anymore the village received electrical power only two or three hours each day. It was almost as if the area was possessed with a will that despised such intrusions of technology in its backyard.

Still, power failures or not, life in Jhattipuri was hardly going to be affected all that much. Basically the same habits and lifestyles that had sustained the village's ancestors of a thousand years back, or more, were going as strongly as ever. In a place like Jhattipuri, where the meals were still cooked over smoking dung or twigs on the ground outside, electricity was probably much more of a luxury than an actual necessity.

All that day had been spent with Ajad and his excited friends, touring their farm fields, their homes and, most fascinating, the separate boys' and girls' schools. As in most other areas along the walk's path, the detachment of the people from modern technology was almost too great to be believed. Almost all of the farming of the land was still done by oxen-pulled plows. Water for the homes was still pumped up from wells by hand or pulled up in buckets by the sinewy arms of the women. Animals, from pigs to buffalo, still wandered freely about the streets, and the school children still did their work on hand-held slate boards. As with the homes, the schools had been virtually unfurnished, unheated, badly overcrowded, unlit and with almost no windows. All the children sat on the floors of the schoolrooms, just like at home, or else they sat outside on the dirt, where the weak winter sun provided some semblance of warmth.

Though a thousand Jhattipuri-like villages have come and gone before me on my walk around the world, the primitiveness of each has never failed to leave me astonished. The gap between the lifestyle and thinking of their inhabitants and those of my own homeland is so vast as to seem absolutely improbable. It just seems too incredible to think that in an age of mass media, instantaneous information dissemination, and rapid transport, people still do things like ride buffalo-pulled carts to market and wash their clothes on the rocks of rivers. And it's not just some of the world that lives like that, but most of the planet's inhabitants.

That a very small part of the world could be instantly cooking entire meals with microwaves, doing much of their problem solving on computers, and even launching themselves and their robots into the solar system, while the rest live in a shadowy world largely unchanged from centuries before, seems to be more the stuff of science fiction than reality. Yet such is how it is, with the gap growing more profound each day. So great is that difference I can't begin to see it being narrowed or its growth arrested.

At dawn, a shivering Ajad roused me from the depths of my sleeping bag. In his hands were a tin cup and a large pot of hot buffalo milk. I drank all of it, hoping it might keep some of the morning chill away when I left the stable to continue my journey eastward. While I drank the turnipy tasting liquid, dozens of village boys crowded among the cots and cud-chewing cows. Last night they had been overflowing with questions about American society, now they simply wanted to see that I had a warm send-off.

As is my custom, I asked Ajad for an address to which I could send his family a postcard whenever I reached home. He wrote it down and handed it to me along with twenty rupees.

"What's the money for?" I asked.

"Please send a gift of your country to us, when you can. We want something from America we can show to our friends," he explained in a hopeful voice.

"And," he added quickly, "I will pay any duty."

I smiled. Twenty rupees was worth just under two dollars. Nothing it could buy would fetch any duty fees.

"Sure, I'll send a gift," I said, shoving the money into my jacket.

He told the others in Hindi, their native language, and they talked excitedly among themselves. Slipping into my pack I worked my way through their midst and out onto a gray street of housewives with pots on their heads and children leading dull-eyed buffalo toward the nearby fields. Ajad and the others accompanied me to the Grand Trunk Road.

"What should I send you—anything you want in particular?" I asked Ajad upon reaching the still quiet highway.

He gripped my hand and held it firmly. "It does not matter. I only care to know that I have a friend who has made it back home."

"You have a friend," I said, "and I'll make it home. Don't worry."

Then I walked away toward the east and a future I knew could never be ordinary.

Steven

Choma, India
December 31, 1984

Dear Folks,

    With 15,000 extra police manning the election polls in New Delhi on the December 24 elections, peace reigned in that crowded megalopolis over the Christmas season. Still, I cried. In a phone call to home on Christmas night, I learned my father is no longer with us. After years of struggling, his heart finally surrendered last Thanksgiving, my mother told me softly.

    Not wanting to talk, yet not wanting to be alone, I have walked these past six days in silence. More than anything, I have wanted to end what seems like a silly, stupid journey, and go home.

    As my family has become little more than a long-ago memory, I find myself increasingly gripped by terrible bouts of homesickness. I reflect often how all through South Italy and the Moslems' paternalistic societies, I had watched the close, lifelong bonds between the sons and fathers with a deep envy. Now, my own father is no more. He will not be waiting at home for me. And there is nothing I can do.

    Dad had been ill for many years with heart trouble, and there was no way of knowing when the end would come. I had gambled he might outlive my walk, just as he had so many of his doctors.

    In the final weeks leading up to my departure from home, I had spent every evening with Dad in his bedroom, watching the television news programs. Afterward, we'd spend a long time discussing the woes the newscasters had shared with us that day. Though I never allowed it to show, those few precious hours we had together meant more to me than any others. And, by the way Dad would stall me from rushing back off to my typewriter or maps, I realized that he, too, feared we would never see each other again.

    One day last September, in a little town in Turkey, a small group of excited telephone linesmen braved a fierce rainstorm to secretly present me with a free, though probably illegal, telephone call to home. While lightning crackled and a cold northerly blew, the bravest of the group scrambled up a pole in a back alley and somehow connected their ancient field phone to a mess of wires overhead. After dialing and re-dialing for what seemed like an eternity, he finally got a distant ringing tone. A loud, happy shout went up from our soaked bodies.

Concentrating so hard that I forgot all about the water dribbling down my mustache, I silently prayed that through some miracle our fragile connection might hold. The ringing stopped. From another world far away came a teeny voice, like that of a child . . . "Hello?" . . . It was Dad.

"Hello?" he repeated.

I screamed, I shouted, I ranted into the handset gripped in my fingers—but it was no use . . . for some reason he couldn't hear me.

Then, something happened that will haunt me to my own deathbed. There was another very weak . . . "Hello?" . . . a long pause, then . . . crying . . . so soft, yet so clear over all those months of distance.

"Steve?" the trembling voice asked.

"Steve? Is that you, son?"

Then . . . he was gone . . . blown away by the howling wind. It would be our very last contact on this world.

He had cried only once before that I could remember. It was on the cool April morning that I began the Worldwalk. Though he was so weak he had been confined to his bedroom for over a year, he somehow found the strength to greet me standing when I entered his bedroom to say goodbye. We stood before each other, unable to speak and barely able to look at each other. He suddenly reached for me, as if to hug me.

I had to grab him to steady him. He sagged into my arms weeping like a boy of six, not a man of over sixty. "Please promise me one thing. Promise me you'll place a rose on my grave when you come home," he said. I promised, hoping that such a scene would not come to pass.

No one who watched me leave home that morning knew of the horrible pain and sadness gripping my insides. All they saw was a confident and smiling young adventurer. No one knew the truth—no one, that is, except for the gaunt little man behind the crying eyes I noticed peering down at me from an upstairs bedroom.

Steven

Top; Drawing water from the well is a daily chore in rural India.
Bottom; Muscle and teamwork help this farmer and his wife to irrigate
their fields every day, a method of irrigation that dates back thousands of years and is still common in the poor rural areas of India.

Agra, India
January 7, 1985

Dear Folks,

My ears were struck by the shrill of a single cicada—brilliant, eerie, a sound as sharp as two finely-edged swords brushing in midair. Gingerly, I pushed a hand-stitched blanket of burlap from my eyes. A farmyard of silvery moonlight and statuesque oxen, still tethered to their clay feeding bin, floated into view. The largest of the bulls, Zebus, a veritable giant with a floppy hump as thick as a fat monkey, turned his long neck ever so slightly, and the small bell secured to it tinkled with a beautiful subtleness.

Beside me, on another blanket spread on the same straw-covered dirt floor, a black-skinned boy stirred uneasily in his sleep. He was of the lowest caste, a "Shudra," and I wondered if perhaps the ox's bell has stirred in his subconscious a fleeting image of all the udders to be drained by his hands in the morning. The gentlest of breezes kissed my forehead. Mother Nature's sweet perfumes momentarily transfixed me. Images of the farm I had explored beneath a pink evening sky drifted into my mind—a bent and toothless, ancient grandmother squatting barefoot on the cold, finely-swept dirt beside a broken clay pot, churning milk in the pot as she sings—a shy young mother plucking ripe guavas from branches bent to moist clay because of the sunny fruit's abundance, as her baby clings papoose-style to her rainbow-colored dress—lean, beautiful children, playful and friendly, taking my hands and walking along, oftentimes stopping to burst into somersaults and laughter.

How easy it feels to be superfluous in such surroundings as this farm, and the region I have passed through the past ten days in no haste and not in want of any gainful destination. This is the land where it is said the Hindu god Krishna played and teased his love-struck human friends over five thousand years ago. Where, as a boy of indescribable charm and disconcerting smiles, he played his flute and danced with the cow herder girls, the "Gopis," his almond eyes agleam with the sparkle of heaven and flowers.

In many of the meticulously-cared-for farm fields, the

time-darkened ruins of formerly graceful temples have stood as numerous as the stumps of an old and great spiritual forest. Many of the keepers of those temples, still topped with prayer flags, have somehow sensed my passing and had me come behind their walls to be fed and sheltered from the foggy nights. Never have I found heaven and its God to be of so many forms, nor so many confidently hopeful, happy, obedient devotees.

The members of the various religions have been as different and colorful as the innumerable tropical birds swarming through the forests like winged kaleidoscopes. They have ranged from one group that dresses entirely in burlap sacks, to one that is heavily financed by American pocket change, and whose well-mannered, cologned disciples live in spacious, sterile apartments and dance wildly to sequin-covered deities housed in an enormous palace built of the finest marble and crystal chandeliers dollars can purchase.

I even had an audience with my first "saint," although I must confess that, after humbly raising my eyes from my bare feet to his gleaming white beard and gown, I could not bear to gaze upon him for very long. His nervous eyes revealed, all too painfully, the real reasons for his six automobiles and all the immense property he had lately felt in need of acquiring.

India, it is said, is a religious experience. I can vouch for that. Self-serving saints and monied statue worshippers aside, there is unquestionably something here that plays with attentive minds and souls. This has been particularly true in the countryside, where the hard glare of technology is practically nil. There, mixed with the pastel shades of yellow mustard flowers and wispy, green eucalyptus leaves, a clear and subtle illumination of the *oneness* of existence does reach the spirit. As simple and uneducated as most are, the farmers and their families bear the calm of contented monks. They are happy, and Nature reflects that joy. The people laugh so naturally, so effortlessly, as do I when watching with delight the many wild monkeys and peacocks each day.

What a pleasure to again see man and woman as equals, to not see the women cowering and hidden away like inhuman objects, as they are in the staunchly male-controlled Moslem societies. In this serene and indiscriminate domesticity, there murmurs a common pulse of being—there is no hesitation to tie up a loose blouse or roll up a sleeve and help another with his or her labor, or for the animals and their keepers to work together.

My eyelids closed, heavily, slowly. Sounds of a world not quite asleep trailed across my fading thoughts . . . the soft rhythm of a baby swaying in a wicker basket, the dogs' paws scampering to—or maybe from—a suspicious moon shadow, a field mouse scratching curiously inside my backpack, a housewife in the heart of one of the mud huts clustered in the farm's center chanting prayers before a simple altar, her prayer beads rustling nervously every so often. The sounds, as much as all the glories and love I've experienced in my past 8,300 miles of walking, assure me there is much more to life than the obvious.

And yet the tears fall . . . again. My spirit is still so numb from the news I received on Christmas night that Dad had died, that he no longer will be anxiously awaiting my figure to come back up our long driveway. I cry because I loved him, still love him. Because in spite of all the miles between me and home, I can feel too strongly the void his sudden absence has brought to my life.

As I suspect too many other children do with their fathers, I took him so much for granted. He broke down and cried when I left, so afraid he'd never see me again. His intuition proved correct. Now it is my turn to weep.

I have plodded along in a state of amazement, sometimes smiling, sometimes weeping. One must have a stout heart to follow the unusual road I have taken, for it is long and full of sacrifice and decisions to be made. But something tells me the road I follow is no more "heroic" or difficult than that road the parents of a large family must take to see their children become responsible adults.

Perhaps, like me, Dad also sensed there is a source for the deep restlessness that stirs the human soul, and that the path leading there is not a path to a strange place, but the way to our real home. Now perhaps he is walking the path home himself—maybe he's already there. I hope so. For, God willing, we may yet embrace each other one more time.

Steven

Top; A group of beautiful Indian girls gathered to see the tall, red-haired American walking through their village. *Bottom;* Muddy streets, oxen-pulled carts, and vendors squatting on the ground beside their produce make for a typical scene along the route that I took across northern India.

Varanasi, India
January 27, 1985

Dear Folks,

Thunder boomed. Water drummed relentlessly against water.

Rushing bodies and weaving bicycles, their movement intensified by the pitch blackness and angry horns, surged against and past me. It was all I could do not to stop, turn my tired leached body around and become another piece of human driftwood. How tempting to let myself be swept back down the G.T. (Grand Trunk) Road to the quiet little side pools of mud huts and banana trees where most were undoubtedly heading.

They were anxious, not so much to escape the cold wind-driven rain, as they were the mire of painted flesh, bad-sweet odors and ankle-deep mud in which they had spent much of the day. Over two million, all Hindu and mostly very poor, had made the pilgrimage to the holy city of Allahabad in the past week to celebrate the festival of Mankar Sankranti. From all over India they had come, most with babies in both arms and pots and blankets on their heads.

Mother Ganga, the Ganges River, had called their souls. It was the time of the new year to bathe body and spirit in her oily, muddy flow, to wash away sins and give the gods reason to smile once again.

Krishna, Rama, Shiva, Ganesh, Durga—all the countless lords and goddesses of a Vedic past, dating back millions of years, danced in all the brown eyes tumbling by me. Even in many of the lifeless eyes, so pervasive in India, there glinted a hope of new energy.

Beneath a heaven exploding with lightning, the tumbling river of humanity and its many tributaries flashed intermittently into billions of sharp-contoured details—ragged vagrants huddled between crumbling temple columns, broken-spirited horses, bent-back dogs, scavenging sows scurrying ecstatically from one littered shop front to another, their little ones scrambling to keep up.

In the darkness following each flash of lightning the vermillion tikka dots and candy-colored stripes on the foreheads of the pilgrims glowed with eerie vividness. Like sailors with freshly tattooed anchors, they wore their beacons proudly. It was their outward proof, along with their exhilaration, that they have journeyed somewhere special.

Later, while slogging through flooded streets in search of a non-existent hotel bed, the haunting image of a pretty child leapt at me just before another crack of thunder. Behind a smiling face, like a broken stick doll, she was dragging bent useless legs. As soaked and sunken as I was, I couldn't help feeling that the lack of bitterness in her eyes was the blessing she had received.

Morning came cool, misty, pure, and rapidly changed into warmth, and the usual spring-like sun shone. In late afternoon I wandered on, glad to be free of Allahabad's choked streets, but sad to leave the fatherly bearded Sikhs who rescued me from the stormy night. Soon after leaving their fortress of a temple, I was at the Ganges herself. Crossing over her on a bridge of mufflerless three-wheeled taxis and rattling window-less buses were more pilgrims, coming to catch the end of the month-long bathing festival.

On the mud flats along the roiling river current was the largest number of tents I had seen in my life. The patched angled canvases of Mother Ganges's brood left no gaps between myself and the far flat horizon. The notes of flutes and playing children floated up to me, along with the smoke of all the campfires. The squatting lumps ringing the fires took me back to the gypsies of Turkey. Those seclusive but friendly nomands never traveled as lightly as these Indians. Their camps had been of warmer teepees, grazing pack horses and the smells of wool, leather and roasting corn.

The gypsy camps had been small enough to be romantic, but such camps as the one beside the Ganges were too over-whelming to be anything but a spectacle. I continued east, contented to leave such places to other explorers less loath-some of crowds and noise.

Four days later, downriver from Allahabad, I came to Varanasi (or Benares as most still say in deference to its ancient name). Where Allahabad was a place to renew the soul, in a sense be reborn, Varanasi is reserved for the dead. Here is where the Hindu faithful have their spent bodies of this incarnation consumed by fire and then tossed into Mother

Ganges. It is a returning of themselves to the All.

Yet, ironically, the very magnitude and, alas, profitability of an industry as stable as death has attracted to Varanasi a greater clamor of life than is found in most cities several times its size. Swept along by the tide of voices and crying babies, one nearly forgets about the pyres burning nonstop along the river. The wistful shouts of the religious paraphernalia vendors, the streets choked with rickshaws, the children charging from everywhere to practice their school English on a lone "Bora" (white) made death seem a has-been.

"Good morning, sir!"

"What is you name?"

"Sir, my name is . . . "

Down at the river, at the smoky gate to death itself, there is the greatest display of life anywhere. Curly-tailed monkeys screech from temple walls, children rake embers from spent pyres for their mothers to prepare dinner on, cows savor marigold garlands that have decorated the deceased, and brightly dressed old women cackled delightfully at each other's stories in voices far more vigorous than the crackling logs. And, as if to show death once and for all that it is not to be in the least taken seriously, the people splash merrily in the same spot where the ashes and charred remains of the dead are raked into the river.

In the evenings in Varanasi, the sun becomes a perfectly round orange dot of immense beauty, like a sort of celestial tikka dot. When it set, it left behind a flaming world and a din that never softens until just before the sun rises again. The sky at dusk, turning the color of the ashes around the pyres, reflects off a wide, slow Ganges of criss-crossing rowboats and junks. Silently the black, featureless forms of the boats drift past the flames like restless roaming spirits, freed by the pyres, but still reluctant to leave behind all the laughter and merriment.

On my final day in Varanasi, I stepped from my back-alley hotel to take one more good look at a city that, much like India itself, is too lively to ever begin to know. Just outside the door I was stopped by the smiling round face of what was surely the most exotic being yet on the walk. The smile and eyes of this ancient man in robes spoke of more mystery and beauty than perhaps anything I've experienced. My heart was pounding with excitement. What a source of delights this world is!

Politely, kindly, the monkish, Chinese-like figure told me in halting English that he was a Tibetan lama. With him were two of his Buddhist devotees. They were the most compelling humans I have seen since leaving Europe. On their backs were crude packs of board and cloth—they had journeyed from the hidden reaches of the Himalayas to learn more of the world below their solitary monastery.

"What is your name?" the holy man asked softly, all three bowing toward their tattered sneakers.

"Sir!" my voice rang out, like an excited schoolboy, "my name is Steven!"

Steven

The river's edge in Varanasi teems with life. Children play in the Ganges where only moments before the ashes of the dead were strewn.

Dhanbad, India
February 10, 1985

Dear Folks,

I shall never forget the roses . . . so large and regal as to be from the pages of a tale, each flower a perfect sculpture of nature's poetry.

Nor shall the kindly image of Baba, "The Elder," be easily dismissed from my mind. His mysterious figure had guided me to those roses . . . and to the very special gift of love they watched over.

It was in a raffish jungle where my worried eyes first met the little citadel of silence and humility that others respectfully called "Baba." At the time I was over seven hundred miles into India and should have been advancing toward my final destination of Calcutta, almost an equal number of miles to the east. Instead, I was hopelessly lost.

Foolishly, I had wandered from the Grand Trunk Road to follow the banks of a small river channel that had seemed to parallel the road from a distance of about one half kilometer. However, it soon veered sharply to the south, and I had little choice but to plunge into a thick forest of bamboo shoots and banyan tentacles in the direction I hoped the road still lay. Soon I was snarled in the vine and root cords of the leafy net draped about my stumbling figure, haunted by the approaching night and unseen wild cries. Worse, I was in the region of Uttar Pradesh, home of the deadly fangs of hissing cobras and the growling of man-eating tigers. Just the day before I had read of a veteran British guide being killed in the bush of Uttar Pradesh by one of those fearsome animals.

As dusk became thicker and every trail I stumbled along led me only to more fleeting shadows and confusing swamp, I began to wonder if the maze in which I was trapped might be my last vision of this world.

Then suddenly, as composed as a monk and looking as if he'd been patiently awaiting me, there stood Baba, around a curve in the trail. To my relief, a glint of recognition shone from his peaceful eyes at my mention of the elusive highway. Uttering not a single word, he turned and glided away down the footpath, having simply nodded that I should follow. And yet, even after all I'd been through, I hesitated—a strange creeping tingle pricking at my mind.

I suddenly realized my monkish apparition was being swallowed by the jungle. I raced toward the fading shadow, the forest's thorny fingers grasping at me desperately. As I teetered from my pack's weight, tripping over the feet of trees and slipping along greasy trails, my eyes clung to the steady form always just ahead and out of reach.

Finally, we were out of the jungle and came upon an enormous checkerboard of inlaid sky mirrors and squares of golden rice speckled with snow-feathered herons. We splashed and splished our way over the paddies to a distant vine of asphalt and broad shade trees. Then was when a divine scent enchanted my senses, and I looked across the still road to the magnificence of the roses growing prolifically on the front wall of a house.

Leading me past the roses, through a tall gate and under an inconspicuous sign which read, The International Guest House, Baba guided me up onto the columned veranda of a beautiful European-styled villa. Completely uninhabited, it was the quietest and cleanest home I'd seen in India, indeed, along the Grand Trunk Road.

Waving away my wallet, my guide-turned-host handed me the home's keys and wandered off. Inside the double doors I settled down in a luxury of wicker furniture and privacy, all the while marveling that such a beautiful place could be in such a secluded area, a place where foreign visitors were surely rare. I reclined and was soon sound asleep.

I took my bath the next morning in the same manner I have had to do all across India—quickly emptying pails of icy well water over my loudly protesting bones. But in this particular bath I had good reason to celebrate, and to even take an extra baptism or two—*privacy!* For the very first time I had no large crowds of gawking villagers for bath mates. Only me—*me!*

It was the first bath in a long time that I came away from feeling totally cleansed. Awash in perfumed mist, warm sun rays, and the sparkle of watery diamonds dripping from the petals all around me, I set out to see who was responsible for this secret paradise. My answer lay but three strides away, around the nearest corner of the house in a little garden of gold roses.

Beneath the sheltering branches of a wizened old mango tree stood two ordinary headstones. One on the left was etched in the flowing script of Hindi—the one on the right in the stoic characters of English. Humbly and with tears stinging my eyes, I read its special message:

"The divine souls of an extremely simple couple of this area, who symbolized the ideal of love, compassion and selfless service to mankind, are resting here in peace.

"This place has been constructed by their son in the memory of his most ideal parents, as an expression of his extreme devotion and love towards them. Having founded this memorial he has made a meek effort to give concrete form to his parents' feelings of 'welfare of all.' "

What an honor to have been invited into such a home, one built entirely from love and devotion! And what a strange coincidence that the one man who holds its keys had been there in the jungle when I'd needed shelter the most. I picked two wildflowers and gently placed one on each grave.

That day stretched into three, and never a single rupee of payment was wanted, or even accepted, from my willing pockets. To the Hindus, one of the saddest tragedies anyone can suffer is that of being separated from one's family, particularly one's parents. I have noticed that in India particularly, most sons never leave the area of their parents. And so it was that many farmers and villagers, some with small gifts of fruit or vegetables, visited me at the guest house to let me know in their own subtle way that I was still among a family of sorts. Some stopped by just long enough to ask where I was from and where I was going (as if they didn't already know) while they puffed on one of their crude, bitter "bitas"— cigarettes. Others stayed for hours and took their turn trouncing me at chess, deftly capturing all the pebbles we had standing in for absent pawns and rooks. Usually in the background there were laughing children, playing another one of their unusual badminton games in which marigolds were substituted for birdies and hands became rackets.

Eventually I learned bits and pieces about the devoted son who had built the guest house. He had lived in West Germany, having gone there many years before as a young man from a nearby village, and had been fortunate enough to land a good job with the government. However, having found the material riches he'd hoped for, he was still plagued by homesickness. Acutely aware of how it was to be alone and in a strange culture, he'd had the home built to shelter and provide comfort to any foreigner who should need it. They would not, he hoped, feel so far away from family and friends as he had all those gray, rainy German evenings.

The night before my departure I sat up late reading the messages of gratitude contained in the guest house's log book. Since the house was but three years old and unknown to all except the occasional foot or bicycle traveler who chanced upon it, there had been only a few guests inside its walls. Smiling broadly, I noted I was the thirteenth, a very lucky number in India, where many associate the meaning "giving to all" with it.

I was also the first American, though most of the writing was in English, the common tongue of the world anymore. One passage held a particular fascination for me, written by another foot traveler, dated July 9, 1984. Shozo Nakamura, a Japanese from a city named Gifu, had written:

"I'm walking around the world. But yesterday I got sick. Maybe I caught cold. So when I reached this International Guest House, I was real happy, like oasis in the desert . . ."

The rest was in fluent Japanese, of which I know nothing. But then that hardly mattered, you see . . . for I had no doubt that the very same emotions and thoughts of joy that he'd gone on to express would soon be flowing from my very own heart and pen.

Steven

Baba, "The Elder," who guided me to the "International Guest House," and a young village boy of India warming themselves in the early morning by a stick fire.

Calcutta, India
February 23, 1985

Dear Folks,

The slow waters of the Ganges cast back the sun's last light like some old dirty mirror. This was, I pondered sadly, perhaps the final time our meandering paths would ever cross. For behind me were the entire width of the Indian subcontinent and the fifteen hundred miles of the Grand Trunk Road.

I was done, or nearly so. Calcutta, the "Royal Route's" eastern-most anchor, was but a few hundred meters away at the end of the bridge on which I'd paused. It was so hard to believe I'd actually done it, actually made all those supposedly "deadly" and "diseased" miles between the Afghanistan border and Calcutta on foot and alone.

Gripping the bridge railing and standing tall, I looked back toward the land to which I'd just given so much of my time and emotions. A river breeze tousled my hair and tickled the stubble on my cheeks. I laughed aloud, causing a rainbow of parrots to stretch out over the river. How utterly absurd to think that all I have seen, learned and felt these past months could ever be put into ordinary words! No words existed that were extraordinary enough to describe my time here.

I watched in awe as the sun settled onto the lance of a poor farmer's rake to burst into the heraldic rays of a magic wand. Was not all I'd seen the greatest magic possible? Surely every second was a miracle. A rumble to my right caused me to turn. There, with its smokestack horns flaring and its dark labyrinth snarling, lay the "Black Hole" . . . *Calcutta.* The black of never-ending poverty stirring restlessly inside its hulk, it looked to be the most evil of urban pain. But it didn't scare me in the least. If I am sure of anything, it is that fear is an unnecessary part of life. Oh, to be sure, there were dangers inside that beast, but I also knew from my journeys that they would quickly flee in the face of boldness.

My walking has shown me that fear need be a reality only to those who don't care to see past man's false world and experience the universe as it really is. So much of what we have been told in ignorance is taken for granted, when all we need do is look for ourselves to see that what we had feared is really absurd. Why, I wondered sadly, do so many end their pilgrimage in life with empty eyes, when all those years they had been surrounded with so much wonderment?

India had shared much with me, and not all of it was beautiful, particularly the widespread bribe-taking, police brutality and horrible public education and illiteracy. Yet, I also knew that even those had been invaluable to me, if I realized that those things were not to feared, but to be viewed as a challenge.

An infant democracy of only thirty-eight years, India's philosophy for its eight hundred million people is taken from Mahatma Gandhi, a simple villager who became a dominant figure in their war for independence from the British. As had our Martin Luther King done later, Gandhi stressed non-violence and peaceful co-existence. Because of my being from the nuclear superpower America, I found myself continually having to answer for the current nuclear race madness between the United States and the Soviet Union. India, the leader of the Third World (or the "third superpower," as they like to say) forced me into being a sort of "backroad diplomat" more times than I cared for.

All across this world, even in some of the most isolated spots, I have found the vision of a dead planet, charred by nuclear war, to be on most people's minds. Their sense of fatalism and their staunch conviction that nuclear destruction from the arsenals of America and Russia is a certainty is enough to shake the confidence of even the most naive optimist. In India that sense of doom was the strongest yet.

Unfortunately, I had no answers for their worried faces. I have no clear idea of why the superpowers keep building so many nuclear weapons. I could, however, share the words of a village sage I shared tea with one night.

"My child," he said slowly, staring into a campfire, "if you want peace, look not at others' faults, but to your own. You and I and the rest must learn to understand that none is a stranger. The world belongs to all. When we seek only for goodness and the beauty God has placed in every single man and woman, then will evil lose its hold. Then we will know peace."

Of all the treasures India gave me, surely that sage's words are some of the most priceless. They were nothing new, of course, for these same words have been said in a million other ways by countless men of peace. Yet, the truth in those words still rings out as crisply as ever.

Now, if only more would have the boldness to live those words.

Taking one last look at an Indian sunset, then at a garland swirling down the Ganges, I shouldered my heavy pack . . . and continued my journey.

Steven

A last look back at the river of life, the great Ganges, in whose waters the spiritual life of India flows.

The walk thus far

675 days
April 1, 1983 - February 23, 1985
9,198 miles walked

SOUTHEAST ASIA

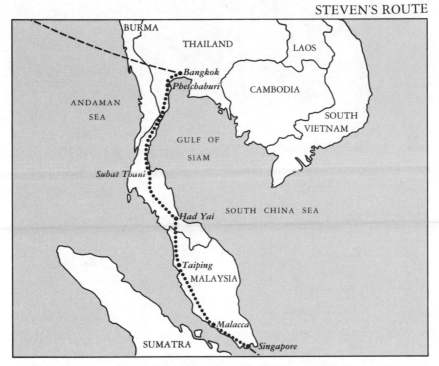

After walking across Pakistan and India, I had wanted to continue my journey by walking across Burma as my entry into Southeast Asia. But Burma has a policy of limiting visits by foreigners to a maximum of seven days and would not make an exception in my case. Because I would have needed at least three months to walk across Burma, I had no choice but to fly on to the next country, Thailand, where I continued my walk on into the jungles of Southeast Asia.

The walk ahead through Southeast Asia

126 days
February 24, 1985 - June 29, 1985
1,231 miles

Many scenes of former Thai daily life are to be found in this traditional mural painted by Phaptawan Suwannakudt. This mural is a good example of how every character in such art is supposed to have something to teach the viewer and how the action is continous and numerous.

Bangkok, Thailand
March 8, 1985

Dear Folks,

The thick Bangkok traffic rolled up to the red light. Engines roared impatiently. Drivers stared intently through swirling fumes like racers on some colossal drag strip.

Along the edges of the six lanes of asphalt jostled another jam of humanity. Dressed mostly in American-styled jeans and T-shirts, the mob pulsated to the comings and goings of overloaded buses and over-amplified American rock music. Though hardly a lip knew a word of English, many a chest displayed such messages as "Pittsburgh Steelers," "Laurel High School Wildcats," or—as one unknowing boy's did—such faddish cliches as "Cute Girl."

Red —

Yellow—

Green—*Vroom!* The race was on again!

Lurching and darting, the racers zipped along their tracks of concrete or asphalt to wherever it is crowds are always scurrying. While some of those encased in the sleek Japanese steel and chrome bumpers might eventually somehow find a familiar garage or parking space, many of those on foot spun off into lush, multi-storied malls to be surprised by the latest punk designer fashions, or maybe an innocent-looking bleeping, blooping computer. Yet others would speed on tirelessly, peeling away from the pack only to replenish their tanks with Big Macs, Kentucky Fried Chicken, A&W root beers, Dairy Queen banana splits, Shakey's pizzas, or, as one pit crew's sign simply put it, "American Fast Food, Hot Hamburgers, Served With No Waiting."

Designer jeans, knobby cassette players, wide-striped running shoes—anything and everything in a department store manager's wildest dreams—rushed past me at dizzying speeds. I stumbled backwards, as feverish from culture shock as from the Thai summer heat. From the open door of a fancy discotheque came Hank Williams' "Cheatin' Heart," while the giant figures of Clint Eastwood and Burt Reynolds stared down at me from a marquee.

Dumbfounded and soaked, I collapsed onto a lawn chair

beneath an umbrella of Civil War flags. Why hadn't anyone told me America now had fifty-one states? Was this what the travel posters had meant when they had said, "Thailand—Asia's most exotic country?"

"Drink, sir?" purred a waitress straight off the cover of *Cosmopolitan.*

I couldn't answer, at least not verbally—my eyes were pressing too tightly against my upper lip. On her tray, glaring at me, like some haunting specter of a long forgotten past, was a Budweiser.

"Maybe you like watch American football?" she asked. Then pausing as if to wait for my eyes to plunk into my lap, she added, "Today, inside on big screen, we have Super Bowl."

Super . . . Bowl—the Super Bowl? In Pakistan and India hardly anyone had ever heard of such a thing. But now, in a land I had expected to be the most primitive yet, I was being offered the most sacred of all American spectacles as casually as I might have been offered a cup of coffee in a Park Avenue eatery.

"Ma'am, is this really Thailand?" I wanted so much to ask.

What I had forgotten to take into account were the effects on the Thai society of a recent bit of history known as the Vietnam War. Though probably not well known by most Americans, Thailand was a major part of our military's logistics in that protracted conflict of Southeast Asia. Separated from the long length of Vietnam by only Laos in the North and Cambodia in the South, the ancient Buddhist kingdom, formerly known as Siam, was a strategic place to put bomber bases and supply depots and to provide recreation for battle-weary soldiers.

Thailand is still an extremely popular "R&R" spot for the U.S. Pacific and Indian Ocean naval fleets. As such, the Thais have been subjected to a continuous influx of Western culture not known by many other nations. Like Japan, South Korea, and Taiwan, Thailand has taken eagerly to the overwhelming American culture. Unlike India and most of the Moslem countries I have walked across, the government here has not gone to any great trouble to stem Western materialism or influence. To the contrary, the Thais have taken to both the good and bad of American culture with a fervor that makes their Asian counterparts seem mild by comparison.

The more I explored Bangkok, the more that question I had wanted so much to ask the waitress kept creeping to my lips. As I roamed the interiors of what seemed innumerable new malls, department stores, jewelry shops, banks, and hotel-restaurant complexes, I was amazed to find a contemporary architecture and luxuriousness that often rivaled anything in the very heart of Los Angeles.

Unquestionably, the Thais' willingness to take Americans to their hearts and tills had brought them wealth that otherwise would have been unimaginable. Instead of the largely poor, chaotic, and backward society I had expected in Thailand, I was surrounded by perhaps the most modern, efficiently run and monied society I'd seen outside of Europe.

Nowhere outside of my own country, not even in London, Rome, or Athens, had I seen such a concentration of consumer and luxury goods from all over the world, particularly America and Japan. It was almost as if those two economic behemoths had found in Thailand a perfect arena in which to do battle for the consumers' bank accounts. Without a doubt, Bangkok was the "great shopping paradise" of which I'd always heard, but had never really found.

With the prices for luxury and electronic items reputedly being some of the very lowest in the world, Bangkok was filled with Europeans and Americans scurrying about exercising their credit cards. With their arms loaded down with everything from fake Rolex watches to alligator-emblemed country club polo shirts to gaudily-carved elephant tusks that would inevitably end up in an attic, these red-faced shoppers seemed to have an awful lot of "friends" back home. At the main post office, which conveniently had an entire department set aside solely for the rapid fire packaging and mailing of tourist purchases, the Western shoppers could hardly stand to take the time to scribble down their mailing addresses before rushing off again to load up on more twenty-four-hour-made silk suits and whatever.

For the serious shopper, Bangkok was a dream come true. From sapphires to Mercedes, they were there—and cheap, *very cheap*. To many Germans and Americans I talked with, flying to Bangkok to do several days' of shopping and bargaining (an accepted and expected part of any purchase) was as ordinary to them as it might have been for me to hop in my Jeep and drive to the closest shopping center.

Steven

Bangkok, Thailand
March 22, 1985

Dear Folks,

My original visa for Thailand was, another American traveler pointed out, good only for two weeks, not the two months
I had thought. Having learned this unexpected detail only the
day before the visa was to expire, it was all I could do to catch
the next express train out of the country.

By one of those bizarre quirks of foreign bureaucracy that
I'll never quite learn to appreciate, one could not obtain a visa
extension in Thailand. Rather, one must go clear to another
country to obtain a new visa, at one of Thailand's foreign
consulates.

On the thirty-six-hour-long train ride to the quite un-Ma-
laysian sounding town of Butterworth (a vestige of Malaysia's
days as a British colony), I discovered, to my pride's relief, that
a large part of the packed train was made up of other foreigners likewise hurrying off to Malaysia for Thailand visas. Indeed, I learned that the same train always was rushing off
dozens of new visa aspirants to the otherwise lonely fishing
village of Butterworth. It was to the point anymore that any
Westerner who stepped into the Bangkok train station was
automatically directed to the ticket window for the southbound
express.

Now maybe I was wrong, but I certainly couldn't help
wondering if the Thai king's treasury didn't have a veritable
genius when it came to figuring out how to make the railroads
and foreign consulates pay for themselves. At twenty dollars
for a new visa, it wasn't too difficult to understand how the
consulate in Butterworth (actually in a nearby island city
called Georgetown) could be housed in such a magnificent
mansion.

Still, his majesty's treasurers were mere amateurs compared
to others far more experienced, like the Italians, who could
make you smile broadly no matter how many traveler's checks
fell prey to your signature. So I decided to let the others do the
huffing—I would settle down and make a point of enjoying
what otherwise seemed to be a very special sort of journey.

Sitting in the only real "air conditioning" of my air-conditioned coach, the breeze blowing over the outside steps at the coach's end, I watched with growing pleasure the tropical scenery passing by. Though it was the hottest time of the year in Thailand and far into the dry season, a dark rainstorm swept off the seas to cool things down and make the setting seem all the more a part of some high adventure. As if trapped inside some demonic cyclone, the train sliced through winds that howled in my ears and set my mind to imagining all sorts of intrigue.

What might be watching us from the heights of the spectacular limestone monoliths rising like sudden bergs from the jungle blurring by within arm's reach? From where did that wonderful scent come? Perhaps from the bright orchids waving at us from the edges of bamboo hut villages.

How beautiful and proud the tall lone palms seemed, so aloof from the tangle far below. And yet, could not there be pirates plotting on the beaches under those arched trunks? After all, only the day before I'd read in the newspaper that pirates in the seas off Thailand had killed at least four hundred people, mostly Vietnam boat refugees, the year before. Certainly there was the possibility of bandits stopping this very train in some remote stretch and robbing all of us by holding long curved knives to our trembling throats. Well, it does happen, you know—more than once I'd read of bandits in the same part of Thailand stopping and robbing the tour buses. Why, only the previous week, the police had found another foreigner's slain body beside the road!

Who knows? This very evening, in the dining car over a glass of wine and a flowery vase, I might meet some enchanting and sophisticated lady. Perhaps, just perhaps, she might even give my heart a good jolt by leaning over the tablecloth and asking softly if I, too, might be heading to a quaint and romantic little place called . . . Butterworth?

I sighed, leaned back against the top step and let my thoughts be carried away by the rhythmic clickity-clack of the train over the tracks.

Americans, by doing away with the long-distance passenger trains, are missing out on an invaluable opportunity to slow life down just that little extra bit so necessary to fully enjoy it. On a train there is more freedom to strike out down the aisle and start up conversations with total strangers. And, in a setting like the dining car, who can help but come away with some good memories?

Oh, to be sure, not all cross-country train rides are a joy. In Morocco the train I took from my month-long stay with the Jaquiths in Marrakech back up to Rabat, the starting point of my North Africa trek, was like a scene from an exaggerated disaster film. From the way the train station's mob in Marrakech rushed the incoming train even before it stopped, most screaming hysterically and shoving everything from babies to suitcases to wives through the open windows, one would have thought that Sahara city was about to join Vesuvius and Mount St. Helens in the annals of great catastrophes!

Stepping off that train after spending a bitter cold night squeezed between snoring soldiers was probably one of the highest moments of my life, although I crashed to earth quite abruptly when I found I was missing a pair of new shoes and my food.

But, good or bad, one thing is sure to come out of any long train ride . . . *stories.*

After all . . . where do you think this one came from?

Steven

Bangkok, Thailand
April 5, 1985

Dear Folks,

The train ride to Malaysia to obtain a new visa for Thailand turned out to be as much a blessing as a hassle. In addition to procuring an extension of three months for staying in Thailand, I also received the break I had been needing from the shock of finding myself suddenly so deeply back in the materialism of American culture.

While the same obsession with Americanism that I had noted in Bangkok was present in the rural areas I passed through to and from Malaysia, there was also much evidence that the Thais' own ancient customs were still strong and alive. Though the rural people might often be wearing surplus U.S. Army gear or bright T-shirts, they still spoke only Thai, still smiled and bowed, and still prayed reverently each day before the highly elaborate little "spirit houses" they had in their shops and homes. They may have changed much on the outside, but spiritually and emotionally they were still little different from their elephant-riding ancestors.

"They are the hardest people to convert. We've had the least success with them," remarked a Christian missionary from Wichita, whom I met on the train to Malaysia.

"Always so polite . . . always listening so well to all you have to teach. But inevitably . . . always going away with that strange smile on their lips, to pray to Buddha," he sighed wearily.

The train ride through the villages and towns reminded me that if I hoped to discover the exotic Thailand I had always dreamed of, I was going to have to start looking for the little things and stop letting all that was loudest or biggest or brightest grab my attention.

With that in mind I set about again to explore the streets of Bangkok, only this time with a keenness that had been missing before. What I discovered, particularly on the quieter side streets and in the less hectic hours of the dawn and late night, was a fabric of modern society literally teeming with threads of fantasy.

As beautiful as they are in the golden sunlight, the graceful and intricately-adorned spires and columns of the temples, or "wats," actually took on a far greater fairy tale quality in the late hours of night. Then, the brightly-colored porcelain, ceramic and gold that adorned each temple reflected the city's and the moon's lights with a sparkle that left me wondering if they had been dusted by a magic wand or built of multi-colored fireflies.

In the earliest gray of the dawn, stepping noiselessly, almost furtively, along the empty sidewalks on every block were the orange-robed Buddhist monks performing the ancient custom of "bintabat," the taking around of a bowl in which to collect the day's food from the faithful. So vividly did their bright robes stand out against the mist that I could not help thinking of them as pieces of the sun still trying to collect together for the sunrise.

I stumbled upon many oddities that might have gone unnoticed had I not kept a sharp eye. One of the more unusual was on the meticulous grounds of the British Embassy. There I found women and young brides praying fervently to a statue of Queen Victoria, who the locals believed to be generous in the dispensing of pregnancies. It was all I could do not to laugh aloud. It's not that I thought the women were so absurd. But, rather, that they could not have chosen a more frightful hulk of stone and metal to pray to for something as sweet as a baby. Be it in Belfast or Nottingham or Bangkok, Queen Victoria never ceased to be the most stern-eyed statue imaginable.

However, of all the new exoticness that opened up to me, perhaps the one that took on the most meaning was one I found in a park by the Grand Palace. Tired, soaked and resigned to the idea that I would never get back on the correct bus, I slumped onto a bench in the park, in the shade of a small tree. Leaning back to rest, I saw that perhaps the most special bit of exoticness had been right above my head all the time.

Kites! Hundreds of them! All fluttering about on the sky's currents like graceful, long-tailed tropical fish struggling on the ends of fishermen's lines.

Were there any kites to be purchased in the park? Yes!

Timidly I released a striking little paper fish of my own into the currents, then marveled at how strongly such a delicate creature could struggle for its freedom. Memories of a windy spring spent on an old farm in upper Pennsylvania as a child came back to my heart. Was that really twenty years ago? How could I have gone so long without again knowing the thrill of coaxing a kite into the clouds!

Abruptly I was again in Bangkok. My kite string had snapped—my fish was escaping!

Frantically I zigzagged through a maze of fruit and soda pop vendors in a futile effort to keep up with my fleeing kite. Panting I dashed into the grounds of an enormous wat where I felt sure the kite had gone to hide. I looked high, low, and . . . then I started laughing. Cradled in the lap of a tall, golden, meditative Buddha sat the little kite, as if to say to those who cared, "This, my friend, is the real Thailand."

Steven

Phaptawan Suwan-Nakudt, twenty-six, daughter of Tan Kudt, sits on her studio floor in front of the mural she is painting. The subject of the scene just above her left shoulder is the baby Buddha in a garden with his mother. The Buddha is the white haloed child figure walking on the path of lotus flowers.

Phetchaburi, Thailand
April 11, 1985

Dear Folks,

To have visited another country and not explored its art is, to me, like going into a new restaurant only to look at the menu. As the expression of a people's inner dreams and fears as well as their history, art can become a thing of remarkable beauty and mystery. Perhaps more than anything else, art provides an intimate glimpse of a culture.

One modern master of Thai traditional painting was a rugged, energetic little man known as Phaiboon Suwannakudt, or, in his last years, "Tan Kudt" (Noble One). So highly prized was his skill at depicting with great intricacy scenes of Thai history and the 547 Jatakas, or previous births of the Buddha, that today his murals can be found in such lavish places as the royal family's Phuphing Palace and Bangkok's Montien Hotel. Some regard him as one of the greatest masters of Thai traditional painting.

But this is not the story of Tan Kudt. Rather, it is of his shy young daughter, who at the age of twenty-three, was asked by the dying Suwannakudt to complete his greatest work. In the main lobby of what was soon to be Bangkok's newest showpiece hotel, The Peninsula, he had been working for over eight months on a traditional mural of over nine hundred square meters. He, however, would not be able to do any more on the half-finished work for he was bedridden, dying of kidney failure.

There were but seven months remaining before the hotel was to open. The mural had to be finished by then, in time for all the dignitaries and royalty that would be coming to gaze at Thailand's latest addition from the twentieth century. And besides, Suwannakudt had said he would have it done in time. Like any real man of honor, he always kept his word, even when death was but hours away.

One could not have blamed Phaptawan, his daughter, if she had fretted and refused to obey the scribbled note he handed her from his death bed, which asked her to complete the Peninsula mural personally. But in the Asian style of devotional culture, there never was a possibility of her refusing the awesome task. In Thailand, as in all Asia, a parent's wish is the same as a command. To disobey is a shameful deed. For the time being, her own artistic ambitions would have to be put aside.

Having studied under her father since the age of ten, Phaptawan was about to find out what it meant to be a serious artist. When her father died a few days later, she was left with a name to be lived up to, six unemployed mouths to be fed, a difficult project to be professionally completed in too little time, and a big, old, open-walled barn for a studio, which was often reverberating with the honks of two mischievous geese and the yawning of a lazy collie.

Many times I have left a work of art wondering who was the person behind the hands that created such beauty or fearsomeness. While often enriched by having experienced a great work of art, I felt as if I'd really seen only the surface by not having come to know the creator too.

That same feeling haunted me after viewing The Peninsula's lobby. However, this time fate apparently decided it was time my curiosity got its answers.

It was through a jovial older journalist named Charlee Sodpraset, whom I met completely by accident, that I got to meet the human behind the Peninsula lobby's enormous mural. Charlee ran an art studio for beginners near a house where I was staying with a group of hospitable Indian monks. For no reason other than to be friendly and invite me to have a glass of that horrid concoction the Thais call tea and a plate of—*gulp*—squid, Charlee talked me away from the curb into his studio. There I met Phaptawan, who taught one of the Sunday evening classes.

Visiting Phaptawan's father's old studio later that evening was like visiting the Wizard of Oz himself. So this was what was behind the workings of that great spectacle I had stood in awe before a few days previously. . . paint-smeared cloths, brushes made from everything from tree roots to the hair of the inner part of a cow's ear, wicked-looking mixtures of minerals and earth pigments, and strange-sounding binders made from seeds baked and mashed and boiled, small porcelain clubs in crusty bowls, lizards scuttling over creaky floor boards with lumpy toads the size of my fist hopping right behind . . . .

You mean to tell me that from these things blossom such beautiful creations? What sort of sorcery is this?

Apparently a very good sort of magic, if the murals of traditional Thai scenes Phaptawan was presently working on were any indication. Filled with detailed miniature scenes of Thai history, religion and daily life, the murals showed that she had mastered the manner of making the actions on the murals continuous, while not letting them merge into one another. Those in which she had so carefully created designs in gold leaf and black lacquer were as stunning as any art works I'd seen in the grandest of buildings.

Typical of Thai painting, there was no use of shadows, none of the European perspective of the fixed point and vanishing point. Time was not stopped at any particular point. Action was seemingly worked into every inch of the man-high murals, no matter from which angle they were studied.

Though some of the works, at least the smaller ones, might be sold at exhibitions for $200 to $400, there would never really be any sort of decent monetary compensation for all the time (weeks) that went into each mural. Most, she explained, were simply too large to be practically displayed in the average Thai's small flat. The larger works would have to go to the temples, which could pay but a pittance of their actual value.

But she didn't mind. She knew that the role in life with which she had been entrusted was too important to dwell on money. Though young, she already knew that the secret of happiness was not money or possessions, but having a purpose to fulfill.

What had been her thoughts on the day before The Peninsula's opening, when she finished putting the last stroke on her father's mural?

"I felt . . . I felt as if my father's life had been completed then," she said slowly. "That he hadn't quite gone away until he was sure the mural was finished completely."

Steven

Subat Thani, Thailand
May 3, 1985

Dear Folks,

The eyes of the two young men narrowed and swept back like those of two hateful tomcats. Their arms cocked and their fists challenged the other to advance. Bare feet danced nervously over straw-covered dirt, as the paws of those same quarreling cats might have on a tin roof in the heat of the day.

The light from a bulb hanging from an overhead tree limb made the thick sweat on the men's dark, farm-hardened bodies shine like grease. Their chests heaved and their heads moved from side to side with wariness. The inner spirit peering through each pair of glass-like eyes was totally oblivious to the deafening shrill of the cicadas in the jungle surrounding the crude boxing ring's ropes and fencepost corners.

An invisible, unspoken spark flashed from one fighter to the other. The cumulus of moths and bats around the bulb exploded. A roar erupted from the crowd around the little battlefield. Raw muscle charged, collided, pounded. Guttural cries burst from bruised lips. In the background, tom-toms and a raspy Java flute tried frantically to mimic the battle's tempo. Feet slapped against skulls, knees pushed into stomachs. In Thai boxing, every limb and body joint is part of the fighter's arsenal.

At last a straw-hatted scarecrow leapt onto a horse cart and wildly beat a spoon against a metal dinner plate. *Clang! Clang! Clang!* End of round four! End of round four!

Their nostrils gasping desperately at the steamy midnight air, the boxers sank backwards into corners of worried and zealous faces. Such beatings they had taken with hardly a flinch! And still one more round to go. Surely they had to be wondering by now what had ever possessed them to step from the crowd into this gypsy camp ring in the first place.

Neither man had refused a punch or kick. No doubt could there be that they were equals. How easy and shameless it could have been to retreat to the ropes or the straw. What stamina! What courage!

And yet—there it was, glazing their gladiator eyes as surely as the veins bulging from their necks . . . fear.

Fear . . . of what? Of losing? No, it couldn't be that. Each hurt too much to think of anything other than surviving. And there was no prize to be won or lost, other than perhaps boasting rights. Though that, too, meant nothing anymore, with each having proven his courage and fighting skills.

What a strange thing fear can be. We can tolerate such pain and loneliness, achieve great success, even master the secret of being at peace with the universe, and still fear remains as entrenched as ever. Convince ourselves and others all we might of our fearlessness, laugh in the face of death a million times, and still it is with us when the test comes.

I took my eyes from the fighters, closed out the excited crowd of spectators and listened to my own inner trembling— the fear that had been growing inside me for over eight days since I was attacked by two bandits who charged out of the jungle's black heart, machetes swinging.

The attack had been near midnight on an empty stretch of moonless road south of Phetchaburi. Everyone had warned me gravely not to journey along that road, even in daylight. "Gangsters are everywhere," they said, and they would kill me for my watch. But still I'd gone, even defied the police's orders, for it was the heat of the summer that drove me from Bangkok to Petchaburi, and I hated it so much I was willing to chance any robbers. And, besides, how many countless times had I heard the cry of "wolf" before?

But this time the wolf was there. Me and it. Or, rather, *them.* And no one to hear my screams but blackened pineapple fields and the thickly-muscled men behind the knives.

So quickly did everything happen that the nightmare seemed in flashes—a pair of lone passing headlights betraying figures crouching in the weeds below the shoulder of the road—the dull glint of the knives, the figures springing up and coming directly for me—my flight down the dead road crying aloud, "No! No!"—heavy footsteps rushing from behind, the sickening feel of death—sure death—in the guts—the larger man closing in from the left with his knife up for the kill— someone pulling me around—metal striking the large umbrella I was flailing about in a desperate bid for a few more seconds of life, the mind pleading to God and then fleeing the body to avoid the pain of the knives. Then—*headlights!* And the "wolves" scrambling for the weeds, to stop and crouch only a few yards away until the next sweep of darkness.

At last the pin lights are blazing suns—a door is flying open—arms are grabbing me and pulling my head past a row of huge eyes—a breeze blowing over my legs—my pack stuck on the door frame. Will the robbers pull me back out? Or stab my legs? My heart pounding, pounding, pounding.

"I'm alive. I'm alive . . . *alive* . . . Oh, thank you, God."

Only later did I fully realize how closely death had brushed past. It was the closest—only mere inches—that the walk had come to the tragic end so many believe is inevitable. Just the tiniest change in the way the drama had unfolded—say, the truck arriving only half a minute later, or my not seeing the ambush in advance—and I'd surely have perished. It was then that a very tired and familiar voice inside me begged again, for me to flee all the danger and pain still ahead.

"There is nothing to be ashamed of in quitting," the voice always tempts sensibly. "Go home, Steve. Why risk your life like this? And for what?"

As usual I had no answers. Just that to quit solely because of fear of things unseen and not yet experienced somehow seemed "not right." Some things in life can't be explained in words, and fear is one of those mysterious clouds of the human spirit. Mysterious, too, is why some are its slaves and others choose to challenge it to the last round.

The spoon pounding the plate brought me back to the present. The faces screamed. The fighters charged and staggered, charged and staggered. Until, in the end, there was a winner, and a loser.

And no more need for showing fear—for awhile, that is.

Steven

Had Yai, Thailand
May 19, 1985

Dear Folks,

The frail, saffron-cloaked monk paused at the cave's dark entrance. Slowly he slipped his calloused old feet from their sandals. Then he feebly tugged at his toga-like garments, as if by doing so he might chase away a few of their innumerable wrinkles. In the pale glow of an evening sun shrouded in rain forest and high cliffs streaked with dampness and vines, it was hard to see what message his tiny dark eyes might be flashing. But there was no mistaking the inviting nod of his shaven head.

Like beacons on a distant shore, the flames of several candles beckoned us from the other end of the large and still interior. A sweet fog of incense smoke wafted across the small sea of darkness. While on our sides, large squat Buddha statues, some with heads and arms long eroded into dust, passed by like ancient, lifeless islands.

At the cave's end the monk lit another candle and sat on a straw mat beside four other monks who had silently been awaiting the elder's arrival. Respectfully, I eased myself onto the cold earth behind the five men, keeping just outside the globe of the candle's glow. With much inner groaning I tried to coerce my stiff legs into the lotus position favored by the monks.

From atop a low altar in front of them, a golden Buddha with feline eyes, long ears and a benign smile gazed down upon the disciples and the many knickknacks that had found their way to the altar over many years.

While the monks' attentions retreated inside themselves, my own flitted about the temple, eagerly darting from shadow to shadow to see what surprises this holy grotto held. And there were many—a pair of long deer antlers protruding from a skull like gnarled stalagmites—enormous spider webs stirring in the drafts of nature's own soul, their handsized spiders not at all fooled—over a dozen framed scenes of the Buddha's mortal life in India 2,528 years ago, the cheap prints now moldy and stained as much as if they'd been hanging in that cave at least that many years—mysterious blank slips of paper and squares of gold-colored foil stuck all over the statues—and the portraits of the king and queen dressed in the costumes of their ancestors, looking like players in some Shakesperian play.

A rustle of rough cloth brought my eyes back to the monks. They were bowing low, as if in response to some unspoken command. Deep chanting echoed throughout the cave.

A Buddha-like smile played across my own lips. Before departing Bangkok I had felt so sure that I would be having very few, if any, close encounters with the religious community of this nearly totally Buddhist society. The Buddhism in Thailand is of a very quiet and private nature, quite introverted. There is none of the loud singing and dancing of deity worshipers in a seemingly endless carnival of worship as in India. Instead, there is only peace and pleasantly taciturn monks coming from or going to their mostly secluded temple grounds, or "wats."

However, the distance between myself and this almost imperceptible religion was to be greatly narrowed as a result of the attack by the two armed bandits near Phetchaburi. Ironically, it took an act of violence to cause me to enter into what has become one of the most serene and fascinating chapters of my journey. Suddenly more heedful of the rural people's warnings that the thieves in southern Thailand liked to slit the throats of their victims while they are sleeping, I thought it best to seek refuge in the sanctity of the wats each evening, whenever I had no family to take me into its care.

While a few of the eleven wats I stayed in since that frightful night have been large and centerpieced with a tall and glittering temple, most have been a tiny cluster of stilt-legged huts deep inside the forest at the base of some half-wild mountain. Gardens of tranquility, these little wats are normally occupied by only a handful of monks who have sought an undisturbed place to spend their final years. Occasionally there may also be a lone "maichee," or nun, also old, shaven-headed and humbly dressed. And always there is the small army of stray dogs, cats and chickens.

Though rarely visited by anyone other than the village children and farmers' wives bringing food and idle conversation, the monks never shied away from my unexpected appearance. Like kind fathers they would show me the bathing well or stream and later wave me up the rickety steps to their one-room bungalows for hot chocolate or a meal of rice, fish and boiled bamboo. Furnished with only a sleeping mat on the floor, a mosquito net, a small altar, some old books and religious prints, their abodes reflected how temporary they view this worldly existence.

At most of the wats my stay was no longer than a memorable evening and night, though at one, Wat Suan Moke, near the city of Surat Thani, I stayed for over two weeks. Its head monk, the Venerable Buddhadasa, is said to be one of the world's "greatest living masters" of the Buddha's teachings. From the monk just under him, the Venerable Poh, I received an invitation to pause and explore what is inside me, for a change.

What followed was one of the most grueling periods of my life, mentally and physically, during the days of long and intensive meditation and teaching. I was made to disassociate myself from all my normal habits and my own ego, as it became taboo to ever speak or make eye contact with anyone other than my teacher. Even stepping outside of the wat area or reading or listening to music was discouraged, since it would distract my mind from what was going on inside of me.

In the end my mind proved too restless to study. Nor were all the scorpions and snakes that liked to surprise one on the paths of that forest monastery helpful to my concentration. Yet, while I may have been something of a dunce at meditating, I did come away with a profound respect for some of the teachings of the Buddha, who gave up the rights to his father's kingdom to become an ascetic in search of the causes of man's suffering.

And, too, I came away with a better understanding of that mystery named . . .

Steven

All during the long, humid afternoon leading up to the ritual, I had watched the preparations with a keen eye and asked many questions. But it had not been all that easy to be studious. Promenading through the gaily-decorated courtyard of the small temple had been many women of graceful elegance. Beneath the bright sun, their colored silk skirts and saris had shimmered like patterned rainbows.

Every so often the spell of the women was broken by dark men in white dhotis coming forth to invite me to the feast in an adjoining field. There, small mountains of rice and string beans were continually being ladled onto banana leaf "plates." Sometimes the shrill of a celebrant's flute caused my eyes to dart, or the jangle of loose jewelry on a mother and daughter, bowing to the black stone Mariamman and symbolically washing their faces in the flames of her holy fire, would distract me.

The only outsider at the festival, I was constantly surrounded by others eager for me to share their joy. Once a young man dipped his thumb into a bowl held by a bare-chested priest and smudged gray ashes onto my forehead. Delighted, his friends danced around this "orang puteh" (white man) who was now like them.

Then the energy level burst onto a higher plane—coconuts thudded against the temple in another appreciation ritual—artifacts from the worshipers' homes were waved before the statue's wild eyes—the flutes grew more piercing—a replica of Mariamman was draped with more garlands and paraded for several dusty minutes in a sort of back hills Mardi Gras.

Finally the procession wound its way back and the moment of climax, the time for the magic of walking on fire, had come.

My heart was pounding as the first fire walker lifted his leg to step forward. I was positive there had been no doctoring of the men's feet or the coals (which had started out as a tall pile of flaming logs). And the heat from the pit was still so great it would have boiled water in a minute.

Each fire walker's face seemed to register great pain as he crossed the coals in a quick dash. Only one man actually walked, and his steps were long indeed!

At the end of the pit, helpers immediately grabbed each walker, as he literally collapsed into a shallow small pit for soaking the feet. The soaking fluid was milky-colored. A few of the walkers looked about to faint. Was it from pain? Or were they overcome with emotion? Or had they snapped out of the trance they had put themselves into through fervent praying and fasting?

I examined their feet very carefully. Some of the soles were as soft as an office worker's—not a single scar or blister—not a speck of redness. Each coal walker smilingly swore there wasn't the slightest bit of pain.

Was it all extraordinary, or a quite normal event? The priests and walkers repeated their earlier conviction that it was possible only because of the intervention of the heavens.

Steven

Malacca, Malaysia
June 17, 1985

Dear Folks,

The morning sun rose slowly through the long fingers of
the coconut leaves. The one-lane road was still lacquered from
a midnight shower. Snaking down the date palms were many
vines, while around a bend in the road to Malacca lay a
massive limestone outcropping, like something from a Chinese
painting.

Beside the road were flimsy, family-run stalls with all sorts
of freshly-picked fruits, from purple mangosteens to heavy
succulent papayas, to tart star fruit, to hairy red and yellow
rambutans, to the spiked durians with their rotten odors. Past
the stalls, further to the west, was a sky still colored with
dawn, hugging a green sea peppered with old fishing boats
going *"tuk-tuk-tuk-tuk."*

Dipping into a marshy swamp, the road was surrounded by
a den of mangrove roots and high branches rustling with
fleeing monkeys. Stepping around a freshly-killed snake the
width of my arm (How many is that now? One hundred? Two
hundred?), I caught my breath at the sight of a crocodile
sliding off a stream bank. Then it was back to the rice paddies
and buffalos, including one slumbering in a mudhole, his
swept-back horns being used as perches by several large birds.

At noon, a fishing village on the banks of a chocolate river
appeared. Wooden shack homes leaned crazily upon stilts stuck
into the water. Planks pungent with fish smells formed the
sidewalks.

The road became a narrow Main Street, squeezed between
shop homes—Chinese medicine sellers—bookstores with newspapers in Malay, Chinese, Arabic, Indian and English—a cof-
fin-maker hand carving his newest order—a husband and wife
pounding, in perfect rhythm, a piece of glowing iron into the
shape of a parang knife blade—a general store with rows of
canned sardines, fresh cabbage, salted fish and tin boxes with
glass fronts so you could see what was inside.

My pack suddenly felt too heavy and my stomach very
empty. Ducking into an Indian coffee house, shaded by bamboo porch screens, with wobbly ceiling fans swooshing over-

head, I ordered lunch. The chipatis (unleavened Indian bread) were sizzled on an oil drum stove by the shop's open front. A Kickapoo soft drink was placed on my table.

Meanwhile, the village's inhabitants spilled in and out of shops and homes, which had entrances framed by collapsible metal gates with padlocks the size of my fist. They were a study of chaotic contrast—bustling Chinese matrons in flowery pajama suits—demure Indian girls in shiny saris—moslem Malay men in long cotton tunics and new kopiahs (small black felt hats)—cherub-faced schoolchildren, the boys in green knee socks and shorts and white shirts, the girls in white telekungs (a head covering similar to a nun's habit, worn by the Moslem schoolgirls).

A Chinese man who had known fewer than ten words of English paid for my meal without telling me. I continued along the empty beaches toward the south, hearing the call to Allah coming from a distant golden bronze dome. And still fresh on my contented mind was the sight of a tiny Chinese Buddhist housewife setting fire to a pile of play money in an alleyway. (To make sure their deceased loved ones are comfortable in the spirit world, the Chinese send them everything from money to cars to entire houses—all made of paper and transported via smoke.)

As I had done ever since leaving Bangkok, I shaded myself from the harsh tropical sun by an umbrella. Peering from behind a group of coconut tree trunks, several young children didn't know what to think of this strange man plodding past. With a quick twirl of the umbrella and a crossing of the eyes, I quickly had them laughing—a *mistake*.

"Hello! Hello! Hello!" rang out their voices, for an eternity.

In the afternoon I settled like a lazy cat into the eternal dusk of a rubber plantation forest. So cool, and always deathly still and quiet. The branches met high overhead like the arches of a cathedral. I nodded, then nodded again, then drifted to sleep.

Hours later I eased back into a world of growing shadows. Men in sandals and plaid dhotis stood in their yards to watch me pass. More often than not there was a child in each arm. Momma must have been cooking dinner.

That evening my hosts filled me with sirap (rose-colored

sugar water) and all sorts of dainty Hari Raya cookies and cakes. Hari Raya is the Moslem equivalent of our Christmas. It marks the end of the month of fasting, during which no food or water must pass the lips between sunrise and sunset. Observed during the ninth month of the Moslem calendar, it is to remind the faithful how the poor often feel. Afterward gifts are given.

After a dinner of rice and spicy mutton, I retired to the high wooden front steps to sit and listen to the violins of the crickets. Far, far away, a crescent moon smiled through a starry night.

"It's been a nice day, hasn't it?" I whispered to the Old Man in the Sky.

He just kept smiling.

Steven

The walk thus far

801 days
April 1, 1983 - June 29, 1985
10,429 miles walked

AUSTRALIA

STEVEN'S ROUTE

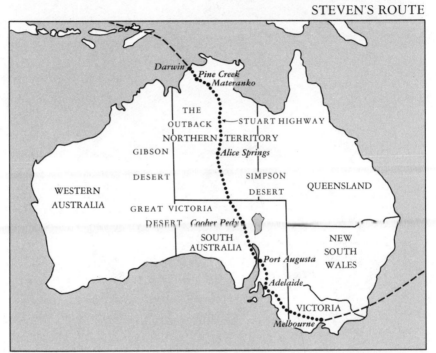

The romantic in me had hoped to lace my way by ship through the lush tropical islands of Indonesia, but, alas, I was to find that now, because of the cheaper air fares, the boats have all but disappeared. And so, I suppose, like a normal tourist, I dropped out of the sky onto the old, cracked runways of Darwin, Australia's most isolated city, on the edge of the great deserts of the Outback.

The walk ahead through Australia

355 days
July 1, 1985 - June 20, 1986
2,338 miles

It wasn't fancy, but Roo, the buggy I used to haul my supplies across the Australian deserts, was a life saver. For the first thirteen thousand miles of my journey, my backpack Clinger was all that I needed, but in the Australian Outback where temperatures often reach 140 degrees, and settlements can average three hundred miles apart, I had to revert to using a cart that I built from an old golf buggy to carry all the supplies I would need in the desert.

Darwin, Australia
July 17, 1985

Dear Folks,

Those with the most wrinkled faces still refer to it as "The Track." Others, much younger and more domesticated, prefer the less colorful, if more reassuring, name "Stuart Highway."

All I know is this—that endless, narrow, dusty snake of rough asphalt and dirt should soon be leading me into the most challenging adventure I have ever faced.

Incredibly, the Stuart Highway is the only lifeline from Darwin's location overland to the rest of this enormous island continent. In fact, it is the only road from here that leads to another town, which just so happens to be a mere two hundred miles away.

The loneliest highway in all the world, it knows fewer inhabitants along its 2,200-mile route than a Main Street would in the average small American city. And the vast empty spaces that keep the most untamed region in this half of the world—the great Australian Outback.

One can count on one hand the number of towns on that road between Darwin and the next city, Alice Springs. Of course, some may object that 20,700 miners and cattlemen clustered together in the middle of a desert hardly qualifies as a city. But then by the time I drag myself into "Alice," Darwin will be 1,100 miles behind and the next city just as far ahead!

Now, why would anyone with half a brain wish to travel on foot across such a sea of solitude?

Good question. Perhaps Mark Twain hinted at the proper answer when, in *Following the Equator*, he wrote with a chuckle: "Australia history does not read like history, but like the most beautiful lies. And all of a fresh, new sort, no moldy and stale ones. It is full of surprises, and adventures, and incongruities, and contradictions, and incredibilities—but they are all true—they all happened."

Australia is still very much a frontier land—a place where experimentation, sweat, fearlessness and being different from "the rest" are, for many, the keys to survival. Somehow, being normal in such a place just doesn't seem sensible.

The Northern Territory region, which will occupy the first

half of my trek from north to south, has an area of 1,346,200 square kilometers, or one-sixth of the Australian continent. Yet less than 140,000 people inhabit it.

Of the 1,200 miles I'll cover in the "Territory," around 1,000 fall in the torrid, semi-arid zone north of the Tropic of Capricorn. The remainder will be harsher—sand dunes and claypan deserts, part of Australia's "dead heart."

There are but two seasons—the "wet" and the "dry." Presently it is the dry or winter season. From now until October every day will be exactly the same—cloudless, dry days followed by starry nights with freezing temperatures. Traveling this same road in the summer season, from November to March, would be impossible much of the time. In those months the torrential monsoon rains bring unrelenting heat and humidity and turn the interior into a swampy inland sea. Where only weeks before, a parched desert stood, rivers suddenly swell up with waters deep enough to sweep away semi-trailer trucks. And beneath the swirling, muddy waters swim thousands of crocodiles and even sharks that have come down hundreds of miles from the northern coastline.

Alas, there will be no jumping into any of the "billabongs" (ponds) I happen upon the next several months. While almost all of the water from the wet season eventually evaporates, very few of the "crocs" and sharks ever do.

Untamed, rugged, wild, even deadly—the land along "The Track" can't help but be lonely. But that doesn't stop me. For, as I've said, such a place breeds a special sort of person. And what few of them I do meet these next months should be fascinating enough to make up for all "the rest" I didn't find in between.

Steven

Pine Creek, Australia
August 10, 1985

Dear Folks,

Like an egg yolk oozing across a pale blue china plate, the setting sun stained the sky a greasy yellow. Ever so slowly, its glow was ingested by a never-ending plain the color of a brown paper sack. The crackle of something parting the tall, brittle spear grass on the right side of the still road made me stop walking. From the broken reeds, a long head with curiosity-filled eyes poked its way into the clearing. Behind it followed the tawny form of a wild dog.

I held my breath—a dingo!

Startled at suddenly finding his dreaded foe—man—mysteriously standing mere yards away, like some ominous spectre, the large dingo sprang in one leap across the roadway. Instinctively, the beautifully healthy creature's figure zig-zagged effortlessly through the ghostly, white-trunked gum trees speckling the other half of the road. Fearful, perhaps, that I was some pale giant of the Aborigines, he avoided looking back until his flanks were out of range of any spear or arrow.

Once again I was alone, left to inch my way across an empty vastness that smelled of brush fires and spoke occasionally through the squabble of the large parrot-shaped cockatoos. The words of Matthew Flinders, an explorer in the early 1800's, came to mind. Once scribbled thoughts on a diary's pages, they had been the frustrated observations of a young man who had come to the north of Australia full of dreams, but who—like all the others before—had eventually fled away from this "poor dried-up land afflicted by fever and flies, fit only for a college of monks whose religious zeal might cope with suffocating heat and musketos which admitted no moment of repose."

I swatted for the millionth time at the swarm of flies crawling into my eyes and nostrils. Ever since morning—or had it been an eternity?—the horrid pests had been fighting over every drop of moisture my flesh had surrendered to the blazing sun. Glancing around at the hundreds, maybe thousands, of other flies clinging to the supplies lashed high onto a cart I was pulling, I thought a part of my soul might break into a rage. But, instead, I encouraged my thoughts to drift back to sometime more happy and sane.

Five days before, on August 5, I had taken the first steps into this latest chapter of the Worldwalk, one which I knew would be the most physically severe yet. Though excited by the thought that the long trek across Australia was finally starting, it was with a nervous eye I sometimes looked up at the crisp morning sky. The last time the heavens had yielded any water to the parched Outback had been in March. No longer would being thirsty be just an inconvenience, but a way of life, or death. With the walking distances between each station (ranch) in the Outback anywhere from two to seven days, I had no choice but to carry along many gallons of water, in addition to a large supply of tuck (food). For the first time since leaving home twenty-eight months ago, my big, weary, frame pack, Clinger, would not be proudly weighing me down. Much as I'm sure he felt insulted about it all, he would have to spend the next several months ingloriously lashed with all the extra supplies, to the creaking frame of an old golf cart of an equally cantankerous demeanor, known as *Roo* (Australian slang for kangaroo).

Nervous as I was, I still left Darwin a very hopeful and happy adventurer. The thirty-five days I had spent preparing for the Australia walk had left me with much to smile about. For starters there had been Don Zoellner and his lovely wife, Ardys, who both had graduated from Bethel High School (in Bethel, Ohio) just a couple of years before me, and thus were the first familiar faces (out of all those millions) I had seen in over two years.

When not with the Zoellners, I was often with another exceptionally hospitable couple named Leon and Yvonne Roberts. Open and friendly, like most of North Australia's "Territorians," they cared for me as they might have one of their own sons. Like Neil, the teenaged boy who gave me his golf cart, and Jan, the television newscaster who had gone to much effort to let people know I would be crossing the Outback's deserts, the Roberts showed that Darwin, population 65,000, was still not too big to forget its frontier spirit.

Margaret, Leon's spry eighty-nine-year-old "Mum," gave me old-fashioned meals and tales of an Australian past that revolved around homesteads and sheep. As much a piece of Australia as that dingo was, her sparkling blue eyes let me know that no matter how rough the land might get, I could always look forward to the next Aussie.

Steven

My only source of shade in the Outback were boulders like these. I would huddle for hours in their shadows, moving with the sun.

255

Mataranka, N.T., Australia
August 30, 1985

Dear Folks,

The tall, dark Irish publican leaned his angular frame over the cluttered bar counter. A devilish grin pulled back the corners of his big eyes. His thin fingers rose to eye level—pinched between them was a golden stone the size of a blacksmith's thumb.

"Now, maybe, mate, you be thinkin' this rock a wee bit bonza (first-rate), eh?" his voice crooned.

I was wholly mesmerized by the shiny nugget. That it was a dandy nugget, there could be little doubt.

Six other motley men, and one woman, crowded about the lonesome little roadhouse's counter.

"Ya . . . Nice!" a stocky bundle of syntactical eccentricities known as "Joe the Bouncing Czech," whistled.

"And what you thinking now?" he asked me, plunking a yellow-latticed quartz rock into my hands.

Though no bigger than a fist, the jagged rock felt like it weighed a small ton.

"The boys say there's likely four ounces in that thing," the woman, Carolyn, said.

My brows worked their way closer to my hairline. At five hundred dollars an ounce, that was . . . .

"You say there's heaps of gold on top of the ground around here?" I heard myself wondering aloud.

"Fair dinkum (true)! Mobs of it!" a twenty-eight-year-old prospector of lanky height and giant energy exclaimed.

Charlie, a sixty-nine-year-old retiree from East Liverpool, Ohio, laughed with zest at the boyish enthusiasm of young Greg Germon. Too tickled to say more than, "Aw, gee," he slapped a grungy baseball cap against a pair of youthful legs.

Nearly-forgotten memories of enormous gold-leafed murals in the cathedrals of Venice, and a covered market in Istanbul with dozens of shops dealing exclusively in breathtaking gold jewelry, whirled again in my mind's eye. *Gold!*

A raucous roar erupted from a crusty creature four stools down. It was Dickson, the orneriest, most bush-blooded of the lot—and, the most successful. He thumped a tin of baked beans wrong side up on the counter. The publican gasped. Gold nuggets, not beans, lay everywhere.

Predictably, the morning sun rose soon enough to find yet another excited soul chasing the rainbow. And—sigh—perhaps even more predictably, it would set twelve days later onto one more would-be tycoon with nary a speck of golden riches weighing down his pockets.

Yet, it was not without some riches that I continued on my way south to Katherine, across that haunting and bedeviling land of broken promises. Though my nose for the gold may have been clogged with a bit too much red dust, and flies, and just plain inexperience, that motley group of gougers and diggers gave my mind memories and stories far, far more cherishable than perhaps any yellow rock could have.

There were, of course, those sorts of adventures that most of us can only delight in while seated in a darkened cinema house. Such as, for instance, the day Wickham and I snuck down the musty passageway of an abandoned mine shaft, only to suddenly be besieged by millions of mosquitos and, to my frantic shouts, a legion of fanged fruit bats with wings the length of my flailing arms! And where was "D for Dog," Wickham's "trusty" mongrel, in our moment of peril? Why, at the entrance, of course, leaping with abandon at all those furry squeaking "birds" escaping out of that giant snake hole.

Best of all, however, were all those evenings tucked around a crackling wood fire—a skillet of tucker (food) sizzling, a billy (can) of tea bubbling, and the crisp starry night echoing with prospectors' lore.

"There's hundreds right now blipping all over the old gold fields with metal detectors, like we're doing," explained Clive, a scholarly sort, on whose claim we were camped, and whose campfire we shared.

"It's another gold rush, what with Pommies (Englishmen) and rubbernecks (tourists) joinin' the fray," blasted Dickson.

"Why—why there's thousands lookin' fer the lode," he expounded.

"Fair dinkum!" came the chorus, above an orchestra of mosquitoes.

Clive adjusted his glasses upon his large face and continued, "Millions of dollars of gold is being found each week by ordinary blokes, like us, with detectors. Australia is the only place in the world where much of the gold is in nuggets, right on top of the ground and spread throughout every part. The detectors have made it possible for anyone to be a prospector. New patches are being discovered so regularly that it's impossible to catalogue them, although the majority of finds are in old gold mining areas, where they go back over the old diggings."

"Ya! Dis no bluey (joke). In paper I see where two years before, two men with detectors find 851 nuggets, weighing sixty-three ounces," rattled an excited Joe.

"Mind yer, that ain't ever time that happens," Dickson said.

"A find of one to two ounces a week is doin darn good. Why, there's many the times when several weeks pass by without any cries of 'Gold!'," he added. It was no secret that while the others were on a dry spell, Dickson had added at least $3,000 in nuggets to his hoard in the past two days.

"There's tens of thousands of square miles of gold country which hasn't been gone over with a detector. There's more than enough gold to support thousands of full-time prospectors in each of the mainland's states," Clive concluded eloquently.

Germon leaped into the rare pause in conversation.

"My girlfriend and I prospected for two months in the Western Australia deserts and came back with $96,000 in gold nuggets. And that was after my dad and brother came back with $100,000 worth from the same area, after spending five months looking," he related with a twist of pride.

One nugget alone weighed some nine ounces and was shaped like the island state of Tasmania. As is a popular custom in Australia, one of the casinos offered an inflated sum—$15,000—for the novel nugget. Altogether, Germon had over $400,000 worth of gold nuggets to his credit since he started prospecting with a detector at the age of seventeen. But keeping to the lifestyle of his kind, that huge, tax-free fortune had been sunk into the search for more gold.

"If you're willin' to stand the heat and the loneliness, you can pick up $50,000 within a few months," Germon talked on confidently.

"It was a four-day ride to any sort of settlement, and I was bitten by a scorpion while digging a hole—but I just got a bit sick and recovered. The whole area was alive with wildlife, including emus and kangaroos, as well as pythons and lizards galore slithering around the workings. And during that time, we didn't meet one person who hadn't found gold," he added.

Charlie heaved an enormous wild buffalo dung patty on the fire to smoke away the mozzles (mosquitos). And long into the warm night the tales kept coming, and growing. While I settled back against my pack and grew ever wealthier.

Steven

Dear Folks,

Bright red dust billowed from behind the pickup truck in which I was riding. On my right there was a thin line of gum trees, their droopy branches silhouetted against a darkening horizon purpled by dusk and the smoke of uncontrolled grass fires. To the south, on my left, a "willy nilly" was visible inside the dry depression of what a few months before had been a large billabong (lake). Its violent funnel churning every twig and dead leaf in the lonely old pond back into life, the small but powerful twister seemed unable to decide which direction to head.

It was, for me and my driver Bruce, the winding down of another cloudless day spent in the repair of miles of barbed wire fences damaged over the years by such natural vandals as rust, wild buffalo and trees toppled by frequent winter fires or termite legions. Sadly, this was also my last bumpy ride back to the Western Creek Station's cozy homestead, with the home-cooked meals and long evenings of storytelling from the depths of over-stuffed easy chairs. After two weeks of helping the Roses spruce up their newest home, it was time I hit the road once again, if I were to reach the south coastline before my six-month visa expired.

A painful rawness in my hands made me glance at the fingers I was resting atop a black cowboy hat on my lap. Bloody, blistered and as encrusted with dirt as nearly everything else in this thirsty land, those hands suddenly seemed too abused to really be my own. Like the ranch's old wood fenceposts and the thickly scarred and beaten faces of the many aborigine women in every town through which I'd passed, those hands looked wanting of rest and someone who cared.

The abrupt lowering of the truck engine's roar, along with Bruce's own fingers grabbing at the gear stick, snapped my attention back to the environment outside the Land Cruiser. Just ahead were several deep tire ruts. Their baked erratic courses were stark reminders of just how swampy this same near-desert world would be in the approaching wet season.

Once past the miniature canyons, Bruce seemed to visibly relax again. The gear stick was eased back into fourth and we and the aborigine stockman hanging on for dear life in the back bed of the truck, were rushing once more at the vanguard of an endless column of dust clouds.

The older of two sons of Western Creek's new American owners, thirty-two-year-old Bruce continued his fascinating account of all the obstacles the family had had to overcome in the three years since they'd acquired the Rhode Island-sized spread in a bankruptcy auction. (Western Creek is quite ordinary-sized by Australian measures—where a ranch bigger than the state of Texas existed up until a few years ago.) Trying to transform Western Creek into a profitable operation had involved taking on challenges that would have beaten anyone ordinary at the end of just the first year.

Many of the difficulties—among them isolation, cattle rustling, fires, worthless equipment, theft, destructive and diseased, wild-born cattle ("clean skins"), antiquated property laws, and broken promises of financial assistance from the banks—reaffirmed my earlier thoughts that in a setting as unyielding as the Outback, only the most courageous settlers could hope to last long there. They were hundreds of kilometers from any actual town, out of range of any television or radio, and linked to the outside through a small shortwave transmitter wired to car batteries on their front veranda. Conditions many would consider indispensible social amenities were, for Bruce, Gerry and Darlene Rose, infrequent luxuries.

But then, they seemed to thrive on this. For the elder Roses particularly, both now around seventy, overcoming dangers and challenges was a way of life. Listening to them recount at the dinner table each night their lifestyle of the past forty years was like being privy to one of the most incredibly plotted adventure novels of recent time. Never with such frequency have others managed to still a fork between a plate of food and my lips.

Before their marriage, after World War II, Darlene had already survived—*barely*—several years as a P.O.W. of the Japanese on a jungle island. Though managing to just avoid the beheading her first husband (also a missionary) had suffered, she had been decimated by hunger and illiness by the time she was rescued. Then, for most of the next four decades, she and her next husband, Gerry, called the largely unexplored interior of New Guinea their home. There, living and preaching among cannibals who had never before seen white men and who knew nothing of metal or alphabets, Gerry put his medical background to use treating a constant stream of horrid tropical diseases and spear or arrow wounds. (He often had to dodge spears and arrows upon encountering many of the unknown tribes.)

And still they had somehow managed to find enough energy to raise a family and two highly bountiful coffee plantations, both of which were taken away from them, with little more compensation than a ticket out of the country, by corrupt governments.

However, the Roses did not let the confiscation of their latest home by the newly-independent Papua, New Guinea government in the late 1970's force them permanently back to America's security and the easy retirement others said was the only sensible thing for them to do at their advanced age. Instead, they reacted as only pioneers know how—they repacked their few belongings, leaned once again upon the staff of their unwavering belief in themselves and God, rekindled their sort of magical flame of energy and courage, and were off to conquer yet another part of the world that others found too intimidating to face directly.

Meanwhile, their sons, who were attending colleges in Casper, Wyoming, and Seattle, Washington, were feeling the same itch as the parents, and it was not long before they were hurrying back to the challenging lifestyle of less civilized lands.

"I wish very much you had come just a few months later, during the wet. Then everything is so lush and green you wouldn't think it was the same place," Bruce said with a sweep of his thick arm over the station property on the morning he was driving me back to Larrimah, the nearest settlement.

"I know it's not so pretty now, all brown and dried out, and that things aren't going well for us . . . but . . . I really love it here. There's freedom here. This is my home," he said softly.

Some part of me understood and knew what he said was the truth. There really was something spiritually and naturally beautiful in this rugged wilderness. It is only man, not nature, I have found, that is ever ugly. Home is anywhere we want—if we have the guts to believe so.

Steven

The Australian landscape, except for the coastal areas, was always harsh, but also had a haunting, mystical beauty.

Alice Springs, Australia
October 15, 1985

Dear Folks,

The inevitable question put to me by all who come upon me in the vast solitude of the outback is, "Aren't you lonely?"

It seems almost as if we dare to spend much time by ourselves, we must be unhappy for some reason. Apparently the "rugged individualist" is okay to read about, but in real life he, or she, is something to be pitied. Strange, isn't it, how you supposedly can't be happy nowadays unless you are surrounded with security and all sorts of gay and boisterous friends?

Well, for those who are interested, I am not in the least lonely. And I am not at all itchy to leap back just now into the mainstream of civilization. If anything, I am reveling, not drowning, in the infinite cocoon of sky and earth I have been crossing for the past fifteen thousand kilometers.

The most serious problem of the Worldwalk has been the great lack of privacy I have had to suffer through in the heavily populated Third World nations. In these societies, where I have spent most of the past one and one-half years, there was hardly a day that I didn't have to contend with large crowds of the curious. Most people in those nations of Africa and Asia still depend upon their feet or animals to get from one spot to another. All of which meant, of course, that even while I was moving I usually had "companions."

The most important reason I had for routing my journey through the almost unpopulated interior of Australia was to give my mind and body a badly needed break from man's general chaos. After two and one-half years of intently studying man, it was time to take my eye off the microscope's lens for awhile. Time, in other words, for some peace and quiet.

It is important to me to study each society in both its new and old forms. To find the latter side always meant walking deep into the rural areas whenever possible. In the poverty and conservatism of the countryside, I thought I would find society's real roots and soul, and perhaps its most time-tested valuable lessons to be learned about our existence. However, by wandering so openly in areas where normal day-to-day life has few diversities, I knew the risk of my sudden appearance generating tremendous excitement.

The trouble was, I did not realize just how overwhelming it could become in reality. From the huge numbers that often rushed to me and the amount of commotion that swept over all, you would have thought I had two heads or a convoy of circus wagons behind me. Sometimes in rural India so many screaming schoolboys and young men would sweep over any shop I entered that all outside sunlight would be blocked out. The madness of it all made no sense to me, especially when they climbed onto each other's backs to get their faces closer to the doorway or the window bars. More than once a squad of police charged violently into the crowds to find the cause of the sudden mass "riot." During those times it was my own body that those flailing arms and shouting heads were pressed against. It was all I could do not to faint in the crush.

Two nights ago, on the television of the host with whom I am presently staying, I saw the film *Gandhi* for the first time. I had to chuckle. In the scenes where Gandhi is walking through the countryside and towns the people, though quite numerous, were standing in an orderly fashion along the sides of his route. That was certainly not the real India!

Many were the chilly mornings I was abruptly awakened by some big-eyed brown head poking unannounced through my tent's door flaps. Even more common was having the entire populace of some small village crowd around me while I shaved and bathed at the local well. A few times I had a bit of fun by breaking into a wretchedly off-key, but high-spirited, song and dance number, before all those perplexed faces.

Other times, though, the scene was not so amusing, as the months of having little time to myself wore my nerves thin. Right now, in a certain farm village in northern India, it is likely that one of the stories being told beside the crackling dinner fire is of the wild-eyed, red-haired giant who—blood streaming from his face—chased everyone home with his thunderous fury and slashing disposable razor.

I have now walked over 11,200 miles across nineteen nations. When my imagination and spirit stop to reflect upon all that I have done and wondered about in those miles, I can't help thinking, or fancying, that I have been blessed with another whole life at the same time I am living the original. So many times my eyes have seen the sun and moon rise and fall. Surely more raindrops than there are stars in the heavens have played on my face. Who could count all the friends, all the laughter, all the tears of love lost and love gained?

Why would I ever be lonely?

Steven

South Australia Border
October 30, 1985

Dear Folks,

I lowered my book. My heart was pounding. Goose bumps were rising on my arms. Something wasn't quite right outside the storm pipe in which I was hiding from the rain. My nerves tingling, my ears straining, I concentrated all my attention on the odd sound of gravel or rocks tumbling against one another.

"That's not a car driving on the road!" screamed a voice in my head, when I suddenly became aware that the rocks were making an awful lot of splashing sounds, too.

My guts twisting, I bolted from my sleeping bag. Bent double in the low, long pipe, I scrambled to the far end and stared out wide-eyed into the dawn light. Flood! *Flash flood!*

"Oh my—" My body didn't give my mind a chance to finish. In a second I was thirty feet back, grabbing madly for any gear lying loose around Roo and flinging it onto the sleeping bag. Already a foamy brown flow was swirling around my ankles. Like some horrible nightmare, my escape route was blocked by the cart—gear was being swept away and death was inching its cold, watery hands up my legs. Now the water was tearing at my calves!

Wild with fear, with images of my lifeless body entangled in the cart in that dark and roaring hole, my mind screamed. Bulling forward, I shoved Roo out into the rapids, which were fed from the flood waters gushing from six adjacent storm pipes. I leapt into water up to my thighs, shuddered at the bolt of iciness, and heaved the sleeping bag onto the nearby bank's rocks. How lucky that I didn't sleep last night in one of the center pipes! The roar was deafening, the lightning and thunder exploding in my head. Where was my cart?

There! Let it go, the water's nearly waist high. I'm slipping—get it now or get out!

My hands lunged for a part of Roo. Fingers latched tightly onto slippery metal, legs strained, strained, *strained.* The wheels were caught! Without a thought I was under the filthy flood, ripping away roots and boulders. I couldn't let the flood win—all my records, films and camera were on this cart in my backpack, Clinger.

At last the unseen grips loosened. Falling, splashing, lunging, I reached the bank with the cart in tow. Like a pair of muddy beasts, we tumbled awkwardly onto the rocks. I took no notice of the rain starting to fall more heavily—it was but a mist in comparison to what I had just escaped.

I had no idea a flood could be so swift and vicious. And I was sure not enough rain had fallen overnight to even soak a decent-sized sponge, let alone drown me! Where I grew up, it usually took a whole day and night of pouring torrent to get the tributaries of the Ohio River to flow halfway fast.

Many Australians had told me stories of the notoriously sudden and deep Outback flash floods. It was not unusual, they said, for the Stuart Highway to be completely cut off for weeks in spots where normally not a drop of water would be found. Tales were abundant of motorists being stranded in the middle of the desert for days, cut off from an unknowing world by flash floods behind and in front of their vehicle. Other times, planes had to be used to drop supplies to cut-off roadhouses glutted with hungry stranded truckers, or to station houses, with all their vehicles and animals, mired in the thousands of square miles of muck surrounding their isolated locations.

With the rainy season approaching, I would now have more than just heat to worry about. With the ground too hard and baked to soak up the water, even the lightest of rains in the Outback could conceivably cause flooding. As fate would have it, I splashed myself into Alice Springs to spend the next eleven days.

There it was through Alice's lone street sweeper, Bob, whose job entailed having eyes that always looked down, away from the sky, that I came to be in the fascinating company of Peter Strickland, his thirty-eight-year-old younger brother, a meteorologist. Through him I learned an expert amount about the moods of the wild weather conditions which often characterize the Land Down Under, particularly the wide-open Outback.

Fifty-four-year-old Bob had met me several days before my arrival in Alice Springs, or "Alice." Then he had been out testing a new motorcycle he had just purchased from an American Air Force worker who was returning home from the highly secret Pine Gap "satellite spy" base in the desert west of there. He had heard of me from others and invited me to be his guest while in Alice. True to his word, the extremely kind Bob showed me the way home, when I walked into the pretty downtown and came upon him and his cart with its two trash cans and brooms. Peter, also unmarried, lived in the same house.

For Peter, working as a meteorologist meant working for the government, and all the usual shuffling from one far-flung weather post to another every few years. After seventeen years of watching the world's roof, he had also seen nearly every corner of Australia. It was in Alice, however, that he felt he'd finally found home. There, surrounded by more sky and land and space than was possible nearly anywhere else, he found his life-long infatuation with both the day and night skies soaring to new heights.

And through his enthusiasm I rediscovered that part of my own past, when as a young boy growing up in the shadows of Cape Canaveral, I had dreamed of someday following those heroic astronauts to other planets and the stars. My imagination, as it fed on Peter's extensive science books, circled across his weather radar screen at the airport, and listened keenly to his scientific explanations of the universe, was again electrified by the thought of just how incredibly immense and intricate creation is, not to mention all that which is still unseen and unknown.

The discovery, thanks to Peter, that what I had thought were clouds in the night sky are actually entire galaxies of millions-upon-millions of suns, and that my eyes were beholding not merely hundreds-of-millions of stars but *billions*, could only leave me wondering—how can all this be possible? Where could so much infinite matter have come from?

If only we could look around our world, or even at that part just around us, with the same enthusiasm Peter does when he gazes out from tiny Alice Springs into the vastness of the surrounding Outback with all its surprises!

"Here around Alice, Bob and I can roam for endless miles without seeing others. I am alone with both this world and all those stars, and no one to tell me I can't see this, or do that, or go here or there. Tell me, where else can you enjoy all this and still be so free?" Peter asked.

I nodded, secretly wishing for the day we would be even freer.

Steven

From this rocky hill, the Outback seemed to stretch endlessly in its harsh arid beauty to the distant horizon.

Mintabie, South Australia
November 7, 1985

Dear Folks,

Since crossing from the Northern Territory into South Australia's even harsher and less populated outback deserts, I have become perhaps the most physically isolated of all travelers. Here in the dead heart, or Never-Never, of this empty continent, both the land and the sky have become infinite planes virtually devoid of mankind's traces. Rather than airplanes, or autos, or telephone and electric poles, it is only death, sand, clouds and an awesome sense of freedom that swirl past with each tick of the universe's clock. There is not even a speck of asphalt upon the sand-drifted ruts of this much feared, and avoided "South Road" of the Stuart Highway. There is nothing but lizards, snakes, grotesquely gnarled scrub, and unhindered spaces so clean, virgin and sensuously overpowering.

During the day I am often a prisoner of the sun, and with weakened body I labor to pull Roo and Clinger through the sandy traps. The land can then seem cruel, scorning my intrusion by offering me only my own shadow in which to hide. Yet at night, as if to reward my persistence, I find myself elevated to the company of the gods themselves. It is only here in the Southern Hemisphere that the whole of the Milky Way can be seen.

I was 433 kilometers (almost 300 miles) south of the little city of Alice Springs and still 300 kilometers north of the next town after Alice, Coober Pedy, when Johnny B. Coolie's clunky old Holden auto roared at me from out of the damp, blood-red dunes. Putting his big-bellied and wide-hatted aborigine body through the absent windshield, he shoved the usual beer into my hand and virtually dared me to go with him to some isolated little camp of opal miners situated some 50 miles off the Stuart Highway.

There, off to the west in the Gibson Desert, was a "Wild West" camp of around two hundred fifty prospectors and individual miners sitting on the richest opal claims in the world, he boasted. Mintabie was its name, a refuge from all that is civilized and tame. Johnny was convinced it would be unlike anything I had ever seen.

I was more than a little bit hesitant to load myself and my cart into Johnny's battered tank. There were those who had told me people actually lived and worked in that giant bleached sand carpet, but what I could see from the road was outrageous. Still—it was inevitable, my succumbing to my curiosity. A million missed heartbeats later I came racing on a cloud of dust and smoke into Mintabie's unusual gathering. Here I met my main host, Ron Elliot, in an amazing way.

A reader of my *Capper's Weekly* stories in Melbourne, Peg Matthews, had told me in a letter to ask for a person named Ron Elliot when I go to the Marla roadhouse. He was the son-in-law of a close friend, and she knew he'd look after me. Well, just before I got to Marla, Johnny Coolie picked me up and brought me to Mintabie. Going into the pub there, he introduced me to his best mate, Ron. Ron was my first Mintabie "native," and I was quite taken aback when he stroked his beard calmly and looking at me closely out of one eye, asked if I should, by any chance, be walking around the world.

"Yes," I replied, astounded that this total stranger should ask such a question right away. How did he possibly know what I was doing?

Well, as you might guess, Ron was Ron Elliot. He had already been told by letter from Peg Matthews that I was coming through his area, and he had simply put one and one together when he heard my American accent and Johnny said he'd brought me to Mintabie from the Stuart Highway.

That Ron and I met at all is so characteristic of the luck with which this journey seems to be blessed. If I had not accepted Johnny's invitation to go bouncing off across the desert to that isolated place I'd never heard of, I'd never have met up with Ron Elliot, for Marla lay along the Stuart Highway, more than fifty miles away from Mintabie where Ron was now camped.

Through Ron, I met Ian McClellan and Ron Gregory. Although they may not look it, these three forty-year-old plus adventurers, who gave up security in the city to chance opal prospecting, are very likely to be future millionaires, having found their claims full of the high grade opal gems. But then maybe all this isn't unusual (at least to them). Called the three "Silly Gooses" by others, they used a "divining rod" to find their "El Dorado" where all others said no opal could possibly exist.

Now, six nights have passed since I arrived at the opal prospecting camp of Mintabie. Tomorrow I will be leaving, forced to stay ahead of approaching summer, with its promise of 140-degree temperatures. It will be with sadness that I continue on my way back to civilization. Johnny Coolie, who brought me here, was correct about Mintabie's colorful lifestyle. For once I had met an Outbacker who told as much truth as tall tale.

Mintabie's motley collection of lean-tos, trailers, cave shacks and woolly-whiskered gougers comes close to fiction. With the thumping of pick axes, the millionaires in grimy overalls, the tens-of-thousands of dollars changing hands nonchalantly in bets, Chinese buyers scampering around carrying as much as a million dollars with which to buy a man's opals dug during the past month, the Yahoos and the smack of knuckles against chin, Mintabie is indeed one of the few genuine "last frontiers." It is a place which still makes millionaires out of penniless and illiterate immigrants, where the customs and laws and especially the pettiness of civilization have no place. Because of its location and the reluctance with which its hard bowels surrender their treasures, only the courageous dare come, and only the strongest and most determined will stay.

A breed quite unlike any other soldiers of fortune I have known, the Mintabie prospectors and miners are strangely open and easygoing. Even though their tunnels and open pits are crowded together, no one seems to bother keeping the secrets of his claim intact from others. There are no threats, no No Trespassing signs, no glares, no shaking of fists or raised voices or stony silences. Incredibly, in spite of their varied backgrounds and temperments, an almost uncanny order prevails, from the merriment of the beer guzzlers in Luka's Goanna Grill to the human moles in the cool narrow tunnels.

"It was the lifestyle that drew me here," remarked Ian McClellan, a giant of happiness and the claim partner of my host, Ron Elliot.

He stroked his rich dark beard, then pointed at several others in the noisy pub. Just around us, he said, were twelve Yugoslavians, mostly Croatians, and several other nationalities. He himself was originally from Liverpool, England.

"It's amazing, but we're like a family here. Everyone's so different, and still you rarely see trouble. We don't even have police of any kind," the forty-year-old ex-bus driver from Adelaide continued.

"Some of those you see came here penniless and hungry, but not for long. We do things our own way here, and no good man is going to go wanting. I think perhaps the men realize we are different. We're proud to be our own bosses. It gives us a good feeling to know we could come to a place like this to try and make our own fortune. It shows in how we look after each other."

His apple-red cheeks rose ahead of a huge smile, upon which he added, "We care for each other, because out here you never know when you might need another man's help. We all do, at some point."

Ian's wife and children live thousands of kilometers away, along the coastline of the continent, as do those of most of the miners. In Mintabie there are very few trappings—no television, no radio, no power except by individual generators, no daily newspaper, no shops, no school, not even a medical clinic. Mail sometimes came in twice a week in the back of someone's pickup truck. Once a month the plane of the Flying Doctor Service drops in on the dirt airstrip. For most, the only time with the family was during the ferociously hot summer months of December, January and February, when the heat forced a halt to most mining, and everyone retreated to the sea's breezes.

The prospect that the next swing of the pick ax might be the El Dorado of their dreams keeps most from dwelling upon their lack of family and comforts. After a year of meager results, Ian and Ron's claim had suddenly opened up its prized gem cache. In the past two weeks alone, they have extracted over one hundred thousand dollars worth of high quality stone (worth maybe ten times that when cut and polished). Their turn has come. On another claim belonging to Ian's wife, some other prospectors have confirmed the presence of much opal there, too.

On this last evening in Mintabie, in the crude, though comfortable, stone hut of one of the camp's unrecognizable millionaires, I was allowed to roam my eyes over the young opal miner's private collection which he'd dug and polished himself in the past few months. Reputedly he had several fifty-five-gallon drums of this striking gem still stashed away. I would not have wanted the task of adding up his worth of fifty and up a carat and perhaps sixty carats to an ounce. And still, like a true Mintabian, he enjoyed—even preferred—living in his three hundred dollar handbuilt dugout and driving old beatup "Abo cars."

This was my first close encounter with opal in its finished state. I was at a loss to describe it. Australia produces most of the world's supply of this mysterious and little-known gem. Mesmerized by what flashed at me from within its glassy flesh, I couldn't help agreeing with the Romans of Christ's day who prized that gem above all others. It was as the Roman scholar Pliny said in the first century, "Of all the precious stones, it is the opal that represents the greatest difficulty of description, it displaying at once the piercing fire of ruby, the purple brilliancy of amethyst, and the sea-green of emerald, the whole blended together and refulgent with a brightness that is incredible."

In each of the black, velvet-mounted stones I saw not only the colors of Pliny's gems, but something far more special and beautiful—from beneath its very sands and scrub, I had within my hands concentrated proof of the Outback's beauty. And yet I would have to let it go. It was not to have and take with me. I had little money and many miles yet to go. Sadly, slowly, I placed the stones back into their mounts.

Suddenly, an enormous hand was closing the stones' case. Yet in my hand was still one stone, a gorgeous milky tear-shaped opal. I looked up, startled, to see Ian giving the millionaire several fifty-dollar notes. He promptly forced those same crumpled notes back into Ian's pocket.

"I appreciate what you are doing—but I can't accept such an expensive thing," I protested, trying to hand the stone to its rightful owner.

Ian seemed almost as embarrassed as I was. But he was not

about to let me lose out to my pride.

"You got a mother?" he asked.

"Yes, but—"

"No 'buts,' Mate! You give that to her, you hear?" he ordered.

"Ian, I can't take some—"

"Oh, yes you can! This is Mintabie and that's the way we do it here."

Perhaps I might have continued to be recalcitrant, if only Ian had not let loose with one of his giant laughs. Or if he had not reminded me that I was not in a place where normal rules apply.

So I smiled and tucked away, safely inside my shirt pocket, my little wishing stone that some may try to tell me is nothing more than just a pretty piece of Australian opal.

Steven

Coober Pedy, South Australia
November 14, 1985

Dear Folks,

The many gifts given to me during the Worldwalk have often been as special as the person from whom they came. Those special tokens of friendship and love have included such things as a Spanish policeman's badge, a young Appalachian girl's beloved talisman, a broken-hearted French poetess's self-published verses and the only blanket of a penniless, homeless street bum in New York.

Each and every single present, of course, has earned my lasting gratitude. Many of those gifts had a practical function and served me well for months or years. Other gifts, particularly of an edible nature, quickly disappeared and now have faded into delightful memories.

However, there are a few gifts that will probably never cease to titillate my imagination, no matter how long I live. In the seemingly innocent nature of those particular gifts there is something that, were I not supposedly an "intelligent" man, I might be tempted to call a magical sort of power. Not content to be simply the end piece of some interesting story, those gifts became themselves the protagonist of an even more fascinating tale.

Such was the case in the past ten days with the little, tear-shaped opal stone I carried away from the remote desert camp called Mintabie. The epitome of the mysteries and wonders of the Outback's Never-Never, from whose soul it had been wrenched, that brilliant masterpiece of the earth which I spoke of in my last letter was the instigator of one of the Worldwalk's most incredible stories. But first, true to the "bad luck" label opal has had since the late eighteenth century, when it was blamed for famine, pestilence and even the fall of a Spanish monarchy, I had a most villainous form of evil befall both myself and my treasured "wish stone."

At the end of the first day after departing Mintabie, I found myself at a small collection of sunbaked buildings labeled on my maps as Marla. As is usual in the Outback, there was not any actual town, but merely a roadhouse with a pub and cafe, an attached motel of sorts, a tiny police post, some neglected petrol pumps and a house or two. As almost always is the case in such "bush towns," the kids' schooling is through a teacher's voice on a shortwave radio, Mom's shopping is done from a mail-order catalog, Dad's mail comes, and goes, on the Greyhound bus twice a week—*maybe*, and each family's television is limited to the occasional video movie rented from a town (one of the handful of "real" towns), probably several hundred miles away, when the grocery shopping is done. About the only thing that differentiated Marla from the rest was that intersecting it were *two* Stuart Highways, the present dirt one which I had been struggling to pull Roo over for the last one hundred miles and the future paved one that will be opened in another year.

It was down the paved one I ventured the next morning, even though it meant I would be largely on my own and out of sight of the old Stuart Highway's traffic for most of the remaining two hundred miles to the two highways' next intersection at Coober Pedy. Also, the pavement was only sixty kilometers (thirty-seven miles) long, before it changed back to construction dirt.

The heat and sun all that day were some of the fiercest yet, and by noon I had no choice but to retreat from the scorching thermals and choking duststorms. Sweating half-to-death in a storm pipe under the roadway, it seemed to me that every tree, every rock, even myself, were teetering on the brink of self-combustion. It wasn't until the sun set that I again continued southward. Then came the monstrous thunderclouds with their winds and terrifying electrical storms. And then, just an hour shy of midnight, something even more dangerous suddenly came up from behind.

The drunkenness of the road construction workers in the truck that pulled alongside me was obvious from the very start, when in a slurred voice the massive driver started cursing me for being some "Lying Yank Greenie" (conservationist). As red-neck as they come, the much older man couldn't seem to spit out enough obscenities, criticism of Americans and hatred of journalists in general. It was his belittling of America—something that seems to be quite fashionable with many Australians lately—that in the end got my hackles rising. The moment had come to let the idiot know just how ignorant he struck me as being.

Suddenly his ape-like form was confronting me, then lifting me and threatening to snap every rib in my body. I had no choice but to let the punches fly. What followed was a frightening cat-and-mouse game in which he tried to grab me and make true his vow to kill me. All the while I sneaked in a punch now and then in the hope of making him forget the abandoned Roo. But it didn't work—soon he was making a wreck of the cart and, worse, screaming at the other man in the truck to load his shotgun.

"I'm going to kill you!" he growled to me over and over, in not quite so nice a manner.

There was nothing left to do but flee as quickly as I could across the open black Outback. The flight was like a horrible nightmare with the rain pouring, my clothing in tatters, thunder rumbling, lightning exploding, my body falling painfully onto the boulders and mud. Patiently his vehicle waited my return to the shattered cart, but I was off to the road construction camp, another thirteen miles to the south. By 1:30 that morning I was on the radio telephone in the camp, speaking to the Marla police sergeant's sleepy voice. He'd be out the next morning, he promised. In the meantime the camp's foreman brought me back to the cart, where I spent a restless night beside it.

The assailant escaped. All the policeman and I found of his truck and trailer at the construction camp was an empty space. Very conveniently, he had, in the early morning hours, been "transferred" to another work site at Port Lincoln, nearly one thousand miles away.

"He didn't even pick his tomatoes in his little garden," the young policeman noted with a touch of wryness.

Two days and one hundred miles down the road from where I had been roughed up and my cart broken, I realized my opal was missing. I was heartbroken—I had hoped to use that stone in a pendant for a mother who has worked so hard on my behalf these past two and one-half years. Far more than just an opal had been lost to that lonely stretch of dust and wind. And in such a senseless and cruel manner!

There could be no going back to search for it. It was too far to walk back and there was no one with whom to hitch a ride back.

But then, another two days later, came the most incredible bit of luck . . . or magic.

Two opal prospectors on an old mine site twenty-three miles north of Coober Pedy, upon sighting my lone walking figure in the distance, joined me in the shade of a drain pipe for some conversation and to share a well-appreciated cold beer. As forty-two-year-old Ralph Martin put it—"I looked at Paul (Wundersitz) and said, 'There are three crazy people out in this heat today—you, me and whoever that is way down there with that cart and umbrella.' "

Upon hearing my story of the attack and the missing opal, Ralph shocked me by immediately offering to drive me back to where the attack had occurred. Paul agreed without hesitation. I thought their offer far too generous, for it was quite a distance, the roads extremely poor, and the chances of finding the opal were a million-to-one. To spend most of a day and so much petrol on my lost opal, at "no cost in the least" to me, seemed foolish. Yet, to my inner joy there was to be no talking them out of this bit of sudden adventure. In no time at all we and Ralph's old heeler, Sally, were racing off to the north in his dusty big Holden car.

The petrol and the beer grew low, and the bumps and ruts ever constant. Never, however, did the two men's high enthusiasm for finding the opal waver. I almost pinched my arm to make myself believe this was really happening. Ralph, an earthmover and former professional kangaroo hunter, and Paul, an engineer on oil rigs, were hardly acting the tough-guy image normally associated with such occupations. Indeed, at one point they stopped to observe some finches through binoculars and even told of sometimes leaving water along the road for thirsty lizards! Certainly, not a nicer pair of men could be found anywhere.

At the site of the attack, it seemed that no trace of the lost opal remained. For the longest time we sifted through the sands around where the cart had been flung. Back and forth, back and forth we wandered, probing carefully with eyes and a kick here and there with a shoe. Nothing. Not a single glint of green or blue, only eyes filled with dust.

I was the first to surrender to the obvious—that attacker

had stolen it from my pack while waiting for me to return. More than ever his escape from justice seemed grossly unfair. Knowing that he had the opal, that such a thing of love and friendship was in the hands of something so vile, brought my spirit even lower. All I wanted to do was to leave that scene of bad memories as fast as possible and get Australia over and done. It irritated me that Ralph and Paul persisted in searching after I had gone back to the car.

Then, incredibly, Ralph was holding a little plastic box in his hand and asking, "Is this what you lost?"

I ran to his side. It was the opal's display box! But where was the opal?"

Something distinctly not brown by Ralph's shoe made my eyes pop wider—*yes*—the opal!

"Magic . . . real magic," Ralph mused aloud several times on the drive back to Coober Pedy to get some "snags" (sausages) and "grog" (beer) for a happy celebration. Each time he repeated those words, I could only nod in agreement and again gaze at the gem clutched in my hand. My heart certainly knew there was something out of the ordinary going on, and my mind wasn't too far behind. Considering how slim our chances had been of finding that stone, its recovery seemed almost a miracle. There had been our chance meeting, the remote locale, the opal's tininess, and the fact that Ralph found it on the opposite side of the road from where the cart had been tossed about.

"When I got out of the car, I noticed right away the direction the wind was blowing," Ralph explained. "I figured it would've blown the opal into the opposite paddock (field) if it had been blowin' that direction when you had your trouble."

No one but an experienced bushman might ever have thought of something now so glaringly obvious. Certainly Paul and I hadn't. Again, such a stroke of luck, to have had Ralph's experience along on the search. Could all this be only mere coincidence?

"You know, finding your opal really made our day. It makes me feel good to know you got it back. I haven't had so much fun in quite awhile," Paul said by the campfire that night.

Ralph, his best friend, nodded and poked another stick in

the blaze, before adding, "I always like to look at every little thing in nature and not always be in a hurry and thinkin' only of myself. I don't get much free time in my work, but still I figure I always got time to help anything or anybody that needs it. Why, heck, I'm always jumpin' down from the dozer to move some little lizard or animal out of my way, so it don't get hurt."

Looking up at the gorgeous night sky arching over their tent, and the old opal pit tailings around us, and the alert Sally, I thought of all the love those two supposedly rugged men had shown me, and realized I had been gifted with not one gem that day . . . but three.

Steven

Glendambo, South Australia
November 26, 1985

Dear Folks,

The dead branches of a lone small tree rattled like the bones of a restless skeleton. A dust-laden wind whipped through the white gullies and mounds of the old opal mine. Just overhead, a witch's caldron of dark storm clouds swirled with nervous energy.

Lightning flashed—my eyes wandered. All about me and my cart were the trappings of a world that surely belonged in a bizarre dream—a giant barbarian with horns on his head and an iron hook for one hand, rusting car pipes and mufflers and hub caps wired together into senseless sculptures, an animal skull as large as my torso riding a child's bicycle, and even a mannequin in shirt and cap peering over the lip of an empty oil drum.

Yet, as I stood with my heart pounding in the eerie afterglow of the lightning flashes, I could sense the most unusual was yet to come. Looming before me was a peculiar sandstone cliff erratically festooned with all sorts of oddities, from antique car bumpers to rope ladders. Behind these was the underground dugout home of a Latvian ex-aristocrat, known in the Outback as "Crocodile Harry."

Greeting me at the dugout's entrance was not Harry, but Markos, a wild and dark-haired Swiss of about twenty-five, who was watching over the eccentric property while Harry was in the hospital in Coober Pedy, four miles south. "Poor Harry," the muscular lad said with a chuckle, "tried to stop a drunken Abo gin (woman) from stealing his twenty-five-year-old car and had gotten run over in the process. He has been in the 'World's Opal Capital' hospital for two weeks and is due home any day. In the meantime, would you care to be my guest in Harry's home?"

The name of the nearby small town of Coober Pedy comes from the Aboriginal words "kupa piti." This is said to mean "white man's hole," alluding to the dugouts in which many of the three thousand residents live. It is perhaps the world's most unusual looking community because so much of it is underground. These dwellings were developed to combat the high temperatures and lack of building materials (the nearest supplies are in Port Augusta, six hundred kilometers by dirt and paved road to the south).

Practical, low-cost and often luxuriously comfortable, the dugouts' rooms and hallways always remain a pleasant seventy to seventy-five degrees and are far more dust-resistant than conventional housing. The dugouts, which include churches, shops and motels, are set deep in the low, barren hills known as the Stuart Range. All that can usually be seen are front doors and windows. "Galvo" water tanks, air shaft chimneys and television antennae proliferate along the yellow ridges.

Though the scenery of Coober Pedy may be drab and devoid of greenery, the town's "insides" were very beautiful, as I discovered while waiting for Harry's return. One dugout even featured an indoor swimming pool, something of a minor miracle in Coober Pedy, where until a few years ago water had to be trucked in and cost a small fortune.

It was because of the unusual art forms decorating every room and hallway that Harry's home stood out from the others. The various works, which included abstract sandstone carvings, handpainted wall murals, furniture and shelves carved into the white-painted walls, exhaust manifolds of autos for candle holders and enormous ferro-concrete carvings along the walls, are all creations of Harry's.

During the evening of Harry's first day back from the hospital, after a large dinner, I had my chance to question this man about whom so many wild stories are told. With Markos and Harry's young retriever dog, Prince Ferdinand, also resting around the dinner table, the sixty-year-old host happily shared his past experiences and thoughts on life.

"Greek, Croatian, Russian or whatever, we came here not so much to find a fortune in opal, but to live as free men and to have only ourselves as bosses. Believe me, many here have never found any opal, and yet do you think they would go back to the old country? Though many live in comparative poverty, they will never want to leave the freedom of this type of lifestyle.

"Since coming here in 1968, I have found perhaps twenty thousand dollars in opal—not much, divided into the number of years. Only tucker (food) money, you might call it," Harry continued. "Yet I won't be leaving, for this is one of the freest places, outside of perhaps a desert island, where I could live."

Captured in 1944 by the Soviets, the Leningrad siege veteran was sent to a P.O.W. camp from which he escaped ten days later. After the war he wanted to get out of Europe. Turned away by America and Canada, he found the faraway and barely-populated Australia willing to give him a new home. Thus he found himself in 1951, at age twenty-six, hunting crocodiles in northern Australia.

For some fourteen years the bearded ex-baron dawdled sand through his shoeless toes and slept in the open, as his soul recovered from civilization's atrocities. He had found his paradise. Bronzed and taut, with abundant health, he picked crabs off the Gulf of Carpentaria's beaches or raided turtles' nests for food, walking and sleeping and hunting whenever he wished. Money for clothes, an occasional treat, more bullets, came from the sale of crocodile skins and dingo scalps, many of which he killed by spear.

After a time civilization arrived with mining companies, bulldozers, helicopters and hordes of people with stifling laws and contempt of nature. It was time for Harry to move on.

Nowadays he spends more time decorating and enlarging his white-washed castle's interior than looking for opal. He knows only too well that his claim, like most around Coober Pedy, is probably long played out.

"Things happen all the time which I want to remember," he explained, pointing to the walls and his artworks.

I looked at Markos and he at me. The dugout rang with laughter. We knew what Crocodile Harry meant. He was one person *I'll* certainly remember.

Steven

Adelaide, South Australia
February 15, 1986

Dear Folks,

When I stepped out of the Outback's grasp last December 9, I was ready to call it quits for the Australia phase of the Worldwalk. For the last four hundred miles the wind had tried its best to push my tired body into those empty deserts and salt flats. And as a result of such incessant battering, I was perhaps more tired physically and mentally than I had been during any part of my journey. Certainly there was no doubt that the vast brown giant with which I had been struggling for over four months was the most arduous terrain I had ever experienced.

As I boarded a bus later that same gray, drizzling day to go on to Melbourne for a much needed rest, and to obtain more time on my visa (set to expire in less than two weeks), I had a strong suspicion I would not be returning to Port Augusta to finish walking the remaining 670 miles to Melbourne. For that matter, was it necessary to do them? After all, had I not crossed the entire continent? Surely there was nothing to be ashamed of in not coming back after Christmas to complete my originally planned Darwin to Melbourne route.

There was some concern in my mind that what remained would be too dull, a letdown, in comparison to the raw mysteries of the Outback. Even with the dazzle and energy of the large cities of Adelaide and Melbourne, and the colonialism of the deep south's well-preserved architecture and history, I did not see how a region of mostly sheep and wheat farms could keep me interested, with the cowboys, lizards and red dunes of the Outback still strong in my mind.

Making my decision to return to Port Augusta all the more difficult and uncertain was an almost overwhelming feeling of homesickness I silently suffered during the two months I was in Melbourne. The causes of my strong wish to be in my beloved homeland again were many, and came mostly from sources other than my own heart. They included some two hundred letters from kind supporters of this walk, as well as dozens of cards and cheers from what must be the world's greatest schoolchildren and teachers. And then there was television—a mesmerizing chatterbox of mostly American programs and personalities I had not seen for years.

Wrapped in the warmth and love of the tireless Peg Matthews, a widow with a heart far wiser than her sixty-five years, it was impossible not to think of my own family. Trying her hardest to make me feel welcome in her little brick home on Melbourne's south side—with all its big shade trees and flowers, just like back home—Peg gallantly plied her marvelous cooking skills on such totally un-Aussie dishes as southern fried chicken and pumpkin pie. For a woman more used to preparing the traditional ox-tail soups and strawberry trifles of southeastern Australia, she proved quite adept at satisfying my American taste buds.

Comfortably surrounded by a family as kind as I could hope for, settled over heaping plates of home-cooked meals, and constantly being whisked "live" to the depths of America to watch everything from Presidential news conferences to the Super Bowl, it seemed only sensible that my next steps should be on my native soil, not back to the unsympathetic fringe of the Outback.

But such would not be the case. On January 28—the letters answered, my frame heavier by "a stone" (fourteen pounds), and with my muscles and spirit well-rested—I returned by bus to the little port on the northern point of Spencer Gulf. It was not because I had conquered my homesickness—all those dreams of hot dogs, chocolate malts and baseball—that I was able to resist going on to America. Rather, it was a feeling that I would be departing this nation without really having fully tried to learn about it and its people.

I knew that there was an entirely different side to Australia that I had not found in the harshness of the Outback. To have left others, let alone myself, with the impression that Australia is mostly deserts, kangaroos and cowboys would be very wrong indeed. Beauty and wonder come in countless forms and places. What remains to be explored in this enchanting land might perhaps be much tamer, but that does not mean it will be any less beautiful or inspiring. And to rush off now would leave both myself and all those persons behind those letters I had been privileged to receive all the poorer. Home will always be waiting for me, and there is no guarantee that life would again allow me to venture to this corner of our world.

Those who think of this walk as some act of courage, or a feat of endurance such as sailing alone around the world, are missing the point entirely. The journey has always been, and hopefully always will be, an attempt to comprehend more fully my world and my own self. To come to the understanding I seek, I must expose my mind and body to all aspects of each society, from the exciting to the dull, from the dangerous to the tame. And, as with any relationship to which we give our hearts and minds, haste deserves no place.

Steven

Gary MacDonald's sheep dog, Mandi, lying in a bed of wool, dares the last one in to challenge her. Like all good sheep dogs, Mandi knows who the boss is—and so do her sheep.

Bordertown, South Australia
March 1, 1986

Dear Folks,

My knuckles rapped against the old farmhouse's wood door. No answer came forth, save for the echoes of honking geese and a creaking windmill. I rapped again, more rapidly and more sharply. Again, silence from within.

Into the depths and up onto the summits of this rugged land, I had followed a dirt land all morning that led me to this veranda. With only the stares of uneasy sheep and the black and white crescents of magpies darting from crooked telegraph pole to crooked telegraph pole marking my lonesome progress, it had been a rather haunting sort of journey. Cooled by a wind that hinted of approaching rain, I found my thoughts being swept away by twisting gum leaves and a sea of golden wild oats undulating beneath tumbling clouds of ragged gray. How sad to think I had missed the master of this striking farm. Surely he was lucky to have picked such a beautiful and rugged place for his home.

My canteen, as well as my lips, begged for water. So with little delay I followed the open veranda's shade to the rear of the home. Just as I expected, there stood that welcome trademark of every Australian home, the rainwater holding tank. Suddenly, from the side door of a patchwork shearing shed, emerged a pair of dark coveralls topped by a red beard, ruddy cheeks and the unmistakable, "G'day!" Racing from between the apparition's short, strong legs was the customary work dog. Gary MacDonald was the youngish sheep farmer's name, and as so often happens in this country of strong handshakes, several cups of coffee and an invitation to stay for tea (dinner) and a good night's rest were soon forthcoming.

Of course I accepted. I am only too happy to share time with the world's farmers. I have noted that many who live under the noisy and crowded conditions of the large city seem beset with uncertainty and dissatisfaction. Yet the country dweller almost always is a calm soul. He or she has a more certain sense of what life is really all about. Hence, they have a greater peace and sense of belonging to this world.

It was in search of that peace that Gary MacDonald had

moved from the big city of Adelaide to the beautiful little farm on which I met him. He might have been a factory worker like his father and grandfathers, except for the horrors of man he was exposed to during the Vietnam War. Unable to put those years of fighting in Asia's jungles out of his mind, he returned home to an eventual nervous breakdown. Confined to a hospital bed for three weeks, with his thoughts about life and the future atrophying from confusion and pessimism, he knew he had to find a cure for his dying spirit. It was then that he decided to move to the hill country east of Adelaide and take up farming, even though he knew nothing of such a life.

To some, the farm he ended up buying would be discouraging. Hilly, rocky and able to support only about five hundred sheep, its 350 acres held far more promise of hard work than wealth or comfort. Still, to Gary, it held a way of life that had meaning and purpose. Rather than slaving to another man's whims, he now had only himself and his small family to consider.

His pride and excitement were evident in the way he wanted to share with me all the little surprises of the farm. Things like the gun slit in the back wall of the original homestead, the huge fireplace in the snug shearer's cottage, the root cellar with its roof of twigs and sod, still as cool as the day it was built one hundred fifty years ago. Even the rawness of the land held only magic for his eyes. There were goldfish in the deep dark pools of the almost inaccessible stream, the aboriginal cave paintings in the steep glens, the surrealistic play of the sky's shadows and rays upon the earth's giant swells, and even some extremely rare Yakka plants that had withstood the land's fires and drouths for at least four hundred years.

To stand atop one of those broad hills in the strong wind and watch the farmer and his two-year-old dog, Mandi, herd the sheep from one pasture to another was like watching two children at play. That dog lived to obey her master's simple voice and hand commands. With tireless energy and high enthusiasm, and movements precise and quick, Mandi loved any chance she was allowed to keep those sheep in order. And still after all that "work," she never lacked the energy to leap high into MacDonald's strong arms for a hug and a bit of well-earned praise. Honestly, at those times it was difficult to tell who had the bigger smile, the dog or her proud master.

At one point that day, as MacDonald and Mandi sat beside me on a high ridge, we spied two large foxes fleeing up the side of a hill just opposite us. Zig-zagging from cover to cover, the beautiful creatures went totally unnoticed by a nearby flock of sheep. I asked MacDonald if those same foxes might not eat the newborn lamb we had found along one of the fence lines a few hours earlier.

Yes, they might, he answered. Still, that did not mean he would shoot the foxes. Killing no longer seemed the right thing to him, and it was now his policy never to harm any animal, unless it was a direct danger to his family. Instead of hunting the foxes, we gathered up the lamb and its mother on our way back to the house. They were put into a pen near the house where they would be safe and better fed.

Life, especially its creation and preservation, has to be the most important task under man's charge, I have decided as a result of this journey. That evening, as I held in my arms the quiet, soft form of the lamb, and waited for Gary and Mandi to bring the ewe to the holding pen, I couldn't help feeling a little proud of myself. I had helped, if only for a few minutes, some other creature to survive.

That tiny lamb's heartbeat was the rhythm of nature. It was life as it really is, not as man thinks it should be. Somehow I understood why those who live by nature's clock are so much happier and kind. Their's is a life of sharing—not just taking and wanting only for themselves.

Steven

Ararat, Victoria, Australia
March 15, 1986

Dear Folks,

The rains have been absent here in western Victoria for too long. So long, indeed, that to talk aloud of when they might return is almost considered bad luck. In the last four years there has been but one good wheat harvest in the large growing belt called the Mallee. Yet, to talk too much about 1984 somehow gives the impression that maybe the good times are all in the past. Still, for a man with no money coming from the banks and his farmland dropping in value each day, what other source of hope is there?

Some blame the American President Reagan and the diminishing overseas market for the money problems. Some blame Halley's comet for the record cold summer and the hint of a dry winter. There is talk about another depression, and about small farmers going under and only giant subsidized "farm corporations" being left to grow the grains. Hundreds of family farms have folded to creditors in the past five years. Most of the failed farmers, it is said, have gone to the cities to join the record unemployment, to draw perhaps for the rest of their life the fortnightly welfare check from a government already on the verge of financial default.

"Where is this all leading us to? I wish I could be here just long enough to see who will be left to do the farming," said a seventy-seven-year-old farmer named William Nitschke. And though his seventy-five-year-old wife's gentle smile seemed almost to mock the elderly man's worries, the solemn look in Edith's soft green eyes betrayed her own inner concerns.

I looked over the proud way they held their heads, the tidiness of their small but comfortable home in which they had spent all fifty years of their marriage, and then down at the array of plates and mugs before me. Each dish had, over the course of the long, hot afternoon, held one of the usual farmwife goodies—things like ice cream on peaches, a ham sandwich, piping hot tea, iced fruit cake. Like so many who run this world's farm homes, Edith would never have allowed me to go away with just the drink of water I had asked for at their screen door.

The Nitschkes came from backgrounds rich in farming. Not surprisingly they had devoted their lives to their farm and its growth. It was not only their income and their love, but also their gift to the future. The farm seemed one of the few things around that would always be secure.

Said William, with a slight straightening of his long, lean frame, "Edith and I worked long hours everyday. We cleared the land, built the house, and always saved what money we could spare to buy more land. We didn't borrow money unless it was necessary—like when we bought the land—and then we made sure it was quickly paid off.

"We made up our minds the children, when they grew up, would never have to work as hard as we did. We were sure we were doing the best thing for the three boys. After all, how could farming be a bad choice, when there would always be more people being born needing more and more food to live?"

In time all three sons did follow in their parents' footsteps, settling onto the lands that belonged not to the bank, but to the family. But the security that owning a farm once meant no longer seemed to exist.

"It's a mistake for the government to let the family farms die off," William reflected. "What but waste, lower production and bigger debts can come from all these huge corporation-type farms? Everyone in power says everything has to be on a big scale and run like some factory. But I ask you, who's going to pay for all those high union wages, and all their time off, and coffee breaks and all the sloppiness?

"It costs too much for an ordinary bloke to go into farming anymore. Only the big businesses can get the money and afford those ridiculously-priced machines. Yet do you think those big conglomerates will be watching every expense and always be putting something away for the bad years like Edith and I did?"

He gave a sharp laugh. "Of course they won't, 'cause to them and the men in those huge machines and buildings that farm's nothing special—just another ordinary job. Just look at how they spend so many millions of dollars and still lose money, which, of course, we end up paying for through subsidies."

There was a short, loud rapping on the kitchen screen door.

Outside, kittens rubbing against their pants' cuffs, were two serious-looking men in dress clothes holding bulky notebooks. They were looking for the Nitschke's eldest son. One went to the metal shed William pointed to, the other stayed to talk with me a few minutes.

He explained they had come to discuss the "farmers' troubles" with the son. Apparently they were representatives of a grassroots organization that hoped to bring the farmers' plight to the government's attention. Again, unions, big business, the United States and the "liberal socialist" government of Australia received all the blame. Very wisely, Edith brought to his attention that the drouth was mostly on their minds at the moment. How odd the representative of the "common farmer" had failed to mention such a simple and obvious thing. "I guess everyone will have to switch over to sheep till it passes," the short, wiry man figured.

"Then you got too many lambs on the market at one time," quickly replied William. "And besides, what you gonna feed them when there's no money and no grass?"

"Oh . . ." the man muttered. He excused himself to talk business with the others in the shed.

Back inside, William revealed that he was pretty certain none of the family's farms would pass on to his grandsons. Meanwhile, Edith went off to another room to get something she said I might like to see.

"I see it in the boys' eyes, the way they look at all the wrinkles their mom and pop are growing. They got to be thinking there's a better way to live," said the old man. "The oldest is soon going off to university, to be an accountant. The other's already talking of doing a trade." He gave me a sort of pleading glance. "Don't you think all this making everything so big and mechanical is communism? It can't be democracy to make everyone so faceless and dependent, can it?"

My gift from Edith and William was a strikingly intricate and fragile doll-sized rocking chair. William had made it by hand from a Coca-Cola can. Full of curls and twirls, the six-inch-high rocker looked as if it had taken a tremendous amount of skill to build. However, all he had done was cut off the can's top, snip the can's sides into dozens of fine ribbons, and then curled them into the shape of the rocker. Into the concave bottom of the can, he had set a red cushion made by Edith, to form the seat.

That evening, as I continued on the railroad tracks toward the small town of Stawell, I thought often of the rocking chair safely tucked away in my backpack. I couldn't help thinking of that little handmade gift as being representative of Edith and William's lives. They had taken under their charge something others had not wanted—nearly desert scrubland—and with patience, imagination and work had transformed it into an object of beauty and admiration . . . just as they had with an ordinary piece of litter, the Coca-Cola can.

It is said by many that honest, hard workers are a disappearing breed of people. How frustrating it is to find that for such people life is usually one of constant struggle and few financial riches. But maybe the lessons they pass on, and not material objects, are the most important. Drouths and farms may come and go, but let us hope that every generation will live long enough to go knocking at the Nitschke's screen door.

Steven

Six-year-old Craig Garlic of Warracknabeal looks as if he can hardly wait for school to start again.

Pretty, eye-catching Tenille Sharp in period costume (1800's) at the Railroad Centenary Celebration at the Warracknabeal station.

The local ladies in Warracknabeal enjoying themselves at a round of "bowls." Like a group of white hens standing in a barnyard littered with black eggs, the ladies never seem to grow tired of tromping up and down the bowling green chasing after the bowls in this insufferably slow game.

Here I am standing in the front lawn of the Ward Family, publishers of the *Warracknabeal Herald.*

Warracknabeal, Victoria, Australia
May 27, 1986

Dear Folks,

Warracknabeal, where I have spent the past month, would probably seem to be the end of the world to some of my city-slicker friends. Over two hundred miles northwest of Melbourne, in the center of the Wimmera Plain, Australia's major wheat-growing region, this little, old-fashioned town of 3,200 is a perfect antithesis to "life in the fast lane."

There is one main street, no traffic lights, not even a stop sign. The two rows of one-story shops are all tidy and modest, with square facades bearing such dates as 1883 and 1904. For a good fifty miles around one will find little more than the furrowed fields of the large farms that are the backbone of Australia's economy.

Quite simply, "Warrack" is the sort of place where one needn't look down the street more than once before crossing it. Or where a reporter could cover most of any day's news by simply taking a casual stroll from the cemetery at one end of Scott Street to the Lions Club Park at the other end. I should know, since I have been the local newspaper's photographer all the time I've been here.

It's a long story, but to put it briefly . . . just before the finish of my walk across Australia on March 26, I was contacted by *The Warracknabeal Herald's* publisher and asked to come here during all of May to help run the newspaper. That was so his son, David, could take a holiday. David oversees the general running of *The Herald* because his dad is now legally blind. In addition to managing the chores of the eight staff members, David also chases advertising and does the photography.

His father, Frank, had heard of my walk through another town, Horsham, fifty miles to the south. Upon learning I was an experienced journalist, he quickly tracked me down. In a country where skilled labor is difficult to find, especially in rural areas, and on a temporary basis, he took a grab at me in the hope I might delay my walk long enough to help him out. It was his only hope of giving David his long-awaited vacation and still keeping the newspaper running smoothly.

Stuck all by itself in the middle of what even some Australians would call "nowhere," this unknown (to me) community was of little significance at the time of Frank's invitation. Until it and *The Herald's* plight came to my attention, it was my intention to spend my last Australian months in Melbourne with Peg Matthews, then continue on by jet to my next destination, Vancouver.

As swamped as I was with my own chores in Melbourne— letter replies, lecturing, etc.—I still accepted the challenge to take on the Warracknabeal duties. I relish the chance to explore a people more closely when the chance comes along. What more golden opportunity could there be to learn about a region's people than working on the local newspaper?

So, here I am—behind a hopelessly cluttered desk, a constantly ringing telephone and under a persistent cloud of deadlines. Ah yes, back to the confused orderliness of newspaper work—and in a foreign land to boot!

For those who might think we've been hard-pressed to find a sufficient amount of copy and photo material to fill *The Herald's* sixteen pages twice each week, think again. Though my chief responsibilities have been photography and reporting, I've not really known a day off since my arrival.

What I cover in Warracknabeal may not be as earth-shattering as the scandals and politics I used to chase after as a reporter for *The Casper* (Wyoming) *Star-Tribune*, but that doesn't mean the stories come with any less frequency. The amount of energy spent behind the quiet exterior of a small town is amazing.

If it's not historical celebrations or someone's fiftieth wedding anniversary, then it's some farmers' group meeting or maybe bingo at the local golf clubhouse.

I spent one day riding across miles of sun-baked wheat stubble in a one-hundred-year-old steam train—one morning interviewing a ninety-nine-year-old man who has written five hundred beautiful and lengthy poems since the age of ninety-one and who still has better health than those sixty-year-old whippersnappers—and froze half to death in the old courthouse on other days trying to cover the monthly court session, with the major disputes usually concerning fence lines.

There are many interesting stories I've wanted to share

with you, but my hectic workdays in what I had hoped would be a slow period have prevented my usually prompt correspondence. All those quiet evenings around the camp fire, when I'm on the road, simply haven't existed. Without the peace and solitude I need to compose my letters, I've found it difficult to compose anything I could share with you. Now I think I can understand why Thoreau needed the peace of the countryside.

I apologize for my silence of the past several weeks. With the newspaper work, lecturing and so many people wanting me to visit their families for some good Aussie hospitality, I've hardly known a free moment. And this is probably but a hint of what awaits me after my plane touches down in Vancouver on June 21.

I promise to write again soon and tell more fully of my stay in Warracknabeal. Right now my phone is ringing and there's still a stack of film in the darkroom waiting to be developed.

As we say in this field—news (and the chasing of it) knows no such thing as sleep.

Steven

Godfrey Letts, the longest-working editor in the world. His workplace was as humble and simple as they come, but "Goff" had a stamina for work that was extraordinary.

Melbourne, Victoria
Australia, June 6, 1986

Dear Folks,

There is no need for me to expound on how highly I regard the life of rural people—I have already done that in other stories. Instead, I am going to share the story of a very frail little old man named Goff, whom I met with for a few hours a couple of days ago.

Still editor of the local newspaper in Donald, a farming town of fifteen hundred people only thirty-five miles down the road from where I was working in Warracknabeal, he has, in his own quiet manner, become an example of just how rewarding the country life can be when a person takes to heart his work, his family and his neighbors.

It was a brash twenty-three-year-old Godfrey Letts, fresh from the high pay and fast life of the gold fields in West Australia, that stepped from the steam train at the Donald platform in 1921. As the new editor of the *Donald Times*, he found white settlements with aborigine names like Watchem, Watchupga and Birchip all within his journalistic responsibility.

Undoubtedly his mates tried to convince him that his talents were better served in the big city and big companies than in a far-removed, no-name place scarce in people and money. There must have been quite a few that would have bet their last quid that the athletic and ambitious Goff would quickly see his mistake and come rushing back to something more razzle dazzle.

Well, sixty-five years later Goff is still busily at work behind that same editor's desk. As mentally sharp as ever, though a bit hard of hearing, he still puts in six days and five nights a week to get out *on time* a quality fourteen pages of news and advertising each Tuesday and Friday. And he has somehow managed to find the time to write more than five thousand editorials and do the bookkeeping, too.

Such a pillar of work has Goff been that in April, 1985, he became the longest-serving full-time newspaper editor in the world. It is a record he sees no reason to be ending for quite sometime. (The old record of sixty-three years and eleven

301

months had been set by another Australian editor who worked from January, 1862, to December, 1925.)

Much could be written about all the honors that have come Goff's way for faithful service to others, including being made a "Member of the Order of the British Empire" by Queen Elizabeth II in 1974. Suffice it to say that he still considers his greatest reward to be that of "working for the community" and living the way of life he both loves and "believes in." In a nation that is constantly beset with workers striking over the least discomfort, this almost-unknown eighty-eight-year-old editor still puts himself through a most demanding program in one of the most humble newspaper offices imaginable.

Loving one's work, always striving to treat each person fairly and equally, building relationships of harmony and trust with all in the community, and not forgetting to thank God for the blessing of family and friends are what Goff attributes to bringing him the abundant happiness he has found in what some might think a dull place in which to put down one's roots.

Goff's cheery face and refreshing modesty seemed to reassure me that the best things in life are still those that are the most simple and basic. As I stared idly out the window of the train that was to take me from the Wimmera Plains to Melbourne for one last time, I thought a lot about that old man tucked away in that vast farm country. What a pleasure to realize that somewhere up there, wearing a well-worn suit and typing away in a drafty little office with rickety furniture and ink-smeared plywood walls, was a genuine history-maker.

A chuckle crept to my lips. I couldn't help wondering if some of Goff's long-ago mates had any idea that way out there in the "empty" countryside Goff is now merrily sitting on top of the world—and that he enjoyed every minute it took him to get there.

Steven

The walk thus far
1,156 days
April 1, 1983 - June 20, 1986
12,767 miles walked

CANADA AND THE
WESTERN UNITED STATES

STEVEN'S ROUTE

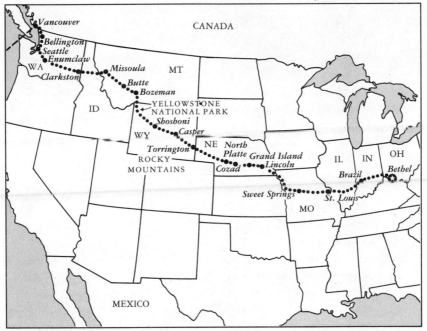

My original plan had been to fly from Melbourne, Australia, to San Francisco, and then follow old U.S. Route 50 across America. But I felt my homecoming would be more meaningful to me if I walked onto American soil, rather than landing in the impersonal hub-bub of an airport. And I was right. Like someone falling in love again, my heart beat faster and the pace of my walk quickened at first sight of the tall, proud firs and sparkling white waters welcoming me back to my homeland.

The walk ahead through Canada and
the western United States

285 days
June 21, 1986 - April 1, 1987
2,736 miles

Mel and Rosalie Eaton beside an old wagon in their farmyard near the tiny town of Veteran, Wyoming.

Vancouver, Canada
June 23, 1986

Dear Folks,

As I write these words my body and soul are flying over this world, somewhere over the Pacific Ocean, at an altitude of 37,000 feet. Yet my heart, I fear, has been left behind at the airport terminal from which this jumbo jet began its journey to Canada many long hours ago.

I should feel nothing but exhilaration, or anticipation, or joy racing through my being at this time, because the final steps to home lie ahead. And so I do. But not perhaps with the same electricity I might have if my heart was with me.

It is not easy to write this letter. Indeed it is saddening, as my blurry vision so vividly reminds me. This, I realize, is the ending to a year-long chapter of enchantment and warm hospitality called Australia.

I hate goodbyes. And I especially hate them when loved ones are involved. Which perhaps explains why it took every bit of courage and strength I had just to hold tightly to Peg Matthews those last precious seconds at the Melbourne airport. As well as why I couldn't hold back the tears, couldn't ignore the sadness in her own eyes, couldn't feel ashamed of the tears that dripped from my chin to her gray hair, couldn't even begin to get that choking frog in my throat to say even as much as, "I'll miss you, Peggy."

Women must be tough, or maybe it's just that they've somehow learned how to live with all of the goodbyes in life. There I was, unable to squeeze out the slightest syllable, while Peg was so calmly able to whisper that I would always be a son to her, no matter what.

Then, all too quickly, the thick, cold, windowless security door of hardened steel was between us. At a time when I should have felt so happy to be going home, I felt as denied as a prisoner. I'll never know Peg's final expression—I was too cowardly to turn back around once the door slipped from my fingers, though I'll never forget the slam of the door behind me.

Below me, through my little square window to the world, the clouds seem almost rooted to the sea. It is hard to realize the swiftness with which everything around me is passing.

Vancouver, the beginning of the Worldwalk's end, is invisibly rushing toward me. It is yet one more door to be opened, then closed.

Australia was unquestionably the most difficult chapter to close behind me, because of the time I gave it and the exceptionally large number of memories and friends it, in turn, gave to me. Peg was the brightest, though there certainly was no shortage of others who wanted to take her place. What I found in terms of love and care at twenty-six Rotorua Street in Melbourne could very easily have been mine for the asking in so many other places. The vast majority of these people I have never been able to share with you in these letters, and some of those I have mentioned, such as the Wards in Warracknabeal, were far too understated in my writings.

Maybe it takes being up this close to heaven to realize the "secrets" of life. It has occurred to me, so I write these words that in all the goodbyes, in all the lands in which I've walked, I was being shown a fact of life of which we are so absurdly ignorant, even though it is staring us in the face each time someone smiles at us and helps us in our difficulties. That fact, of which I am suddenly aware, and which is making me feel so much better now, is this . . . I never did leave home.

Home isn't ahead of me, and it never was behind me. I was there all along. And so was my human family.

Steven

Bellingham, Washington
July 1, 1986

Dear Folks,

Just minutes after landing at Vancouver's international airport I was greeted by one of the most pleasant surprises imaginable—my mother! Never at any time had there been even the slightest hint that she would be waiting for me at the end of my long flight. Needless to say, it was a very happy son who wrapped his arms tightly around dear little Mom and, to the cheers of the crowd, lifted her high off the floor for a big kiss.

Though I never said so in the two days we had together (after which she had to hurry back to her nursing duties), it thrilled me to see her able, for once, to put aside all the home and work chores with which she normally struggles. Try as I might, I could not remember the last time she had any sort of vacation. In fact, I was not even sure she had ever had one. Being the mother of seven children, as well as having to work to make ends meet, she never had the time or money to travel anywhere—or even enough for something as simple as a new dress. And yet I knew how deeply she desired to see other cultures and lands.

Making our reunion all the more special was the fact that it had come about almost as unexpectedly for her as it had for me. It was solely through the sudden, last-minute generosity of a small, family-run shoe company in the Appalachian foothills of southeastern Ohio that Mom found herself going to Vancouver.

Totally out of nowhere, it seemed, came a heaven-sent offer from the William Brooks Shoe Co. Like thousands of others across America, that company's workers and owners have been following me around the world through my stories. It had simply struck them that it would be nice if my mother and I could see one another again. And so they had unselfishly reached into their pockets to send a mother they had never met to greet her faraway son.

While it is true that I have worn their walking boots all during my journey, I believe that company's act of kindness came from the heart. There are, after all, much better ways to sell shoes than arranging "family reunions." And besides, I know well the people in that very special part of our nation. To them, even with all the struggles life seems to hold in those poor hills, there is nothing more important than the family.

Nelsonville, Ohio, where their dark old red-brick factory is located, is only about fifteen miles up the highway from where I attended the university in Athens. Poverty-stricken and high in unemployment like most of Appalachia, Nelsonville needs that factory. Knowing that some two hundred families in that little town depend upon the factory for their livelihood, not the thought of huge profits, is what has kept the company's owners determined to stay in existence when many others would have given up.

Only a few decades ago there were some one thousand shoe manufacturers in America. Today it is closer to one hundred fifty. The massive flood of cheap imported goods has left some American industries hurting. For the domestic manufacturer it has meant surviving on lean capital and learning to be tough. And still, as those in Nelsonville showed, there is room for simple compassion.

So, the next time someone wants to generalize about how evil American business is, I seriously doubt I will be sticking around to hear it. More likely I will walk away with something far more positive on my mind . . .

. . . like, for instance, the excited face of a little graying mother trying to make itself seen above the clamor of a Canadian airport's crowd.

Steven

Enumclaw, Washington
July 17, 1986

Dear Folks,

On June 29, exactly at noon, I walked beneath the striking white Peace Arch on the U.S.A.-Canada border between Vancouver and Seattle. For the first time since July, 1983, my shoes had American soil stuck to their soles.

None of the burly customs officers at the border checkpoint knew me, but when I introduced myself, they were quick to gather around and give my hand a hearty shake. They were the vanguard of what I was sure would be a most magical and friendly last leg of my journey.

However, in the week that I spent getting to Seattle, I was rudely reminded that the American brand of friendliness is sometimes not all that easy to experience. In a society where the auto is so incredibly pervasive, there just simply aren't many people on the streets and sidewalks with whom to strike up a chat. Indeed, in the rural areas between the towns, to see anyone else freely strolling along the roads is almost a shock. And even those you do meet walking in the towns and cities are always in such a rush that you feel guilty asking them for a minute of their time.

I could tell soon enough that, unlike most of the countries I crossed, Americans are not easily accessible. Their life is on too fast a speed, and is spent too much behind doors—car, home or business. When they are not behind a steering wheel, then most likely they are glued to a television set or busily working. Many have become exactly what the rest of the world thinks Americans are—zealots of ambition and almost fanatically obsessed with technology.

The "American Dream" is truly a miracle in terms of its excessiveness. In Australia many a family or community in the Outback would have loved to be able to afford a satellite dish so they could have television reception. Here in Washington's rural areas, having a dish in one's yard seems to be as common as owning a car or pickup. After having been away for three years, I am still having trouble adjusting to how glutted Americans are with material goods.

The average American, because of his preoccupations, will

never be as accessible as, say, the simple Third World person, who has no television to keep him inside or any automobile to drive. And so I must realize that meeting with the everyday American will sometimes be hard work, for lack of a better way to describe it. Gone are the crowds of the curious who flocked to me, the religious who constantly told me it was their "duty" to help me in some way, and the teachers, shopkeepers and village headmen who did not hesitate to spend days at a time, away from their work, as my personal guide.

In a way I was spoiled by the over-eagerness of so much of the rest of the world to help this novel visitor to their towns, villages and farms. Now I am just another American. And perhaps not a very desirable one at that, since I am "evidently" too poor to own a car.

Steven

Clarkston, Washington ✓
August 7, 1986

Dear Folks,

Many times the locals in an area I am crossing have tried to discourage me from following a certain route, instead highly recommending another way that they feel is safer or easier or more exciting.

I received just this type of discouragement a little over a week ago when I steered my feet toward an old and abandoned gravel road that once connected the eastern Washington wheat towns of Dayton and Pomeroy. The sun was too hot and the land too dry to be journeying on foot for so long, some warned. Others took a look at my huge backpack and told somberly of extremely steep grades in the road where it traversed the Tucannon River Canyon. Too difficult, too lonely, too long—take the highway!

Still, I took the way shunned. After all, since when was there a canyon whose bowels did not hold a certain mystique for those who explored them? And so it was with that particularly deep wrinkle of the earth—a wrinkle that some told me is, in one place, the deepest in all the Northern Hemisphere.

Cooled by the premature dusk and lulled by the murmur of the canyon's crystal-clear river, I found myself too mesmerized by the hidden, deep world of the canyon to continue on out of it after that first day out of Dayton. Its beauty and icy drafts felt so soothing to a body and mind that had spend most of the day winding across plateaus of glaring light. Dinner was a fresh trout, caught by luck and a pair of surprisingly swift hands. Bed was a patchy sleeping bag spread on the worn floorboards of an old, forgotten schoolhouse that had only a nearby tidy farmhouse, a stuffed hay shed, a few grazing cows, and the *chuk-chuk-chuk* of an irrigation sprinkler set among sweet corn and potatoes for neighbors.

The whitewashed shell of the two-room schoolhouse had mysteriously drawn me to it, even as the sky's glow was nearly gone and I knew I should be ascending the canyon's opposite wall to someplace warmer and more open. To my surprise, the school's door was neither locked nor bolted. It was almost as if I had been expected.

Inside I found an amazingly well-preserved time capsule of candy-colored world globes, long and narrow blackboards still whispering chalked letters like "Aa," pint-sized desks, dozens of neatly-shelved textbooks from decades ago, with titles like *The New Basic Reader, The Follett Picture Story of the Tale of a Trailer, Rico the Young Rancher—New World Neighbors, Ten Snappy Plays for Girls and Women,* and even an old Remington piano whose ivory keys still spoke beautifully. In the smaller front classroom there was a basketball hoop and backboard hanging above the blackboard, while in one corner a pair of simple, metal-wheeled roller skates with rough leather straps shared space with a box of Crayolas and gummed stars.

Such a center of life that school must have been in its youth, I mused from my bed beneath the stars and desk tops. I could have sworn that even as I rested there, a part of me could hear the glass vibrating to the thumping of sneakers and hob-nailed farm boots and clumsily-bouncing basketballs. I could smell the soap of hand-washed clothes and feel the impatient shuffling of little bodies behind desks that they wished were log rafts or doll houses. How eerie everything seemed! It was as if one day the spring on the teacher's pocket watch had slowly wound down and taken everything alive with it, leaving behind only dust-covered memories.

My turning the handle on the wall-mounted pencil sharpener had seemed so unnaturally loud, where sometime ago its coarse whirring would have been as much a part of the canyon's life as the songs of the crickets.

The next morning, I learned from the kindly old Norwegian farmer next door that the old school had, at the turn of the century, been surrounded by a town of three hundred people. Having spent almost all of his eighty-two years in that spot, he remembered the bustling flour mill, the post office, the two saloons, the stores and homes that had stood in the now-empty fields beside his home and the school. Now, he said, only an occasional hunter or fisherman stepped through the invisible streets of a town once known as Marengo.

The gravel road I had followed into the canyon went "two miles up, one mile across the top, and then one mile down" till it reached the new highway again, said Emil Hourud, with a look of sympathy in his one good eye. Halfway up the canyon's wall, I sat back on my heels in the shade of a cliff and silently studied the tranquil green valley below. How could it be that so much, so many, had come and gone so easily and swiftly? How relentlessly time marches on.

Steven

Missoula, Montana
August 26, 1986

Dear Folks,

"No wealth can buy the requisite leisure, freedom and independence which are the capital in this profession. It comes only by the grace of God. It requires a direct dispensation from Heaven to become a walker. You must be born into the family of the Walkers."

Those thoughts were penned in 1826 by Henry David Thoreau, himself a deeply devoted pedestrian as well as a man of letters. He further observed that, "I have met but one or two persons in the course of my life who understood the art of walking, that is, of taking walks—who had a genius, so to speak, for sauntering . . . ."

Some things have not changed since the nineteenth century, if my observations of the average American traveler these past weeks are any sort of measuring stick. Like Thoreau, I have found my fellow countrymen with their minds and hearts trained not upon the scenery of which they are presently a part, but rather upon some altogether uninteresting final destination. Though they have been allowed by fate to witness some of the most spectacular and beautiful settings anywhere in the world, for all their hurry, the land might as well have been masked in a fog.

No less true today was Thoreau when he remarked, "It is true, we are but faint-hearted crusaders, even the walkers, nowadays, who undertake no persevering, never-ending enterprises. Our expeditions are but tours and come round again at evening to the old hearth-side from which we set out."

Why, I wonder, do Americans so often seem so anxious to get back to the home and job from which they spent so much to escape? Why their odd habit of viewing any trip as being doomed to frustrations and struggle? Why the inability of so many to just relax and, as Thoreau put it, "saunter"?

Incredibly enough, one of the more glaring examples of those of whom I speak is a traveler who should be one of the most free—the long-distance bicyclist. Many have whisked past me on their coast-to-coast endeavors, yet so rare are their cries of "Hi!" or "Bye!" Often as we passed, especially these past weeks in northern Idaho, the settings were nothing less than spectacular, with thickly-forested mountains, roaring canyons, and crystal clear rivers alive with salmon. Our route was the same as Lewis and Clark used to open the West, that which hugs the gorgeous Clearwater and Lochsa Rivers now known as Highway 12.

And yet where were the eyes of those spoked riders focused amid all that splendor? Ahead, always ahead, to some place— *the finish*—hundreds of miles distant. In their pained determination to accomplish their adventurous task, did they ever meet even a fragment of the wild and human things that I did? I don't see how. And what a shame!

I loved seventy-nine-year-old Don McComb's little "Ranch on the River" property, sitting in the cool night in his wife's hummingbird sanctuary, listening to his tales of Shangri-La high in the Bitterroot Primitive Area across the river from his fifty acres. And I became excited at Jerry's recounting, over the Lowell General Store's counter, of how the only neighbor's cat and poodle fell prey to cougars that ventured into the kitchen. And only last week, mind you!

So, too, I am sure those bicyclists would have enjoyed Don and Jerry and all the others who took me into their homes as I crossed 220 miles of Idaho (112 of those miles were uninhabited wilderness).

"Life consists with wildness," wrote Thoreau of his beloved outdoors. "The most alive is the wildest." Not yet subdued to man, its presence refreshed him. Certainly that was true of that long uninhabited wilderness stretch I crossed. Skinny-dipping had never seemed more fun, the springfed streams more refreshing, my elk sausage sandwiches more tasty. How wonderfully blessed we are that the bulk of our states is so fertile and varied in its natural fabric.

How sad, though, that the "Walkers" are a small family.

Steven

Butte, Montana
September 7, 1986

Dear Folks,

Butte, Montana, is perhaps the greatest mining camp history will ever witness. Founded on the "richest hill in the world" under which were billions-of-dollars worth of gold, silver, copper and zinc, this mile-high settlement on the western slope of the Continental Divide was, in its time, unrivaled in its reputation for bold, unashamed, rootin' tootin' hell raisin'.

Its inhabitants came from all four corners of the world, but mostly from Ireland. Their number swelled from around four thousand in 1882 to well over one hundred thousand by the Great Depression. Barons, muckers, preachers, cops, housewives, prostitutes, merchants, thieves—they flooded to this new world of smokestacks and slag heaps to live, work, fight, love and die as only people of a roaring, uninhibited, working mining camp can.

But then came amalgamations, lesser ore finds, a depressed world market, modernization, layoffs. By the late 1970's, the talk was that Butte was finished. By then, fewer than twenty-five thousand of the most stubborn remained.

So what gives? Why has rough-and-tumble Butte, which some call the ugliest city in America, survived when everyone said it must die? How is it that it is even growing and prospering under circumstances that have made total ghost towns of countless other places?

The answer is obvious when one comes to know its natives. Take the case of my present host, thirty-seven-year-old Ray McMillan, who was "born here and will die here." There is, among Butte's residents, an incredibly strong sense of brotherhood and faith, both in their own abilities and in a God too filled with love and compassion to forget them in their troubles.

Ray and his wife Marlene told of such community projects as bake sales for financing cancer treatment for a town resident. But mostly they told of the "Lady of the Rockies," one man's impossible dream that became a reality only because of the entire community's concern and unselfishness.

The story of the Lady of the Rockies, six years in the making, really deserves to be told in an entire book, rather than my brief summary.

The beloved wife of one of Butte's older residents, Bob O'Bill, became seriously ill with cancer. O'Bill prayed for her to be cured, promising at the same time to build a large statue of the Virgin Mary atop the Continental Divide overlooking the city.

Incredibly, his wife was cured, and in 1981 her grateful husband set out to fulfill a promise which seemed impossible, with his own meager resources and the immense natural obstacles to be overcome. For starters, there was not even a road to the top of the seven-thousand-foot-high mountain on which he proposed to build the Madonna.

But O'Bill, a mere laborer, had a strong faith in both himself, his neighbors, and his God. Butte's unselfish side rose gallantly to the challenge, though there was nothing more to be gained than a collective sense of pride. From every religion and social class came volunteers, donations, and offers of the construction gear and raw materials that would be needed.

Finally, on December 20 last year, the "impossible" promise was fulfilled. The golden rays of a setting sun gleaming in her eyes, the fifth and final piece of the statue, the fourteen-foot-high head, was airlifted by army helicopter from the city to the torso waiting on the mountain. Weighing sixty tons and standing nearly as tall as the Statue of Liberty, O'Bill's dream now stood protectively atop one of nature's own forested steeples. On that day very few in Butte felt the cold because of the warmth in their hearts.

From its position, the Lady of the Rockies' pearly white form looks out over every single home and resident of Butte. The statue is visible day or night (when it is spotlighted) to anyone anywhere in Butte. Suspended in starless blackness, the statue looks every bit the fabulous miracle that, perhaps, it is.

Tomorrow, as I continue my journey eastward and pass beneath that statue on my way to the other side of our nation's backbone, I have no doubt I will pause atop the mountains and look down at Butte, too. Butte was never a place to mature gracefully, I suppose. But now maybe all that will change. Now there's a "Lady" around to go with its strength of character.

Steven

Bozeman, Montana
September 28, 1986

Dear Folks,

Call it a lucky coincidence if you wish. I found Walkin' Jim's deep voice entertaining the same group of Montana schoolchildren with whom I was scheduled to visit one sunny morning two weeks ago.

With long sinewy fingers strumming an old guitar, he sang to all of rainbows and frogs and untamed horizons he had found in his many treks across America. With bushy whiskers the color of rich farm fields, and dressed in faded jeans, he was a folk troubadour. And, depending upon the angle from which one chose to observe him, he seemed very much like the mountain men, cougars and grizzly bears that have inspired his songs.

Later, as we sat alone on the edge of the school's small stage and shared our very different and yet very similar walking adventures, it became quite obvious that thirty three-year-old Jim Stoltz leads a most unusual sort of life. As he explained, he has spent several months of nearly every year since 1974 hiking alone through the wild regions of America. After which he then emerges to share in song all the great beauty and peace he experienced in the back country's solitude.

He lives now near Bozeman, high among snowy peaks, but was originally from Detroit, Michigan. Though he remembers childhood summers spent camping with the Boy Scouts and staying with grandparents in the country, it was a two-thousand-mile-long hike over the Appalachian Trail in 1974 that sealed his love of the outdoors. Since then his feet have added another eleven thousand miles, and he has dozens of songs to sing and stories to tell.

Walkin' Jim, as he is known to many rural folks, was primarily interested in being with nature on his early treks. Eventually, though, he found as I did that people dominated many of each journey's adventures, and that they had as much to teach us about life as did any amount of sunsets or flowers. To listen to Jim relate how he has found mankind in his long walks across America was particularly intersting to me. For, though we have gone two entirely different routes on our walks, we had both come together at this particular crossroad in our lives with basically the same wonderful discoveries.

"I tried to walk mostly on trails and railroad tracks. Sometimes I just followed a compass," he said of the first time he walked from one side of America to the other. "The people I did meet were just the folks who lived in the area.

"The response from people was overwhelming. I was totally awed by the hospitality and kindness people displayed along the way. In fact, I can remember a lot of times going across some farmer's land, where he'd come out to find out what was going on, and he'd end up inviting me into his house to spend a week or so."

His experiences with Americans in every state have left Walkin' Jim feeling positive about his countrymen, and looking to a future for our country that is filled with hope and optimism.

"Time was when I first started walking that I didn't want to be around people at all. But I've really evolved since then because of my experiences with all these Americans, and now I find that people make life special."

There is a verse from one of Walkin' Jim's songs that sums up his life as a walker: "I guess I've been a dreamer, I'll admit it all along. But if I didn't go chasing them rainbows, I wouldn't be singin' these songs." And if there was one story he shared with me that I felt summed up adequately the people we both have come to love and call our family, I thought perhaps it was the following:

"In Washington state I was walking down this dirt road, and there was an old farmhouse with the most beautiful flower garden up against the road, with a fence between the flowers and the road. And there was this elderly lady standing in the garden just kind of looking at things and soaking up the beauty," he related in his slow, soft-spoken manner.

"And I stopped and talked across the fence to her. And it turned out her husband had just had a stroke, and they'd been there for forty or fifty years, and now had to leave, to move into town, away from her much-loved garden and home.

"It was a very touching story she told me over the fence, and I was really interested in all she had to say. I just sensed, too, that she needed a friend, so I thought it was so important to stop and talk with her for awhile.

"As I left I said 'good-bye,' and I started walking down the road. But then she cried out and said, 'You know what?' and I stopped and turned around, just as she said so sweetly, 'You know, it's kind of nice to meet a friend once in awhile . . . isn't it?'"

A big smile parted Walkin' Jim's whiskers. Almost as if he were thinking aloud to himself, rather than adding the finishing line to his story, he just spoke a real low, long . . . "Yeah."

And so did I, somewhere deep inside my own smiling walker's heart.

Steven

Bozeman, Montana
October 14, 1986

Dear Folks,

Young schoolchildren have always held a special place in my heart. Just as a brightly colored wildflower never fails to win my admiration, so it is that a young child's inquisitive eyes always fill me with hope. With their budding imaginations caught up in a world that seems more fun than anything, they appreciate much more than adults that this world is still a place of great beauty and enchantment.

By now I have shared this journey with many classrooms the world over—from the uniformed, boisterous Catholic schoolboys of Father Clay's prep school in north Philadelphia, to the barefooted, big-eyed classmates of little Singhs in India, to the straw-haired and sun-scrubbed faces of the one-room schoolhouses deep in the midst of Australia's wheat fields.

As different as all were on the outside, they unfailingly showed themselves, by their raised arms, to be as brothers and sisters on the inside. To all, this world of ours was still a very huge and mysterious place, still a veritable universe in itself of continuous surprises and wonders. If they asked me one question, they asked me ten thousand. They all want to know more about their world.

I can tell from the hundreds of schoolchildren's letters I have received that there are still many teachers out there who realize the importance of extending their pupils' horizons. They seem to understand that we now live in a global society in which no single nation can exist entirely on its own. We have reached the stage where we truly are one big family, and they have correctly pointed it out to their students.

Last February I found, in my pile of mail in Melbourne, Australia, one of the most inspiring letters from a school class. Covered on both front and back by dozens of very intelligent questions about my Worldwalk, it was a giant Valentine's Day letter from the third-graders of Ms. Robin Morris's class at Emerson Elementary in Bozeman, Montana. Measuring three feet by three and one-half feet, the letter was impressive enough to cause me to re-route my walk across America through southern Montana, even though that meant an additional five hundred miles.

The thirty-five-year-old Ms. Morris had been using my stories of the Worldwalk during that school year to help teach her students about other cultures. When I showed up in person one month ago, both her students of the Valentine's Day letter and her present third-graders deeply impressed me with their knowledge of the world's geography and lifestyles. They knew more than most high schoolers I have spoken to—honestly!

Though it has meant putting in ten-hour work days, and a constant effort to come up with new and interesting projects and displays about the world's peoples for her pupils, Robin has hardly minded the sacrifice of her free time. Teaching has always been more than just a job to her.

A year she spent recently traveling on her own throughout Europe taught her just how special we all really are, no matter where we may live. Both the art-filled walls of her big, old, second-story classroom and the open warmth of those children lucky enough to have their minds placed in her care showed me quite clearly the value of her broader vision of mankind.

Something tells me that when I leave Bozeman tomorrow to continue on my journey, I am going to be leaving behind more than just another group of excited school kids. Rather, this time I will be saying good-bye to some very promising future leaders. As well as planting one last kiss on the forehead of a very special and beautiful schoolmarm who has unselfishly shown that she not only cared about her students and me, but about you, too.

Steven

Jackson, Wyoming
November 2, 1986

Dear Folks,

On a cold morning in Yellowstone National Park over a week ago, some forty-four wild bison surprised me in the middle of a bath. At the time, I was far from any roads and chest deep in a hot thermal pool.

Very quickly, those big-eyed animals were crowding around me and unnerving me with their mass scrutiny. It was a bit similar to what the villagers in India used to do by the hundreds each time I lathered up in my shorts at the community well.

Having been warned by one ranger that bison are dangerous and taken to goring funny-looking creatures like myself, I was quite content to stay put for a while longer in all that steam and sulfur. If need be, I was willing to take the time to wash behind my ears a few dozen more times.

Fortunately—unlike the villagers in India—most of the bison soon ceased to consider me terribly interesting. Soon enough they were ambling away to do the kinds of things bison feel living is all about—things like snorting in others' faces, bashing foreheads together, collapsing into cud-chewing heaps, and every so often rolling around in the dust with their thick, stubby hooves flailing in the air, like playful nine-hundred-pound puppies. Unfortunately, they all decided the dead tree on which I had draped my gear was the ideal spot to do all this. As ton after ton of muscle and horn settled down for a morning's siesta, I could feel the backs of my ears getting rawer by the minute.

Normally, thermal pools are far too hot in which to bathe. However, the one I was in was no longer active. It was warm only because of receiving the spillover from a nearby pool that was still being fed from the earth's molten bowels. Still, one can stand to be cooked like a lobster only so long. So I carefully crawled forth from the thick, swirling volcanic fog to walk, hunch-backed and wide-eyed, between all those snorting dark giants.

Viewed from no more than an arm's length, they looked more powerful than almost any other creature I have met on my journey. But, oddly enough, they did not give the slightest hint of being as mean and ornery as described.

Reaching the fallen tree, I deftly slipped into my clothes. With every emotion from fascination to awe prodding me, I spent the next two hours crawling on my hands and knees taking all kinds of photographs. So peaceful and friendly were the droopy-eyed beasts that at one point I even fell asleep for awhile just inches from one particularly mellow fellow.

I must admit I felt more than a little silly when I thought of how much they had initially frightened me. As I walked confidently out of their midst to continue my hike through the park, I realized again that nature is not such a mysterious force with which one should struggle or fear. Respect, yes, but never fear.

On the way back to the road, an old American Indian saying came to mind—"The animals are wild only to the white man." With the bison, I had been vividly reminded that whenever we treat something with kindness and respect—even that which is wild and strange-looking—it is likely to return those same feelings toward us.

Steven

Shoshoni, Wyoming
November 19, 1986

Dear Folks,

Stillness. Utter stillness. With a coldness in the air that seems sharp as a razor's edge.

Such has been my world these past two weeks, as I've walked in the jagged shadows of the Grand Teton Mountains, then melted slowly into the vastness of their captive plains. It has been a time for being alone with ice, snow, and thoughts. And in those thoughts I have frequently seen a dog, a beautiful red collie named Charlie.

He was the only dog I've ever had. I loved him greatly, and it was eleven years almost to this date that he was mistaken from far away for a coyote and shot by a steady-eyed rancher. I think of Charlie now, because not only is this the time of year he died, but also the place.

Then, as now, the Wyoming sky above this windblown junction town had been sullen with early winter, and the sagebrush heavy with snow. I was a twenty-one-year-old uranium prospector. Charlie, who had not yet known two years in this world, was right where he belonged—in the freedom of the outdoor where there was always a jackrabbit to be chased.

Together constantly, and with only one another for company, Charlie and I had spent the summer living one of the most magical times imaginable. Camped deep in the interior of the remote Red Desert, my happy-go-lucky companion and I found ourselves in a setting where space and color still reign undisturbed for the most part.

In such a place of natural wonders, my mind could never rest, nor my soul do anything but grow in size and wisdom. It was the sort of place that makes a man out of a boy, as well as a boy out of any man. I had been sent there to look for uranium, and instead had discovered that fantasy was a far richer treasure than I had known.

But then the early winter, so normal to these mile-high plains and granite ranges, blew in. And with its bitter winds came the sting of tears like none I'd ever cried before.

The rancher who pulled the trigger did not know the dog in his rifle's scope was anything but wild. He did not know it was someone's best friend and only companion. He didn't realize there was anyone else on that remote slope of Copper Mountain. He didn't know, until he came to claim the pelt, and then saw for the first time my anguished face.

I did not hear the shot that shattered Charlie's spine. Yet I can never forget the agony in my voice as I cried out my friend's name again and again all that night. From none other had I known such love and faithfulness, or such delight in sharing life. To Charlie, as well as to me, life had held little pain—until that tragic afternoon.

I sit here staring at the gray hulk of Copper Mountain telling you of Charlie and the Red Desert, because there is more than a mere dog buried up there in all that lonesome scrub and rock. There is also a boy buried somewhere up there, too—the boy that was me before my heart began to harden into that of a man.

I doubt I shall ever quite find that same free boy again or the world he thought was so magical. Certainly there will never be another Charlie.

I might wish to cross the fields and climb that mountain to see the barren ledge with the lone yucca plant where I finally carried Charlie's heavy body to be buried. I had, after all, promised on my knees to come back someday and visit Charlie's pile of stones.

But I can't. I must walk in the opposite direction instead. Because for me memories do not die so easily. For me the snow on Copper Mountain is still too red to bear.

Steven

Casper, Wyoming
December 4, 1986

Dear Folks,

Wyoming has long been characterized as having a boom-or-bust economy, dependent upon the demand for its oil, gas, uranium and coal resources. At present it is in the depths of a severe bust—one that many of the old-timers are saying is comparable to the Great Depression.

So bad has the job situation become in the "Cowboy State" since the downturn began in early 1982, that over twenty-six thousand people have packed up and moved on to other states. For a state that has less than half-a-million residents, the financial impact of such an exodus has been devastating on both the state and local level.

Some towns, like Jeffrey City, have virtually ceased to exist. And even the larger cities, such as Gillette, Rock Springs and Casper, are becoming more quiet and empty by the minute. Stories abound of neighborhoods being down to only two or three families, of family after family selling all their possessions and simply abandoning their homes.

I have been affected by the slump, even though I left here in 1981, while the last boom was still going strong. My friends are gone to California, or more promising places, and even the drilling company I worked for from 1978 to 1981 has ceased to exist.

For me it has been a little bit like coming back to watch some long-time friend suffer a slow death. Pessimism and frustration have seized the land that for three summers during college and for six years afterwards was my dream home of wide skies, tall mountains and great potential. And it is said by most that the situation will get worse yet.

Just a week ago I was to celebrate with my host family here my first Thanksgiving Day meal in four years. While I am sure that Barry and Martha Horn, and most of the others around the table, had much to be thankful for when we bent our heads in prayer, I could still sense that they had known happier Thanksgivings in years past. No one in Casper has gone unaffected by these bad times.

And yet, for all the gloom and doom that is now being

bandied about here in Wyoming, and other hard-hit areas such as Texas, Oklahoma and the farm belt, I can't help but feel most of us still realize we are one of the most fortunate nations on earth. We may lose our job, our car and perhaps even our home. Someday it might even be us standing in the food line at the Salvation Army. But no matter what, we will still have the most precious of all possessions . . . freedom.

Steven

Because of the isolation and loneliness, and the seemingly endless horizon, this Wyoming highway reminded me somewhat of the Stuart Highway in the barren Australian Outback.

Torrington, Wyoming
December 12, 1986

Dear Folks,

Combine the warmth of a wood-burning potbellied stove, the sweet aroma of smoldering pipe tobacco, the snugness of an old farmhouse kitchen, and you have the makings of a most congenial setting. Add to that several cats huddled like fluffy balls outside on the snowy windowsills, some delicious home-cooked smells and a pair of hosts who like to think of visitors as part of the family, and you can't help but feel good.

And yet, for all the homey comforts I have found in my stay with Mel and Rosalie Eaton the past three days, near the Wyoming-Nebraska border, I still could not resist asking them what it is about the prairie that makes them love it so much. I will be spending the next several weeks crossing from west to east on the treeless plains, and to those of us from the woodlands of the East it is a land that, especially now, looks barren and empty.

Many others, including their own ten children, have left the harshness of the open prairie, and more continue to do so with each new farm crisis. In the smaller farming settlements, the voices of youth are seldom heard anymore. And yet so many, like the Eatons, would never live anywhere else but in the depths of what strikes me as so much sameness. Why is that?

"I love the wind," Rosalie said almost right way. "Lots of farmers' wives get really depressed by it, but I really love it. It is my friend. It cleans the air, keeps it clear, prunes the trees.

"Why, I love the way it flaps the laundry on the clothesline, and even how it howls around the chimney—'Listen to that, Mel!' I'll suddenly say when it gets really going."

Thinking of how sharply the cold westerly a few days before had stung my ears made me think perhaps only a fool could love the wind here. But then I realized I, too, had much to like in it. Hadn't its steady, hard pushing at my back made the miles go quickly and easily?

While I tended to look upon the land's immensity as being disturbingly overwhelming, Rosalie and Mel looked at it as being many different personalities, not just one dull giant. Mel, from his lawn chair by the stove, spoke of all the new animal prints in the snow, while Rosalie added examples of her greatest loves in the prairie, the sky and the flowers. Originally from Wisconsin, Rosalie pointed out that there the sky was bright blue only in October, while here in the prairie she had that beautiful color as her roof for most of the year.

"In the spring I just love it when we go out on the range land," she said, just before rushing off to the living room to get a picture book of flowers. "Then there is such a great variety of wildflowers—prickly pear blossoms, violets, primroses, asters, daisies, and lots of blue ones! They don't last very long and are so tiny, some of them. But, oh, are they pretty."

Mel, who at fifty-four is a few years younger than the more energetic Rosalie, couldn't help chomping down with a grin on his pipe's stem and saying, "I've only moved two miles in fifty-four years, and I got to admit I love it being that way. Father wanted to leave like everyone else when the dust covered us in the thirties, but his car was mortgaged and they wouldn't let him take it out of the county.

"I guess you could say I'm still here only because everyone else just up and let me to myself," he added, with obvious pleasure. "Mother passed away. Dad wanted a better climate and moved to California. My brother and sister went into professions. My first wife got herself liberated. And the kids grew up and left to find decent-paying work."

Making his wiry figure comfortable in his "hibernating" spot at the potbellied stove's side, Mel continued with contentment, "All those doctors and lawyers in the cities work so hard all their lives so they can move to a little place in the open country and spend their last few years living like I'm doing. So I figured out early on, why not just stay right where I am since this is what all the others want so much to have in the first place.

"And besides," he said with a twinkle in his eyes, "way out here, I don't have to mow the grass so often."

"Nor have to be keeping up with the neighbors," reminded a laughing Rosalie.

At which point her Cheshire cat husband stretched out a limb or two, opened an eye, grinned almost wide enough to knock the hanging pots off the ceiling rafters, and purred with the greatest satisfaction yet, "Especially when you can't even see them."

And, that, I have since come to suspect, is the real reason so many love to call the prairie "Home Sweet Home."

Steven

I've seen alot of strange customs during my travels, but few stranger than the western Nebraska custom of putting worn-out cowboy boots to rest on fence posts along the roads.

Cozad, Nebraska
December 25, 1986

Dear Folks,

It's late at night. As I sit here composing this letter, another Christmas Day on the road is drawing to a conclusion. Though my hosts, Robert and Vickie Prillaman, and their three young children, Joel, Aaron and Sarah, are now in bed, and all the other guests have long since departed, the signs of a joyful day still lie scattered about me.

For starters, there's the little mop of a pet dog called Rags, passed out in the corner of the farmhouse's living room. Such a day the old gal has had—tracking down tantalizing food odors, leaping wide-eyed around slimy monster toys, enduring constant drafts and competing for affection with some fresh young pup called (hmmmph!) Snuggles.

On the opposite side of the room, over on the upright "no name" piano, I can see the music sheets still askew. With gregarious ol' Faye on her squeaky violin, Clint's medical fingers on the yellowed keys and dear LaVica singing her Sunday best, they may not have been exactly the Mormon Tabernacle Choir, but certainly I will not forget the day's angels all the same. After all, who would have thought "Good King Wenceslaus" and Beethoven's "Minuet in G" had so much in common, sound wise?

Also, I must point to the bright shrapnel of the toys that leapt from so many dazzling packages between the dawn and dusk of this day. Last night it was the Christmas tree resplendent in glitter and surprises, tonight it is the floor. With Cooties, Masters of the Universe, dumbbells, Preppy Bears, moon boots, and evil-eyed robots underfoot, no toe is safe.

Then, too, there is me. My stomach full, my backpack bulging with a few unexpected surprises, and a warm bed awaiting me, I find a new chapter of Christmas cheer being etched into my mind. The tree may be unplugged, the toys' limbs stilled, and the kitchen finally cooled, but certainly I am none of those in my heart.

I had been expecting to spend this day walking alone, then curled somewhere in a farm field during this cold prairie night trying to fight off cold toes and homesickness. Bethel, Ohio, is still over one thousand miles away, and I knew no one living in this part of Nebraska. But then, in another of those amazing encounters that shows just how small this world has become, I found myself being unexpectedly invited into yet another stranger's home for the celebration of this most special birthday.

Unknown to me, Jill Claflin, managing editor of the nearby *North Platte Telegram*, had worked for the *Cincinnati Post* before moving out here. While at the *Post* she had handled the film and dispatches I occasionally send that newspaper. Thus, she had known I was coming into this area, even if none of the other locals did. Thanks to a tipoff from the postmaster of a little town called Hershey, Jill knew I was not only in this area, but virtually on her very doorstep. So our meeting was set in motion, along with her invitation to spend Christmas with her close friends, the Prillamans.

I suppose I am too old for St. Nick himself, but I think Jill and the Prillamans showed through their unselfishness that Christmas itself still lives quite strongly in all of us. And that its gifts always bear our name . . . somewhere.

Steven

Grand Island, Nebraska
January 14, 1987

Dear Folks,

April 1 will be the date I return to Bethel, Ohio. It was, after all, from there that I took the first steps into this journey.

With the final day of the Worldwalk now only a couple of months away, my concentration has already started to shift to the post world walk period. Being aware that there are books to be written and many a speech to be given, my adrenalin is flowing. What comes after the novelty, however, is what has me a bit worried.

Readjusting to normal everyday living could easily become something of a chore if I am not careful. Or, putting it another way, how does one easily settle into one spot with only one set of acquaintences when he knows his real home encompasses dozens of nations and his family actually inhabits a large part of the planet?

Such restlessness, no doubt, has been the post-adventure curse of many a world traveler before me. And so it will always be as long as mankind can transport mind and heart to whatever lies beyond the horizon. With reasoning minds behind seeing eyes, the more we explore, the greater grows our list of questions, thus sharpening our curiosity.

I think, though, that I may have unwittingly found the perfect antidote to such feelings—*a hot shower!* All I need do is think of all the times I would have given anything for a steaming, long, fresh, cleansing hot shower these past four years on the road, and I quickly realize I am doing fine right where I am!

The amenities of normal modern life that so many Americans take for granted (hot showers, washers and dryers, hot foods, cold drinks, a soft bed) have been anything but common for me since Day One of my trek. Not wanting to be separated from normal everyday people by retreating into the comforts of motels and restaurants, I made a pact with myself at the start not to use those facilities except in dire circumstances (starving to death!) Thus, in those stretches where friendliness or people in general have been in short supply, I have found myself relying on my own wits and endurance for maintaining some sense of refinement in regards to personal comforts.

Streams, rivers, irrigation ditches, cattle troughs, even the contents of my canteen, have had to suffice for the hot shower I so often dreamed about. And now with winter upon the land I am crossing, the streams are frozen, and I find bathing more a luxury than ever. It can be quite a test of my sanity at times to see how long I can endure until some kind soul invites me into his home and bathtub.

As for washing clothes, the situation was that I often had to copy the method used by the locals—squatting beside a stream with bar soap for detergent and rocks for a washing machine. And if inclement weather or lack of daylight put a damper on hanging clothing on branches to dry, then it was not all that unlikely that I would use my own walking body as the dryer.

Eating was never easy, either. Depending upon the people in each area to feed me sometimes resulted in a menu of questionable digestive qualities. Ox tongue sandwiches and oxtail soups, which I had early on in the British Isles, seemed dubious enough. But later they would seem almost like candy in comparison to the snails in France, the sheep brains eaten by North African Arabs, the cockroaches and squid tentacles of Thailand, and the monkey innards in Malaysia. Australia might have escaped my stomaches' rumbles had it held to its humdrum use of pumpkin as a vegetable, but no, it too had to surprise my tastebuds with a goanna lizard shared with aborigines in the Outback's dead center, near Alice Springs. How did that lizard taste? Delicious—just like frog legs!

That brings me to the one other bit of my not-so-private life others ask about so often . . . where did I sleep? Well, as any qualified bum might have guessed, my answer is . . . everywhere and anywhere, from abandoned homes to factory steps, churches, boxcars, and bushes to under bridges. And rarely with a lost wink! For as any pioneer woman of a century ago could have told today's housewife, after a day of building fires, scrounging for food, handwashing laundry in cold creeks, freezing in slippery tumbling rivers, and fending off backache, you can't help but sleep like an old log.

Steven

Humboldt, Nebraska
January 27, 1987

Dear Folks,

A little less than two hours ago I was merrily stepping along County Road 105 when a brown pick-up with two friendly faces in it stopped alongside. Even before a word was exchanged between me and the farmer and his wife, I knew I was about to be invited into their home for a spell of warmth and good cooking. For that just seems to be the way of most people in southeast Nebraska, and even more so if they happen to be *Capper's* readers—which, as it turned out, Connie and Eldon Workman have been for many years.

Lunch led to some welcome hours of conversation about such things as their children and—*most especially*—all the grandchildren, the pets, church, the weather, and "Grandpa and Grandma," Eldon's parents, who could hardly believe "Steven" was coming to visit. And there's no doubt in my mind that people will be stopping by John and Helen Glathar's, also *Capper's* readers, when I go to their home in Humboldt for the night!

When I was a journalism student at Ohio University in the mid-1970s, I was taught to avoid making "absolute" statements—such as "He is the best," or "She is the prettiest." Making such blanket judgments would be inviting dispute. I am going to break that rule and write that . . . you are the very best group of readers any writer has ever been honored to know.

I can't imagine people being any nicer than you who have been following my "Letter from Steven" column these past four years. You write to me so faithfully, so often, and in such large numbers. You talk to me in your letters just like you would a son or brother. You encourage me, pray for me, and fret that I may be cold, hungry or homesick. Indeed, it will be well into next year before I am able to get all your letters answered.

Not a day passes anymore that I don't meet at least half a dozen of you on these country roads. Only yesterday, you had me into Moeller's General Store in tiny Cook to meet your ninety-year-old parents (still working as strongly as ever!), then to the high school to share stories with the kids. All that, after having me speak on Sunday at the First Lutheran Church near Avoca, eat lunch at Bud and Virginia Minderman's near Syracuse, and cheer on my favorite Super Bowl team in the living room of Marguerite and Harold Hopp in Cook all that evening.

You make me feel so darn proud and humble in the same moment that sometimes I don't know whether to cry or smile, as happened in Topeka at the reception held for me and my *Capper's* readers on January 22. I have always said the people living in the heartland of America are closest to the pulse of whatever it is that makes this nation so wonderful. You, the *Capper's* readers, are the guts and heart of this greatest nation on Earth. Without your kind, America's strength and soul would quickly wither into something hard and cold. To all who traveled to Topeka, to all who have or will be writing to me, and to all out here on the road who have kept me fed and warm, I say *thank-you* from my heart.

Steven

Sweet Springs, Missouri
February 7, 1987

Dear Folks,

My schoolday memories tell me this is the winter season. The mud on my pants' cuffs and the sweat on my brow, however, tell me differently. Maybe I have just been on the road so long that I have my months turned around, but I would swear on a Bible that last month was May and this month is molting into June. Did, by chance, the new generation of weathermen plug in their computers the wrong way while I was off scampering around in those more conservative foreign lands?

Needless to say, schoolbooks and Pennsylvania groundhogs with phobias about shadows aside, I think this "winter" has been something of a sultry myth. Oh, people tell me they actually saw some snow, for a day or two, over there in good old-fashioned Kansas, and even for a few hours in Washington, D.C. (where going contrary to the rest of us has, I suppose, become a way of life). But I am going to need a little more convincing than that to believe in Old Man Winter again.

With all these "thirty degrees above normal" days, I am naturally quite content to admit spring has already sprung, as the old cliche goes. Neither I, nor any of the old-timers I have talked with, can remember a winter so mild as this. The farmers recount with wistful faces the "good days" when, in January, they trudged to the schoolhouse on snow as deep as the fences. And yet, here I am in mud up to my calves and in enough bird chatter to drive even a fat cat to torment! Certainly we could use some more space shuttle flights, or perhaps another comet, to have a sensible explanation for all this unseasonableness.

Or better yet, why don't we just throw in the mittens and parkas and admit spring is, in fact, here. That way it should be well into summer when I arrive home on, appropriately enough, April Fool's Day.

Steven

Down on the farm with Harold Schippert and his mother Minnie, a *Capper's* reader, near Rock Port, Missouri. *Top;* Here I'm swapping stories with Minnie in the livingroom. *Left;* In the barn, Harold gives me a little "hands on" experience at milking. *Right;* And in the barnyard I'm keeping an eye on a nervous mama as Harold bottle-feeds her newborn calf.

St. Louis, Missouri
March 2, 1987

Dear Folks,

It is with very different eyes that I have been studying my homeland these past eight months. In the years on this journey, they have become older, much more discerning, and perhaps wiser.

It was a disturbing and unsettling enough experience to view my homeland from afar through other societies' eyes. And now I find it a curse to still be seeing my country through those same eyes, even as I am nearly standing back on my front porch. Innocence lost is innocence never to be regained.

Four years ago, before departing to both study and absorb the rest of the world's philosophies and biases, I thought that this nation could do little wrong. I would have gazed up at this St. Louis Gateway Arch and pondered proudly how its soaring grace resembled the great America I knew. I would have seen perhaps only its silvery bow against the blue sky, while ignoring the slums and fear around its base.

I was shocked and hurt to find that many people in the other countries I walked across had absolutely no desire to visit or live in this country. America, they pointed out, has the world's worst track record in drug abuse, suicide, teen pregnancy, crime, violence, abortions, etcetera.

Their viewpoint of America was not a pretty one. But still I was proud, for I knew their negative view was but a small piece in the huge and complex puzzle that is this great nation. I was reared in America and I could not easily forget its beauty and inspiration. Nor could I ignore how much more diverse our society was than theirs.

But now I wonder who was the more realistic. Yes, there is the abundance of material goods. But at the same time, there are more poor, more homeless, and more decay than I realized. And, worst of all, there is so much fear and pessimism.

Every mile I walk now, I listen to America with an attentiveness and intimacy I did not have before this journey. And what I hear is disturbing. Be it in their shops, homes, or on the streets, many Americans tell me they are afraid of strangers, of being out of work, of what's happening to their health from polluted water and air, of terrorists abroad, of war . . . .

I have noticed that it is *fear* that keeps much of the rest of the world so backward and downtrodden. Their fear of rising to push aside corruption, inefficiency, and ignorance has only resulted in those very evils becoming more entrenched and pervasive. To be a dictator is not such a difficult "accomplishment" after all—simply threaten to take away the people's basic wants, and they will fall into line like sheep.

Hopefully, this obsession Americans have with worry and fear will stop. Hopefully, the decay taking over America's heartland communities and farms will be replaced by growth and optimism. Hopefully, the same spirit of adventure, risk-taking, and individualism that characterized the pioneers who headed out of St. Louis into this nation's West will not be discouraged or stifled.

It is fearlessness that made this country the beacon of hope and dreams, that made us stand as tall and proud as the arch in whose shadow I now write this.

Steven

Brazil, Indiana
March 16, 1987

Dear Folks,

Many times when I look into the eyes of my fellow Americans, especially those who have been around for several decades, I (at age thirty-two) sense the feeling that life is no longer anything to get overly excited about. Their eyes seem to say that life anymore is but little more than a daily series of chores and worries. Is that my fate, too? God, I hope not.

Because I took the time to go out from the security of home to see firsthand numerous other faces of mankind, my own society will always be so much more special to me than it was before I left home. These days I find myself unsympathetic to those in our country who would have our freedoms reduced or restrained. It is those very freedoms, guaranteed to each American, that make life here as dynamic and progressive as it is.

Several days ago in Greenville, Illinois, a circuit judge surprised me by asking me to address the jury of a homicide trial he was presiding over. Judge DeLaurenti had met me in the county clerk's office where I was having someone from the town sign my logbook. The two attorneys in the case welcomed the judge's idea, as did the jury foreman and the rest of the trial's participants. So there I was, cap in hand, standing in the old high-ceilinged courtroom of the Bond County courthouse, all worried about what to say to those somber faces in the jury box.

I seriously considered just saying a few harmless words about who I was and what I was doing, then getting on with my walking. But then my eyes caught sight of something that angered me—a look of apathy in one jury member's eyes, a look that said he had better things to do than participate in some stranger's court case. Didn't he realize the importance of his jury duty? Didn't he know he was privileged to be a participant in one of the most important parts of a free society, the jury trial? Perhaps, like so many nowadays, he wanted to believe that guarding and nurturing freedom are the jobs of others.

Immediately I thought of a man I had seen two years ago

nervously pacing the cement floor of a Malaysian police post. According to the police officers at the front counter, their lone prisoner was to be hung within the week. His crime? He had been caught with a pistol in his home.

Perhaps that condemned prisoner had meant harm with that pistol, and perhaps he had not. It did not matter under Malaysian justice. The fact that he had broken the law against firearms meant death.

A free society is a much more compassionate society, I reminded the jury. It has the courage to believe that its citizens are capable, intelligent beings who can learn from their mistakes and go on to be assets to this world. And that is why being able to participate in this trial is all the more a privilege. By merely being there, they were helping keep our freedom alive. They, the jury, through the time and effort they expended in the courtroom, were helping to insure that *we, the people,* still retain the power to decide how free we shall be.

Then I left.

In what other nation could I have had a chance to make such a speech at a trial in which I was neither defendant nor plaintiff? Thank God, we are yet so free that the voice of the little man on the street still has meaning.

Steven

Bethel, Ohio (AP)—Steven Newman, 32, ended his four-year, 20,000-mile walk around the world April 1 with a kiss for his mother on the steps of his family home in Bethel Ohio. He was greeted by the cheers and tears of some 2,000 townspeople.

"I want to say that I love you. I want you to know that I will never forget this day, if I live to be 150," he told the crowd. "As much as other people helped me around the world, you did, too, because you never forget the place where you grew up."

Homes, businesses and churches in Bethel, a town of 2,200 about 25 miles southeast of Cincinnati, displayed signs welcoming Newman home. Some townspeople wore caps imprinted, "Steve Newman, Worldwalker."

About 300 people, many of them schoolchildren carrying flags of foreign countries, walked the final five miles with Newman along rural roads through snow-covered farm fields from a state park where he camped the night before.

Yellow ribbons fluttered from trees and the driveway gate of his home, where Newman arrived with a police escort. His sister, Sandra, gave him a bouquet of roses.

His mother, Mary Newman, 59, paced nervously minutes before the arrival of Steven, eldest of her six children.

"I hope the rest of them don't put me through this," she said, adding that she had followed her son's odyssey by sending him letters to prearranged places.

Mayor Roger Hardin later led a welcoming ceremony, and well-wishers repeatedly stopped Newman to shake his hand or snap his picture.

Newman started his Worldwalk from Bethel on April 1, 1983.

Bethel, Ohio ✓
April 14, 1987

Dear Folks,

Again and again I sat down to write this letter, only to rise once more from my desk in frustration.

It is not easy to write these words to you, for I love you and miss you dearly. And yet this may be the final time we communicate through these letters. A dream has ended—the walk is over. After four years we have come to the end of our journey.

How often we have cried and smiled during those 20,000 miles we walked. How often you worried over me, and I over you. How difficult it is for my heart to accept that there are no more road signs directing me to another "Letter From Steven."

The tears that poured from my soul when I stepped onto the porch to embrace my boyhood home on April 1 were not sudden. They had been falling invisibly since that day's dawn.

When I left this same home from where I now write the final letter, there were those who warned that only a nightmare could come from such foolishness as walking around the world. To be so trusting of so many people was asking to lose everything, especially my life, they warned. Still, I ventured forth—I had to know the truth.

And what is the truth we were to find?

It is that love still lives as strongly as ever. Maybe even stronger than ever.

It is that I am your son and your brother. And you are more than just my neighbor. You are my family.

It is that goodness reigns over evil. That for all the ugliness and hurt we see each day, there are a million times more acts of compassion and beauty silently going unnoticed.

It is that I am lonely without you beside me, sharing in both sadness and the joy of this magic force we call life. For you are my friend, too.

It is that the children will always have a tomorrow to play in, to wake up to. And that this hope should not be cloaked in fear and apathy.

Finally, it is that home sweet home is where I belonged all along. All the riches, knowledge and adventures are empty without a loving home awaiting my tired or excited body and soul at the end of each day.

I realize we knew those truths all along . . . that for all the struggles of this journey, through what seemed a million worlds, I was not to find any new revelations to add to our volumes of wisdom.

Such is the power of love, particularly the love you show. Like a string of pearls draped around the planet Earth, your acts of love still gleam above all else in this tale that has enriched my life.

You were the true heroes of the Worldwalk. You deserved the cheers and tears of my homecoming in Bethel on that crisp, snowcovered morning.

I only walked. You did the much braver act. You loved me—again and again. For that I owe you so much.

Thank you, World, for making your home my home. My heart and mind shall never forget you.

If God is willing, perhaps the separate paths we must now follow will come together again someday in yet another "Letter From Steven."

After all—where is it written that a dream can't live twice? Certainly not in this child's heart.

Steven

AN INTERVIEW WITH STEVEN

Worldwalk totals

1,441 days walking
April 1, 1983 - April 1, 1987
15,503 miles walked
20,017 total miles traveled including boat and air mileage

How did your family react when you first told them that you were going to walk around the world?

My mother hated it. She went, "Oh, no, you're not! You'll die! There is no way you will make it alive around the world!" She was very much against it. My father just shook his head and really didn't know what to say. He probably didn't believe I would really do it. He probably thought I had gotten myself into something that was way over my head.

What did you think about while walking along by yourself all those thousands of miles?

Nothing. I thought about nothing. I was too busy observing all the little things of life going on around me, like the birds or the insects or the plants, or the way the clouds were forming in the sky, or the sounds that were going about me, or the smells in the air, or the people, to bother myself with thinking. I was simply absorbing everything—I was like a sponge on two feet.

What was the most beautiful land you walked?

Well, that is such a difficult question to answer because there is so much beauty I saw all over the world. I think that the most beautiful was the coastline of North Africa, particularly in Algeria. The olive growing regions and the grasslands of South Italy were so mystical and beautiful. Definitely Normandy, Britany, and France were extremely beautiful and lush, and very, very religious-like there with the mist and the fog and the religious crosses along the roads and the cemeteries. Northern India was very mystical also along the Himalayas, and it was very beautiful in Thailand in the rice paddies, and in Malaysia with their rubber plantations. Then in Australia, in the Outback, for half an hour when the sun sets, the temperature would become bearable and the flies would go away briefly before the mosquitoes came. It was very, very much like being on another planet, like on Mars or something—very mystical. I think perhaps overall, again, the most beautiful place in the world was my own country—the United States, particularly in the great Pacific Northwest, in the mountains there. Primarily, because for one, it was unpolluted. You could still drink the water. There was so much pure water flowing in the springs. Secondly, there was still a lot of wildlife and big game running free and loose, like deer and elk and cougars. Unfortunately, most of the world no longer has wild game because the land has been farmed to the point where there is no longer anyplace for the wild animals to live.

Did you ever get sick?

The only times I ever got sick were in Africa, in Algeria, when I caught a bad cold from spending the night in the tree with the wild pigs below, and in Australia, when I drank some bad water out of the rainwater holding tank on an abandoned ranch one very hot day.

Where did you wash your clothes? How often?

I washed my clothes about once a week, mostly in the creeks and the rivers just like the people in most of the countries. Now, that could be very difficult because, at times, the only clothes I had were the ones I was wearing, so I would have to find a nice, secluded spot in the creek or the river to wash my clothes, because I had to take them off. If I couldn't find a secluded spot, then sometimes I had to wash my clothes while I was wearing them. I generally did it with a bar of soap—just washed them on the rocks right in a creek or the river, and then I would hang them on the bushes to dry or on tree limbs.

Where did you sleep at night?

I generally slept outside in the open grass if I didn't have a family to stay with. But if there was inclement weather, or if it was windy, I would try to sleep in some sort of shelter—usually it would be under a bridge or in an old barn. I slept in many, many old barns all around the world, in the haylofts. And that, by the way, was the softest and sweetest place to sleep—in haylofts. And then, I also slept in places like old church buildings, old dilapidated houses, and conduits under the road. I even slept under a parked semi-truck, under park benches, picnic tables, and even on peoples' porches—I would get up in the morning before they got up.

Did you use a tent?

Yes, I used a tent when I was going across the eastern part of the United States to Boston. And then in North Africa because I felt very frightened of the idea of sleeping in the open without any protection, because bandits might sneak upon me and cut my throat. I used a tent in Italy where it was raining a lot, and in Southeast Asia and then in India a lot because of snakes.

How many foreign languages do you speak?

I could speak Russian, Spanish, and English before I started, and on the walk I learned French, which I used, of course, in France and across all of North Africa. I also learned to speak probably several hundred words of Turkish while I was in Turkey.

Did you ever have anything stolen?

Yes. My camera was stolen twice—once in Pakistan, and again in India. Both times I went to the leader of the village and asked that my camera be returned. I explained that it had been stolen from my pack, and both times the head man of the village called all the people together and admonished them and told them that he wanted the camera returned very quickly. Both times the camera was returned within five minutes.I was very impressed.

What was the question most often asked about America?

The question most often asked was: "Why do we lock our parents away in other homes when they get old? Why don't we care for them at home?" That was the number one concern.

How did you find the time to write all your stories and letters?

Well, one of the most enjoyable parts of my walk was how I wrote my stories. I had the "luxury" of writing long hand because I couldn't possibly carry a typewriter or computer with me, and so I felt very often like Mark Twain or Charles Dickens, you know, the old-time writers doing it in long hand. And, for me, that added a great sense of romance and mystique to my walk—it seemed to make my stories more realistic to me and much more meaningful because I was writing in the old fashioned way that seemed to fit so well with the overall adventure that I was going through. As far as finding the time to write, well, that was very difficult because many times I had to write the story in a few hours before the post office would close in the town where I was, or the village, because the next post office might not be for the next sixty miles, which would be days away. Of course, I'd have a deadline to meet, and so I would have to hurry and write the story on the steps of some post office just sitting in the sun, or inside at a table.

How far did you usually walk in a day? How fast was your walking pace?

My walking pace was about three and one-half to four miles an hour, which was very casual for me because I have very long legs. If I wanted to, I could walk as much as five and one-half miles in an hour—I had to do that sometimes when I was in a hurry to get to the post office or the bank or something. But, overall, if you were to average out over the whole length of my journey my miles versus the time that I spent walking, it comes to about thirteen miles a day that I averaged. Now, on a good day when I was trying to make distance and trying to get somewhere up the road, I would always try to get twenty miles. I always thought that was a good distance to get. The longest I ever got was, I think, around thirty-seven miles or forty miles in the Outback one day, and there were many, many a day when I only got one or two miles—so there was no overall rhythm. One day I might get one mile, the next day I might get thirty miles.

How many pairs of shoes did you wear out?

I went through four pairs of Rocky Boots. I could have made it in three pair, but because there was so much publicity on the last part of my walk across the United States, I decided to put on a new pair of boots so I wouldn't look so much like Huckleberry Finn.

Are you the only person who has ever walked around the world?

No, I am the second person to have ever walked around the world. The first person to do it was David Kunst from Waseca, Minnesota. David walked with his brother around the world. I am the first person ever to walk around the world solo, or at least the first one documented to have walked solo around the world. I know a few bartenders in Ireland who say they have too, but have no proof.

Did you encounter many people in other countries who spoke English?

No. I found that it was a great fallacy to think that most of the world supposedly speaks English nowadays or knows of English—that is the farthest thing from the truth that you could say. Ninety-nine percent of the people that I met in the streets throughout the world do not speak or understand English.

How did you communicate with people?

Generally when I came into a village or town, the people would rush off to find whoever it was in that village or town that did know some English (usually the postmaster or the police commander or a doctor or a teacher), and they would bring them to me or tell them about me. And those people would usually come to me, and would extend their hand and ask me to be their guest while I was there, which I would do—and then they would travel with me through the day and evenings, translating for me.

What was the most horrible food you had to eat?

I think the most horrible thing I had to eat was in North Africa. The Arabs have a very sour drink —I believe it was goat's milk with curds in it, and it is very bitter and sour, and they love to drink it. It is very healthy for you—full of yeast and curds, and all this sort of stuff—but it tastes retched, like somebody mixed rotten cottage cheese in sour buttermilk. They like to give a lot of that to their guests, and the first few times that I was in their homes, they would serve it in a big glass and give me a whole pitcher of it. I would force myself to drink it all, which they, of course, were very pleased to see. The first few times I made the mistake of setting my glass or pitcher back down on the table, and they would fill it right back up again. I didn't realize that in the Arab culture in North Africa, that unless you tell them that you don't want anymore, or turn your glass or pitcher upside down on the table, they would automatically fill it. They considered it rude for the guest to have an empty glass or an empty plate in front of him. It was like a torture the first few times.

Did you ever think you were going to starve?

Yes, I remember a few times when I was very, very hungry, and actually became very sick and weak from hunger. Ironically, the time I probably was my hungriest of all happened, of all places, in Italy. I was in the countryside in Italy, and a religious holiday came over the weekend—there were four days where everything was shut down and hardly anybody was in their homes because they were all off to the beaches, to the coastlines for the holidays. I had no food at all with me in my backpack because I didn't realize a holiday was coming up. After the second day, I was very hungry and very weak. I came to a huge pile of oranges and tangerines that had been thrown away beside this factory that made orange juice, and went through the oranges and the tangerines and got several pounds of them, and just cut off the little bad spots. I lived off tangerines and oranges for the next two days until the holidays were over, and I finally was able to go into a little store somewhere and get some food.

Do you ever hear from people you met?

Yes, I do. I get presents from them still on my birthday and letters from them often. After I got home, I got several letters from all over the world from families I stayed with who saw the homecoming in Bethel on their television sets, or read about me. I'll never forget one letter in particular that I got from a family from Algeria in Africa, where the young son wrote that his mother cried when she saw me hugging my own mother on the front porch. I have found, too, that the lives of many people that I stayed with on my journey have, of course, changed since I was there. I was saddened to learn that Dr. Jaquith, who I stayed with in Marrakech in Morocco has since died. His wife, Rita, has moved back to the United States, and now runs a mission house in Las Vegas for the poor people and the destitute. Also, I remember one man I met in Pennsylvania—Ricky, a black hermit, who twenty-five years ago had given up trying to keep up with society, and had parked his truck beside the road. For the last twenty-five years, up to where I had met him, he had been walking everywhere. He lived in a little tin shack in the middle of a junkyard in Northern Pennsylvania, and he had for a sole companion a rooster named "Billy," whom he named after Billy Carter because he would never shut up. And Ricky, I have since learned, ironically was hit and killed by a truck while he was walking along the road in Pennsylvania. Also, the Spanish couple I stayed with, Pepit Cruells and his wife Imma, have since divorced and gone their separate ways. Very sad. But I also hear very wonderful news from my friends around the world.

Did you ever get lost?

Oh, yes, I got lost many times. Always when I came to another country, I never knew exactly where I was going to be walking. Usually I didn't have a map of that country when I came into it because I couldn't be carrying a lot in my backpack—I had to watch every single ounce that I carried. There were some countries like Algeria where I had to make my way across the entire country by just asking everyday, and usually every hour, asking the people I met on the street—"Am I going the right way to Tunisia? Is Tunisia ahead of me?"

Besides the attack of the wild pigs, were you ever attacked by other wild animals?

Yes. I think the most frightening attack, besides the pigs, happened in Australia. I fell asleep one day under a scraggily, old, gum tree out there in the Outback. I didn't know it, but I had fallen asleep on the pathway that these big ants use. They're called bull ants and they're as big as your thumb—the biggest ants in the world. They're very, very vicious—the most vicious on the face of this earth. Well, I fell asleep on their pathway, and I woke up with a couple of them trying to eat my neck. They had a hold of my neck with their big jaws. I tore them from my neck and I looked down and there were thousands and thousands of these huge bull ants all around me, and they were starting to attack my legs and my barefeet, and I ran out into the hot sun and into the sand. They swarmed by the thousands and thousands all over my shoes and my cart, Roo, and all my gear, and I couldn't get to it because they were holding me hostage. And, of course, all my water and supplies were in the shade where the ants were. So, what I ended up doing was, I had a cigarette lighter (although I don't smoke I had a lighter in my shirt pocket) and I found a tree branch. I set it on fire and tried to jam it into the ants like they do in the movies because I thought that it would scare the ants away. But these ants were so vicious that they actually attacked the flaming stick! They would latch onto it with their jaws and would not let go but would burn with the stick. Well, finally I had to swish it through the ants and form a crude sort of pathway, and rush in and stick the stick into my boot, and throw the boots out into the sand away from the main body of ants. And then go out there and kill the ants off of my boots because they would not let go of my boots with their jaws. It took me hours before I was able to salvage all of my gear from those ants, and each time I would try to go near my gear, of course, they would swarm towards me. It was very, very frightening. By the time I was finished, I was so thirsty I thought my lips were going to drop off my face.

What was the hardest part of your walk?

The hardest part of my walk was coming across the Australian Outback because of the 140 degree temperatures, and the flies that would crawl up your nose and in your ears and into your eyes and mouth trying to get to the moisture in your body, and the incredible lonely distances. I mean hundreds upon hundreds of miles of nothing but barren scrub and sand and harsh white sky. A very, very harsh place to cross. Very lonely.

When were you most afraid?

In Africa, when I was walking across North Africa, because it was my first tremendous culture shock in dealing with poverty and oppressiveness and dictators, and the culture that thought totally opposite of me or very different. I was very scared there because I was an American in a land that had so little, and I knew that most of those people who were looking at me each day as I passed them thought that I was very rich. I was frightened that they might think that I had money in my backpack.

Did you ever think you'd be killed?

Oh, yes. I truly and honestly did not expect to live walking across North Africa, and also, I truly and honestly did not think I would live walking down through southern Thailand, particularly after the attack by the two bandits with the machetes, because I still had 900 kilometers to walk through Thailand, and I just knew that there were bandits with machetes waiting to kill me behind every bush or worse, bandits with guns. That is what was most frightening about Southeast Asia—that, because of vestiges of the Vietnam War, there were guns everywhere. I always knew I had no defense against a gun. But, like most frightening incidences, the one in Thailand turned into a very beautiful story because it forced me to go to the Buddhist monks each evening to look for shelter and safety, and I ended up getting a very intimate look at that special side of life.

Did you find people around the world very much alike?

Yes, very much. All around the world no matter what race, culture, or belief, religion, or lifestyle, everyone is very much the same. We all want very much to improve our lives, to be happy, to be free of pain and discomfort, to have friends, to have loved ones around us. We all worry very much about our family, and want very much to protect our family members. We all want peace. We all want not to see people suffer and to help other people who need help, and we all, all around the world, are searching for God and for truth and for justice.

Did you ever feel like you wanted to quit?

Many, many, many times. More times than I can count. It could be something as simple as waking up in the morning with a slug crawling on my face that would make me want to quit and go home. For instance, in Spain it seemed that no matter where I slept outside in Spain it was always rocky, and rocks are hard and uncomfortable. I always felt like I was in some sort of purgatory in a place like Spain. Or, it could be something as frightening as the bandit attacks, or the times I was arrested by the police on suspicion of being a spy. Or, something as sad as learning of my father's death on Christmas night in New Delhi, India in 1984. All those times, I wanted to quit and go home. But why didn't I quit? I think the reason why I didn't quit was because I knew that as a writer and a journalist, I had responsibilities, and I knew from my journalistic background that if I quit, that would be the only part of my story that people would remember.

Did you drink the water in foreign countries?

I drank the water all the time in all the countries. I drank the same water as the local people were drinking right from their wells or creeks or rivers. And I never got sick from the water in any of the countries, except that one time in Australia from the old rain water holding tank on the abandoned ranch out in the Outback. And, the most amazing thing is that, unlike all other travelers to these countries, I had no immunization shots, no water purification pills of any sort, and did not boil my water. I just drank it cold like the people and I never got sick. Why I never caught anything or didn't get sick is as big a mystery to me as it is to anybody else. I think one explanation for why I didn't get sick, perhaps, is because I was walking and traveling very slowly, my system had a chance to adjust to all the various new kinds of bacteria or germs that were in the different water sources, unlike the normal traveler who comes right in from home where he is familiar with the water, and flies right into a place and is suddenly exposed to all those germs and bacteria.

How has your walk around the world changed you?

It has changed me very greatly. It has made me more patient with other people's faults or philosophies. It has made me much more understanding of people. It has given me great confidence in myself because, by having done something that other people said was impossible, I have proven to myself that very few things in life are impossible once we set our minds to it. And also it has made me a much more fearless and coura- geous person, because I have seen firsthand by experience that most of the fears we carry around with us in our lives are totally needless and absolutely figments of our imagination. It has taught me most importantly to be a more loving person, a more kind person, because I have seen that most of the people in the world are loving people and kind people and that it is really not fair of me and even silly to fear people. I view strangers as friends, and then let them show me through their own actions if I should have any reason to be suspicious of them.

What did you miss about America?

What I missed the most about America was our great sense of adventure and freedom of expression. In most countries of the world, the people are very tightly controlled or are very sin- gle-minded, because they have one dominant philosophy or dominant religion, or one dominant form of government that they have had for thousands of years, or hundreds of years, and so life is very predictable and very stoic in some of these places. But in America, there is such incredible variety, and I think it is that variety in life that I missed so much about my own country. So many people doing so many things and all of us being encouraged to live our dreams no matter how crazy they may be. And yet in other countries, people are not encouraged to live their dreams, but are encouraged more to fall in line.

Knowing what you know now, if you were preparing for the Worldwalk for the first time, what would you do differently?

I think the thing that I would do differently, and which I truly regret not having done on this walk, was I would have carried a photo album of my family and my town with me around the world. I found that that was what most of the people that I stayed with around the world wanted to see and know about more than anything—my own family, my own friends, and my own town. I wish that I could have shared more of my life with them through photos.

What's the most special memory of your Worldwalk?

That is a very difficult question to answer because there are so many special memories on this walk. I can say that because many times when I left a home or a town, I cried because of the love and the compassion shown to me. If I had to pick one special moment, it would have to be something very personal. I would have to say that perhaps the most special moment of my walk was when I came home. I can remember when I turned down North Charity Street and walked those last blocks to my home in Bethel, there was no way I could hold back the tears, because here was the last road, of all the roads in all the world that I had walked on, this was to be my last one, and sitting there at the end of it was the big, red brick house that had been my goal all along, every minute for four years. It seemed incredible to me then, unbelievable even, that I was actually seeing it again. And then, of course, going up on that porch, and giving my mom that big, long-awaited hug.

Now that you have walked around the world, what do you plan to do next?

My plans are to continue walking as a source of adventure, a source of learning, a source of teaching, and a source of stories for me as a writer. This fall I plan to walk the entire length of Japan—I'm very much looking forward to that. I'll be leaving for Japan on September 20, 1987. Incidentally, I will be writing letters about my experiences in Japan for my column in *Capper's*, "Letter From Steven." Later, I want to walk the entire length of the Great Wall of China to study the people who live in the shadow of that ancient structure. I want to walk in the Soviet Union between Leningrad and Moscow, and also, perhaps years later, in places like South America and the Andes Mountains. Also, I very much want to walk through the Scandinavian countries because the Scandinavians have for many centuries enjoyed walking as a form of recreation, exercise, and relaxation—they appreciate walking very much there. Walking, I have found, is the best way to meet the people of the world, because you are so close to them and so dependent upon them that it is easier for them to trust you, and to let you into their homes and their hearts and their minds. For me, walking is a way of life.

*Steven Newman invites readers
to write to him at his home:*
450 North Charity Street, Bethel, Ohio 45106

December 23, 1983
MARRAKECH, MOROCCO

Dear Folks,
It was the king of Morocco's birthday. Most of the shops in
MARRAKECH (wh... ...STAYING UNTIL I START MY WA...
IN EARLY J...
THE 9... ...LOSED AND THE STRE...   NORTH AFRICA
FOR NO... ...DOWNTOWN...
W...

February 23, 1985
Calcutta, India

Dear Folks,
The slow waters of the Ganges cast back the s...
light like some old dirty mirror. This would be the...
sadly, perhaps the final time our meanderin...

Dear Folks,
On a cold morning in Yellowston...
a week ago some 44 wild bison surf...
the i... ...e of a bath. At the time...
...roads and chest deep in a...
I was not exactly dres...
...you know what...
...better u...

May 16, 1984
CESANO, ITALY

Dear Folks,
Gone are the wind-brushed fields, the darting lizards,
and the sun-splashed towns of South Italy. In their
places I now have fog-shrouded forests, fat snails, dusty
breaths, and rain.
More rain. And... so much so that the Adriatic Se...
...ed beside the...

To: DOROTHY HARVEY, EDITOR
CAPPER'S WEEKLY
JEFFERSON
KANSAS 66607
U.S.A.

Dear Folks,
My knuckles rapped against the old farm house's wood
door. No answer came forth from its yellowed panes and
thick stone walls, save for the echoes of honki...
and a creaking windmill. I rapped aga...
more sharply. Again, silence f...
Into the depths a...
land I ha...

AUSTRALIA #13
MARCH 1, 1986
BORDERTOWN, SOUTH AUST.

PER VIA AEREA
PAR AVION